"In *40 Questions about Angels, Demons, and Spiritual Warfare,* John Gilhooly responds to many misconceptions, old and new, surrounding the vexing issue of spiritual warfare. Foundational to his approach are: a belief in the final authority of the Bible on the subject; a commendable reticence about engaging in unbiblical speculation; and a conviction that spiritual warfare is primarily about the believer's ongoing struggle with sin. Gilhooly offers robust discussion of a very wide range of issues, and his book will be appreciated by those perplexed by the bewildering and constantly expanding range of unhelpful teaching in this area."

—Keith Ferdinando
Associate Pastor
Woodford Evangelical Church

"C. S. Lewis warned years ago that our approach to demons tends toward disbelieving their existence or becoming fascinated with them. This work strikes a healthy, biblical balance by grounding responses in the Word while addressing debatable contemporary approaches to spiritual warfare. It is a biblically sound, historically informative, and practically relevant resource."

—Chuck Lawless
Dean of Doctoral Studies, Vice-President for Spiritual Formation
Southeastern Baptist Theological Seminary

40 QUESTIONS ABOUT
Angels, Demons, and Spiritual Warfare

John R. Gilhooly

Benjamin L. Merkle, Series Editor

Kregel
Academic

40 Questions about Angels, Demons, and Spiritual Warfare
© 2018 John R. Gilhooly

Published by Kregel Academic, an imprint of Kregel Publications, 2450 Oak Industrial Dr. NE, Grand Rapids, MI 49505-6020.

This book is a title in the 40 Questions Series edited by Benjamin L. Merkle.

The Greek font GraecaU is available from www.linguistsoftware.com/lgku.htm, +1-425-775-1130.

ISBN 978-0-8254-4468-5

Printed in the United States of America

18 19 20 21 22 / 5 4 3 2 1

To my wife

Contents

Part 3: Questions about Spiritual Warfare

Introduction

This book is intended to assist Christians, pastors, and churches to think rightly about the nature of spiritual warfare, as well as the concomitant realities of spiritual beings and occult practices. Writing a book about spiritual warfare involves a number of difficulties, the greatest of which is that spiritual-warfare discussions often take place at the level of folk religion. In other words, the language of spiritual warfare, and the questions that arise about its shape and practice, are often generated in local conversations amongst church people of varying levels of study and experience. If you happen to mention in a church setting that you are writing a book on spiritual warfare, all manner of strange questions and anecdotes pop up. I've spoken to people who claim to have seen Michael the archangel, or live in houses inhabited by demons. However, apparitions of spiritual beings, whether sincere or occult fantasy, are not principally what I think about when I think about spiritual warfare. Neither is exorcism. I think principally about the war with sin.

Of course, such differences are inevitable when working with an umbrella term like "spiritual warfare." It is taken for granted that "spiritual warfare" is a term well-understood and well-attested to by the Bible. As a result, much of our talk about spiritual warfare is unclear.

Perhaps the most troubling tendency in literature on spiritual warfare, however, is the extent to which mere anecdote bears the brunt of the heavy lifting. In other words, many authors on spiritual warfare treat the biblical texts as if they are an addendum to what they have gleaned through experience, whether in deliverance ministry or counseling sessions. In reaction to some of this excess, others reject the idea of spiritual warfare wholesale. Many books on spiritual warfare consist almost entirely of the reporting of stories of personal experience, but experience is not self-interpreting. The best books on the subject fill out the contours of these reports with the data of the Scriptures, so that God's Word becomes the interpreter of our experience.

Even still, these are difficult and weighty matters, and we often find that the Bible does not answer the exact questions we find ourselves asking. In such instances, however, we must ask why the biblical authors chose to address other matters. Perhaps, our speculations about the spirit realm are not always helpful and would be better off left behind. In fact, we are told very early that "secret things belong to the LORD our God, but the things that are revealed belong to us and to our children forever, that we may do the words of this law" (Deut. 29:29). We should be satisfied with what we have been given.

In any case, the paucity of data about some of these matters in Scripture often has the effect of leading to an overreliance on anecdote. Likewise, this leads to another difficulty: Often we find ourselves so desperate for an answer to a question of curiosity that we will "find" answers in texts that simply have nothing to do with the question. Typically, authors accomplish this by allegorizing, spiritualizing, or by word association. However, these techniques are generally disrespectful to the intentions of the authors, since they erode any sense in which the meaning of what the author wrote is determined by the text and not our own questions of curiosity. To say that the text is "for us" does not mean that it is for us to do what we will; it is to say that what the author wrote is what we need to hear.

These worries lead to two extreme responses to spiritual warfare. One is an incredible worry about the dark powers, and an over-suspicion about their involvement in and responsibility for troubles in human life. If all the reports about demonic activity, satanic cults, ritual curses, and the like were true, it might well lead to fear. In fact, Martin Luther argued that we do not see the angels and demons, in part, because we would be terrified if we knew how active they were. But, the fact that there is so much mystery about these activities should not lead us to rely on former occultists for information about the demonic realm, or to an uncritical acceptance of anecdotal accounts.

People who speak as I am doing now, however, are often accused of the other extreme response, which is a mere lip service to the reality of the existence of spiritual warfare. These extremes are not any easier to avoid simply because C. S. Lewis pointed them out so eloquently. Furthermore, threading a middle way runs the risk of being crushed by both sides. Nevertheless, I have attempted to lay out the middle ground in response to many of the questions posed. Again, the middle ground will sound to many like lip service. I will say here at the outset that it is not. My hesitation to buy into fantastic stories of possession and demonic strongholds and the like is based on my reading of Scripture.

On the whole, a key point of this book is that most discussions about spiritual warfare are not based on a robust engagement with the biblical text. At the same time, spiritual warfare is one of the most alluring topics for Christians. This combination is dangerous and has frequently produced excesses and, in some cases, downright silly views about the subject of angels and demons.

It's important to note that the concept of spiritual warfare as we find it in churches today is a very recent invention, not much older than the 1970s. Because it originates in grassroots movements, the term "spiritual warfare" is tossed around with a familiarity and understanding that belie how confused much of the discussion really is. It also disguises the fact that many developments in spiritual warfare—reflected in prayer, counseling, mission, and evangelistic practices—are products of the late twentieth century and not systemic parts of historic Christian theology or (more importantly) the biblical text.

Even when they pretend to rely on historical antecedents, the relationships are tenuous. Hence also, there are strong and significant disagreements among writers on spiritual warfare, even within similar interpretive traditions.

As I have suggested, my own approach to spiritual warfare is relatively muted. I do not deny that the enemy is pervasive and active in his assaults on the Christian church or on Christians individually, but I also see little reason from the text of Scripture to obsess over his activity. Rather, the centerpiece of spiritual warfare should be the gospel of Jesus Christ, because he is the one who "appeared . . . to destroy the works of the devil" (1 John 3:8). John is explicit, in the context of this comment, that sin is the true devilish mark, so it seems clear that the war with sin is war with the Devil in a broad sense.

Fighting against sin, however, is not principally what the phrase "spiritual warfare" calls to mind for most. Instead, spiritual warfare is thought to concern itself primarily with combatting demons and spiritual forces of darkness. It is a mistake on this score, however, to attempt a thick demarcation between the assaults of the enemy, the temptations of sin, and the persuasions of the world. The Devil exercises his reign across the whole of this age (2 Cor. 4:4). Hence, there is little sense in combatting the Devil *as if* this activity were ultimately separate in some way from purging sin from our lives and communities through repentance and reliance on the Spirit of God.

On the one hand, we could think of spiritual warfare in a typical way, namely, as combat with demons. The defense of this line of thinking comes from Ephesians 6, in particular verse 12: "For we do not wrestle against flesh and blood, but against the rulers, against the authorities, against the cosmic powers over this present darkness, against the spiritual forces of evil in the heavenly places." But notice that Paul speaks of something that is already happening, not something that we need to seek out. Neither does he recommend a remedy beyond wearing God's armor and prayer. Certainly, spiritual warfare involves a struggle, a fight, but this is nothing more than the Christian life. To think of spiritual warfare primarily as active moments of intense combat with demons externalizes the ills of human experience and undercuts the sense in which the Devil's authority is united with sin and the whole world outside of Christ. Certainly, if someone in fact is tormented by demons we should help them, but this is an extraordinary event.

On the other hand, we could think of spiritual warfare as an element of discipleship—which is to say merely that our struggle, our wrestling with cosmic powers, is the whole of Christian life. Of course, there are moments of great intensity in this struggle, but the battle is *not* like a traditional pitched battle, where the enemy is over "there" and we are over "here." Certainly, it is instructive to think of the church as a kingdom outpost in hostile territory. It is a bracing image, and one that makes clear the importance of maintaining the doctrinal and moral purity of the church. But the demons and the world are not the only threat: There is also sin. And, sin is on the side of the demons and the world.

Even though there are some key themes throughout, this book does not make a sustained argument for a particular thesis. Instead, it makes many points in response to many topics. First, our discussion of spiritual warfare should begin with a rigorous interaction with the biblical text. Our theology must start with what God has revealed to us in his Scriptures. Second, experience is not self-interpreting. It seems to be in our nature to enjoy stories, especially ones that run to the macabre or fantastic. An unfortunate trend in discussion about spiritual warfare is that almost no amount of biblical argument or theological discussion outweighs the power of one breathless anecdote. But, if we are serious that the Bible is sufficient for doctrine and practice in Christian living, then experience cannot automatically receive higher credence than interpretation. Our enemy is a deceiver; God's law is light. Third, there are more pressing things to worry about than whether an angel appeared to Aunt Sally or whether those neighborhood kids are holding a séance. Frightening as the occult may be, it remains less fearsome than God. "God gave us a spirit not of fear but of power and love and self-control" (2 Tim. 1:7). Angelology and demonology should have a place in Christian theology and doctrine, but it should be proportional to their importance.

This book is divided into three sections. In Part 1, I discuss some broad introductory questions, exploring why the supernatural is so fascinating, the activity of angels and demons, and the various understandings of spiritual warfare. Part 2 comprises questions related to spiritual powers; the angels; the demons; and the prince of demons, the Devil. Some of these questions are exegetically driven, whereas other questions cover various Bible doctrines. Part 3 relates to spiritual warfare theologically, historically, methodologically, and practically. This part concludes with some questions about the occult, which is often a source of fear or consternation in discussions of spiritual warfare. In each of these areas, my goal was to answer the question succinctly; and I have avoided, to the extent possible, reliance on critical apparatus such as footnotes and copious citation. The end of the book contains a selected bibliography for those interested in reading more. I am, like all authors, indebted to everything I read.

I am similarly indebted to my colleagues at Cedarville University for their encouragement during the writing of this project and for their sunny willingness to answer my remedial questions. In particular, I'd like to acknowledge Jeremy Kimble (for suggesting I write this book), Joshua Kira (for mockery and burritos), William Marsh (for barbecue and for Luther), Jason Lee (for employment), Dan Estes (for prayer), Zachary Bowden (for forwarding phone calls about angels), Daniel DeWitt (for coffee and for the dinner on the boat), and Michael Shepherd (for *torah lishma*). And finally, I would like to thank Ched Spellman, who kept reminding me as I wrote that the devil is in the details and the angels are in the outfield. As much as I would like to blame others for mistakes in this book, it is a trope that I take credit for them myself in the introduction. Please know that they are due to my frailty and not to malice.

PART 1

INTRODUCTORY QUESTIONS

Why Is There a Fascination with the Supernatural?

Many secularists argue that supernatural explanations or beliefs are linked with a primitive past that is unbecoming for our modern times. In the past, we all believed in intelligent spirits that inhabited our world from some other realm, with distinct powers over the elements and over the natural world; but it is now widely considered irrational to hold such views. They simply are not scientific. Rather, belief in spiritual or supernatural things is thought to be superstitious. These ideas have even penetrated biblical studies. Rudolf Bultmann famously quipped, "It is impossible to use electric lights and the wireless and to avail ourselves of modern medical and surgical discoveries, and at the same time to believe in the New Testament world of spirits and miracles."[1] Of course, it is not impossible to believe in angels and electric lights—since many persons do believe in both—but some hold that it is inconsistent to believe in both. Nevertheless, it is not at all obvious how use of technology says anything at all about whether spirits exist. Bultmann's point is, I think, a strong example of the tendency to assume that modern developments have made beliefs in angels and demons (or even in God) obsolete. The thought is, perhaps, that our scientific advancements, such as they are, have made supernatural hypotheses unnecessary.

Yet, for all our technological and scientific advancement, belief in the supernatural has not dissipated among the general populace. An atheist might suggest that this fact is due to widespread ignorance of scientific developments or to the inertia of rapidly sinking religions. I think a more likely answer is that there is something to the belief in the supernatural, and that its lingering presence—even after it has become "lowbrow" to believe in things like spirits—can be better explained by other considerations. This kind of

---

1. Rudolf Bultmann, "New Testament and Mythology," in *Kerygma and Myth*, ed. Hans Bartsch (New York: Harper & Row, 1961), 5.

question defies a conclusive answer because there may be many reasons that there is a fascination with the supernatural, but I will suggest a few contributing theological and anthropological factors.

Humans Are for God

Historically, the Christian response to this question turns on the fact that human beings are designed by God for a relationship with him. Hence, all men seek after the numinous (i.e., the spiritual or "otherworldly"), and the prevailing worldview of scientific naturalism does not satisfy this appetite. In the opening lines of his autobiography, Augustine confesses to God, "You stir man to take pleasure in praising you, because you have made us for yourself, and our heart is restless until it rests in you."[2] Augustine is reflecting on the fact that human beings are made in God's image and that God is our proper end. In other words, God is the one—and the only one—who can fulfill our needs and desires. He has made us for himself and for his glory.

At the same time, men deny the knowledge of God that is presented to them. Hence, all men seek to fill their desire for the numinous with something other than God. Men have a need for God, whether they know it or not. This condition leads men naturally to idolatry of various kinds (Rom. 1:18–23). However, the prevailing worldview in the West—scientific naturalism—holds that there really are no supernatural or spiritual entities. The desire for contact with such things is a vestigial sociobiological holdover from a more primitive time. Hence, man's desire for contact with such things is a desire that cannot be fulfilled, according to this worldview. In fact, the desire for God or the supernatural is a desire that we should probably outgrow. Yet, we cannot deny that our longing for wonder remains. For example, even the strongest naturalists attempt to satisfy their desire for the numinous with the wonder of scientific discovery. Some even go so far as to claim that religion shortcuts such discovery and is thus ultimately less satisfying than a scientific worldview.

Such arguments have not been successful in deterring the majority of people from believing in the supernatural. Studies repeatedly confirm that there are widespread beliefs in ghosts, paranormal activity, angels, and the afterlife. These beliefs are independent of commitments to specific religious doctrines, Christian or otherwise.[3] In part, the failure of naturalism to take hold seems to be that its materialism—the claim that all that exists is physical stuff, mere particles in motion—does not satisfy our appetite for wonder and contact with the numinous. It seems to us too reductive to be true.

---

2.   Augustine, *Confessions*, trans. Henry Chadwick (Oxford: Oxford University Press, 1991), 3.

3.   For example, 74 percent of cultures studied in a world ethnographic research project exhibited belief in spirits and demonic possession. See Erika Bourguignon, "Spirit Possession Belief and Social Structure," in *The Realm of the Extra-Human: Ideas and Actions*, ed. A. Bharatic (Paris: Mouton, 1976), 19.

Perhaps for a similar reason, Eastern worldviews are increasingly em-bedded in the thinking of the West. There are more mundane reasons for these developments as well. For example, sociologists have noted a significant increase in the penetration of Eastern religion in the United States, due mainly to the success of immigrant peoples.[4] An increasing religious pluralism has given rise to alternative worldviews that take seriously the presence of spiri-tual realities. Furthermore, recent developments in academia, particularly in sociology and anthropology, have made beliefs in spiritual or supernatural entities less taboo than they have been in the recent past.

The Supernatural Is Exciting

Second, there seem to be no rules regarding the supernatural, which makes speculation free and uncontrolled. A world controlled totally by inflex-ible laws and mechanical reactions feels stodgy and boring, whereas the realm of the supernatural seems both exciting and terrifying. It seems reductive to suppose that there are not greater forces at work than attractions between particles. Furthermore, we are conditioned to craft idols for ourselves because of our sin-natures. Hence, it is not unique to our moment in history that we take delight in fantastic stories about spiritual beings or preternatural occur-rences. However, our materialistic worldview enhances the sense in which speculations about the supernatural serve as an escape from the doldrums of daily life. Since we may believe that there really are not such things as super-natural beings or events, we feel free to craft stories about them according to our own preferences. So, fascination with the supernatural provides both a continuation of the idolatrous tendency in man and an escape from the limi-tations of an unsatisfying worldview. These two factors seem to contribute to our fascination with the supernatural. Supernatural stories are exciting, and it is tempting to think the world is a bit more like our stories.

Not all discussion of the supernatural needs to be ominous. Much of our popular fiction involves some elements of magic or the supernatural, often with explicitly Christian themes, as in the writings of C. S. Lewis or J. R. R. Tolkien. The supernatural elements of these stories increase our wonder and invite us to consider who we are and what the numinous is really like, in com-parison to the characters of the stories. We need to be careful, lest our caution about supernatural practices overturn works of fiction that make use of fairies and goblins to communicate a broader message.

Spiritual Beings, Including Demons, Are Real

Finally, the Devil and his angels are real, and occult speculation provides many lies and obstacles against the faith. There really is a world above the "mundane" experiences of humankind, and much of that world is interested

---

4.   See Diana L. Eck, *A New Religious America* (San Francisco: HarperCollins, 2001).

in directing our attention to anything other than the truth. Hence, fascination with the supernatural is plausibly a means by which the enemy can lead us into temptation. Of course, he wants to do this, so it is natural to think he would stir up unhealthy interests when the opportunity arose.

Once we understand that we are ensouled beings intended for communion with God, who is spirit (John 4:24), the longing for some supernatural contact—or the lingering suspicion that spirits exist—begins to make sense.

Summary

Because God made mankind to have communion with him, we are naturally oriented toward spiritual realities. Unfortunately, our sin-natures lead us to seek replacements for God. When the prevailing scientific worldview denies the existence of the numinous, people search for it in fantasies and occult speculation as well as beliefs in the supernatural and a variety of religious practices.

REFLECTION QUESTIONS

1. How does focus on Christ help avoid unhealthy supernatural speculation?

2. Do you think interest in the supernatural could provide an opportunity for sharing the gospel?

3. What challenges might there be in discussing the supernatural?

4. Does it matter what we think about the supernatural? Why or why not?

5. How might you discuss the supernatural with unbelievers?

Are Angels and Demons Active Today?

Yes! Given what the Bible teaches about the nature of angels and demons, we have good reasons to believe that both angels and demons are active in creation today. In the first place, angels continue their work of ministry both to God and to men. In the second place, demons continue to tempt human beings and spread false gospels.

Angels Are Ministering Spirits

The Bible teaches that angels are "ministering spirits sent out to serve for the sake of those who are to inherit salvation" (Heb. 1:14). Because God's plan of salvation has not come to completion, we have every reason to think that the angels continue in this role. People are still being saved by the finished work of Jesus. But, how exactly do angels minister to people? We do not know all the ways for sure; however, the Bible does indicate that angels have a keen interest in God's activity among men. For example, Peter notes that the revelations that were given to the prophets were of interest to the angels (1 Peter 1:12). Furthermore, Jesus tells his disciples that the angels of God rejoice over a sinner's repentance (Luke 15:10). The ongoing process of salvation through Christ's finished work is a source of wonder for the angels, as it should be for us also.

The Devil Is Seeking Whom He May Devour

The Bible also teaches that the enemy is intent on disrupting God's purposes in salvation. Peter cautions his readers to be vigilant because "Your adversary the devil prowls around like a roaring lion, seeking someone to devour" (1 Peter 5:8). There is no indication in his letter that the threat of the enemy would cease in the near future. In fact, Peter goes on to point out that other Christians are undergoing the same trials as his readers, which would also include the threat of the Devil and his angels. Likewise, Paul exhorts us to "Put on the whole armor of God, so that you may be able to stand against the schemes of the devil" (Eph. 6:11). We have reason to believe that demons are active today because the Bible exhorts us to be faithful to Christ as a means for resisting the "cosmic powers over this present darkness" (Eph. 6:12).

In addition to these reasons, we have also the regular reports of such activity from faithful Christian missionaries, especially in frontier settings. Some of the reports might be mistaken, but we have no reason to believe that all of them are mistaken. Furthermore, many of the descriptions are congruent with the patterns that emerge in the Scriptures. It seems unwise to dismiss all such accounts out of hand, and the number and consistency of the reports seems to provide some evidence of supernatural activity.

Type of Activity

Nevertheless, even though it seems that angels and demons are active today, there is less reason to expect the type of activity among angels and demons that we see in the gospel accounts. In the first place, the period surrounding the life of Jesus was a heightened time of spiritual activity, judging at least from the density of the reports of spiritual activity in the narratives compared to other narratives in Scripture. One might respond, however, that such activity is always as frequent and intense as it is in the gospel accounts, but that the biblical authors simply did not make note of such details in their writings. I think this is a dubious response, both because it argues from silence and because the intensity of certain kinds of spiritual activity wanes as the narrative of the New Testament develops. By the end of the Acts, the apostles and their immediate disciples have become the messengers of the good news, such that the angels (lit. "messengers") are no longer needful for that purpose. Hence, the author of Hebrews can declare that the Father has now spoken finally through his Son, whose gospel he has entrusted to the church (Heb. 1:1–2).

Furthermore, the activity of the angels is not always showy or obvious, even in the Bible. As the author of Hebrews notes, "some have entertained angels unawares" (Heb. 13:2). It seems clear that the allusion is to Lot's encounter with the divine messengers recorded in Genesis 19, but there are other passages of Scripture (e.g., Judges 13) in which angels are encountered in such a way that they are confused for human beings. The fact that the author of Hebrews makes mention of this possibility, however, suggests that angelic activity is continuing.

Demonic activity also wanes in intensity or appearance. In the gospel accounts, for example, the presence of the demon-"possessed" is such a regular and assumed feature of the narrative that it seems that demoniacs were ubiquitous in society. By the time Paul is writing his letters to the churches, however, he makes no mention of exorcisms or casting out demons. Instead, he describes the assaults of the demons in terms of their lies, false doctrines, and temptations to do evil and turn away from Christ. Likewise, John tells us, "Whoever makes a practice of sinning is of the devil" (1 John 3:8). What we are to make of this transition is difficult to say, but it seems clear that any expectation of rampant demonizing or "possession" is an expectation that has focused on the wrong sort of threats. Instead, Christians are charged to guard their thought life and affections in a world of false teachers and beliefs deriving from the Devil.

In fact, apparitions of angels in Scripture occur when God intends to communicate a message to someone, either by a physical manifestation of the angel or in a dream or vision. It would be outside the character of this pattern for us to expect to see angels crossing the street or waving from a street-shop window. Surely, such things could happen, since it falls within the divine power to send his angels where he wishes. Hence, asking whether such encounters could happen seems to be the wrong sort of question. What we really want to know is if such encounters do happen.

Because there is no evidence to show that angels and demons are definitely not active in our world, some rush to the conclusion that they are super-active, and/or active in ways inconsistent with the depictions we have of them in the Bible. As an extreme example, in her book on encounters with angels in the form of dogs, Joan Anderson queries, "If God would use anonymous spirits in human form to work his will, why not in dog form?"[1] This author is sincere that after praying for guidance from the Holy Spirit, she had come to believe that angels sometimes appear as dogs to provide assistance to humans in need.

Is it possible that this happens? Maybe, but I strongly doubt it. Do we have any biblical evidence that it does? None whatsoever. The only evidence we have to go on is the sincere(?) reporting of other human persons. If such reports are congruent with the patterns in the Bible, then one should be more comfortable considering the case. But, we have no reason beyond a series of anecdotes to suppose that angels appear as dogs. We should be cautious about believing stories about angelic activity simply because someone tells us about their experience, especially if the account is inconsistent with the biblical witness.

At the same time, it would be inconsistent to believe that angels and demons are active and then to deny that they ever acted. In fact, to do so would be merely to pay lip service to the mention of the angelic and demonic realms in Scripture. Even though we might debate a particular instance of alleged spiritual activity, the Bible indicates that angels and demons are real, personal beings who are active in creation. While we should analyze reports of angelic and demonic activity with biblical scrutiny, it is wrong to assume that angels and demons are not active in the world, or that all reports of their activity are

---

1. Joan Wester Anderson, *Angelic Tails: True Stories of Heavenly Canine Companions* (Chicago: Loyola, 2011), xi.

made up. They are creatures of the cosmos just as we are, and they are active in the world today.

Summary

Angels and demons are active in the world today, but that does not mean that we should expect to constantly see them or encounter traces of them in the world. The Scripture indicates that we could interact with angels without even knowing it, but it does not encourage us to seek them out or to expect to hear from or see them. Hence, we need to be cautious about reports of spiritual activity, even though we need not dismiss them out of hand.

REFLECTION QUESTIONS

1. Why should we be cautious about believing every account of spiritual activity?

2. Why should we be cautious about ignoring every account of spiritual activity?

3. How should being reminded that demons are active affect our prayer life?

4. What are some ways you could begin to ask good questions about spiritual activity that you hear from others?

5. How does Hebrews 13 encourage us to act in light of the activity of angels?

What Is Spiritual Warfare?

Spiritual warfare is a theological term used to describe the ongoing battle between the church and the Devil and his angels. The term is not used in the Bible but is derived from a conception of the struggle of the Christian life. Paul writes that "we do not wrestle against flesh and blood, but against the rulers, against the authorities, against the cosmic powers over this present darkness, against the spiritual forces of evil in the heavenly places" (Eph. 6:12). The cosmic struggle that he describes is the struggle to which "spiritual warfare" generally refers.

Of course, like many theological terms, the history of the usage of this term shows that it has shifted in its emphases, depending on the situation in which it is employed. In some Pentecostal/Charismatic circles, the term refers specifically to the battle between a Christian and evil spirits (demons). In this setting, spiritual warfare is understood in the context of "deliverance" ministries, in which the goal of the conflict is an exorcism of some kind. Deliverance ministries, however, are generally considered among Charismatics to be broader than exorcism. Likewise, spiritual warfare is something broader than deliverance ministries.

The origin of the term "spiritual warfare" seems to date to the 1970s. Some scholars have attributed its first usage to Michael Harper (1931–2010), who used the term as the title of his book on the Christian's struggle with Satan in daily life.[1] The general concept that God and the Devil struggle over the world and the souls of men in particular is expressed in warfare terminology in English as early as John Bunyan's *Holy War* (1682). In Christian fiction, the concept is found as early as Prudentius' *Psychomania* (AD 384). Even Origen uses the terminology (AD 180). Of course, the Bible also uses

---

1. Michael Harper, *Spiritual Warfare* (London: Hodder & Stoughton, 1970). Harper rejected the term "deliverance ministry," with the concomitant idea that anyone should specialize in such a ministry.

warfare terminology to describe the struggle of the Christian life throughout the New Testament (e.g., Eph. 6:10; 1 Tim. 6:12; Heb. 4:12).

Spiritual warfare is not a distinct brand of Christian ministry. There is not a peculiar gift for "deliverance ministry" or "spiritual warfare" distributed to some by God and not to others. In fact, exorcism is not listed in any of Paul's outlines of the spiritual gifts, nor is it mentioned in any of the New Testament letters. Although it is true that his lists are not intended to be exhaustive, it is curious that Paul does not mention the power to bind demons if such power was intended to be an intrinsic feature of Christian ministry. Furthermore, Paul does intimate that the Christian faithful are involved in an ongoing struggle with spiritual powers (Eph. 6:10–18). Yet, he does not say anything of significance about personal struggles with individual demons—a fact you would never guess from a casual reading of many contemporary books on spiritual warfare.

Nevertheless, the universal commands to resist the spiritual powers of darkness in the New Testament extend to all the faithful. Hence James says to his readers, "Resist the devil, and he will flee from you" (James 4:7). Peter offers the same command (1 Peter 5:8–9). The power for this resistance does not come from some superadded gifting but from the presence of the Holy Spirit in the lives of believers (Luke 11:20; 2 Cor. 10:3–4). The subjection of demonic influences to the Christian is based on the status of the Christian (Luke 10:20). To see that this is the case, we need only compare the effect of the rebukes of the disciples sent out by Jesus (Luke 10:17) with the effect of the self-appointed exorcists at Ephesus (Acts 19:12–17). In fact, Luke is careful to demonstrate, through several episodes in Acts, that the gospel of Jesus Christ is greater in power than the power of magic or demons (e.g., Acts 8).[2]

Models

In later chapters, I discuss a few specific models or views of spiritual warfare in more detail; for now, it will be helpful to sketch out some ways in which the term is used. One way to distinguish between approaches to spiritual warfare is to discuss "high-level" and "low-level" strategies. "High-level" strategies focus on locating and confronting "territorial spirits" who are conceived to be demonic agents that have control over large areas (cities or even nations). Methods for this strategy involve spiritual mapping and "iden-tificational repentance." Proponents of such strategies typically identify with the Strategic-Level Spiritual Warfare movement initiated by C. Peter Wagner and a handful of others in the early 1990s.

There are others who envision a similar high-level strategy, but one that focuses on oppressive and unjust institutions. The reason their focus on

---

2. See Susan R. Garrett, *The Demise of the Devil: Magic and the Demonic in Luke's Writings* (Minneapolis: Fortress, 1989) for a discussion of these themes.

institutional and systemic injustices is because they take language about demons and the Devil in the Bible metaphorically. Such approaches are broadly captured beneath the World-Systems model of spiritual warfare, associated with the influential writings of Walter Wink.

In contrast to these "high-level" strategies, "low-level" strategies focus on individual encounters with the demon-possessed, or with occult practices that give rise to demonic activity in a particular area. These strategies are likewise associated with members of the Strategic-Level movement as well as the myriad deliverance ministry movements. A contrasting low-level strategy is the model of spiritual warfare that focuses its attention on an individual's struggle against the flesh, or with the development and spiritual maturity of local churches. This last model is the one best attested to by the injunctions and emphases of the New Testament.

On the one hand, then, a debate among writers on spiritual warfare is whether we ought to believe and be concerned about the presence of real, personal demons (Satan and his angels) or merely with unjust practices and institutions that are called "demonic" metaphorically. Among those who accept that the Bible teaches that the Devil and his angels are real personal beings, there is a debate about whether certain spiritual warfare practices (e.g., spiritual mapping) are justifiable biblically and whether spiritual warfare literature pays undue attention to the Devil rather than the war with the flesh.

Summary

The term "spiritual warfare" is ironically a contested term, but several principles are clear biblically. First, any power over sin, the world, and the Devil comes only by way of the blood of Christ. Spiritual warfare must begin with personal holiness which is achievable only by believing the gospel and pursuing our Lord. From there, discernment is needed to discuss the nature of demonic or angelic visitations, but the evidence for territorial spirits and various "warfare practices," such as binding demons or breaking seals, is limited almost solely to anecdotes. In later chapters, I will discuss some of the biblical warrant given for these practices. While it is true that Western Christians have a tendency to deny spiritual activity—or at least, to be predisposed to materialist interpretations of "strange" events—it is equally true that Christians from polytheist or animist societies are predisposed to spiritualist interpretation. All of our experiences must be tested against the Word of God. Finally, we should not believe the lie that spiritual warfare is for "super-Christians." All Christians are born again into an ongoing struggle against dark powers and sin. Whatever else it may involve, spiritual warfare is a corporate engagement of the church that involves all of God's people. The "low-level" strategy of obedience to God's commands and the pursuit of personal holiness are *sine qua non* for spiritual warfare. Furthermore, we can all pray.

REFLECTION QUESTIONS

1. What is the difference between high-level and low-level models of spiritual warfare?

2. Why do you think that spiritual warfare is not a specific type of Christian ministry?

3. Why is the pursuit of personal holiness the most important part of spiritual warfare?

4. How might worries about dark powers be a distraction from effective spiritual warfare?

5. What are some ways you can begin to pray, with regard to spiritual warfare?

PART 2

QUESTIONS ABOUT SPIRITUAL POWERS

Questions Related to Angels

What Is Angelology?

The Bible teaches that, in addition to human beings, God has made another type of rational personal beings: the angels. Angelology is the study of those beings. Angelology considers questions about what the angels are, what duties they perform, what their role in the biblical narrative is, and what role they play in the lives of people. A related area is demonology, which studies similar questions about the demons (see Question 9).

There is an oft-quoted remark in C. S. Lewis' preface to *The Screwtape Letters*: "There are two equal and opposite errors into which our race can fall about the devils. One is to disbelieve in their existence. The other is to believe, and to feel an excessive and unhealthy interest in them. They themselves are equally pleased by both errors and hail a materialist or a magician with the same delight."[1] The same is true of the angels. Given the treatment of angels in the Bible, Christians must believe in their existence. Without a robust angelology, however, we have little defense against satisfying our "unhealthy interest" in spirits through speculations of the occult, false religions, or popular conceptions that lack biblical warrant.

Nevertheless, studying angelology is challenging because the Bible contains no sustained treatment of angelic beings. Given what Scripture does say—namely, that angels are spirits, invisible and incorporeal—we cannot study them as we would an ox or a ferret. Their nature is higher than ours, and much of the data about them in Scripture is tangential or obscure. Because the subject matter of angelology is obscure, there is a real concern when discussing angels and demons (and even spiritual warfare) that there is not sufficient biblical data to say much of value.

There is not a concern that one could speculate about such matters. In fact, speculation abounds! Instead, the concern is whether there could really be a biblical angelology, that is, an angelology deeply rooted in what Scripture

---

1. C. S. Lewis, *The Screwtape Letters* (New York: Harper Collins, 2001), xi.

teaches about angels and constrained in some way by that information. Furthermore, there is here an implicit question about what would constitute a biblical angelology. We know that angelology is the study of the angels. But how ought they to be studied?

Brief History of Angelology

The earliest sustained treatment of the angels in Christian theology comes to us in the work of a figure now known as Pseudo-Dionysius. Whoever he really was, he made himself out to be the Dionysius mentioned in Acts 17:34.[2] As a result of his putative near-apostolic authority, his writings were received with a special trust and respect by later generations. His work on the angels is most clearly laid out in a book entitled *On the Celestial Hierarchy*.[3] In chapter six of that work, he explains the nine ranks of angels, how they are arranged and distinguished. In the first rank, he places the seraphim, cherubim, and thrones. In the second rank, he places dominions, powers, and authorities. In the third rank, he places the principalities, archangels, and angels. He draws the names of the types of angelic creatures from the Bible; however, these ranks are divided based on speculation about the intellectual illumination of each type of angel. In fact, the knowledge of the lower angels is thought to be mediated in some sense from the higher angels. He cites as an example the angelic interaction described in Zechariah. Of course, the idea of knowledge being mediated through successive emanations of the One is a standard feature of Neo-Platonic mysticism. Pseudo-Dionysius seems to have assimilated those ideas for his angelology. His idea that there are ranks among the angels is justifiable biblically; his explanation of the ranks is speculative.

Through Pseudo-Dionysius, a robust account of the angelic hierarchy became a regular feature of angelological reflection and cosmology through the Middle Ages. Thomas Aquinas (1225–1274) would give the treatment of Pseudo-Dionysius a critical reappraisal in terms of Aristotelian metaphysics. He argued that the angels of Scripture were to be understood as separated substances, i.e., pure spiritual creatures without any bodily admixture. The viewpoint that angels had no bodily principle had already been codified in the record of the Fourth Lateran Council (1215). Thomas Aquinas' angelology attempted to provide a metaphysical explanation of that claim. Much of his reflection takes for granted the speculations of Pseudo-Dionysius because Aquinas was always hesitant to repudiate the view of a historical church

---

2. The facts about the life of Pseudo-Dionysius remain obscure, particularly because there are some deliberate falsehoods in his writings (e.g., he claims to have seen the solar eclipse at the crucifixion). It is clear that he was a Syrian author from the fifth century. For a discussion of scholarly opinions on his identity, see Ronald Hathaway, *Hierarchy and the Definition of Order in the Letters of Pseudo-Dionysius* (The Hague: Martinus Nijhoff, 1969), 31–36.
3. For an accessible edition in English, see *Pseudo-Dionysius: The Complete Works*, trans. Paul Rorem (Mahwah, NJ: Paulist, 1998).

authority. However, his Aristotelian synthesis is focused less on the overall structure of the angelic choirs and more on the angelic nature as such.

For the medieval theologians, the angelic nature served as an excellent test case for theories about cognition and volition because the angelic nature is simpler than the human nature. All experiments are designed to eliminate as many variables as possible so that the subject of study can be examined under pristine conditions. The same is true with thought experiments. Often angelological reflection was based less on explicitly exegetical grounds than on metaphysical inferences from certain theological assumptions (or deliverances).

The theologians of the Reformation were more mixed in the treatments of the subject. The question of what the angels are had been settled by previous theological reflection. As Martin Luther (1483–1546) says, "an angel is a spiritual creature created by God without a body, for the service of Christendom and of the church."[4] For Luther, the focus of angelology should primarily be the extent to which the angels and demons affect the lives of Christians. He is deeply committed to the idea that angels and demons fight over the Christian: "The devil is also near and about us, incessantly tracking our steps, in order to deprive us of our lives, our saving health, and salvation. But the holy angels defend us from him, in so much that he is not able to work us such mischief as willingly as he would."[5]

In contrast, the approach of John Calvin (1509–1564) to the subject of the angels is much more modest. He writes, "let us remember here, as in all religious doctrine, that we ought to hold to one rule of modesty and sobriety: not to speak, or guess, or even to seek to know, concerning obscure matters anything except what has been imparted to us by God's Word. Furthermore, we ought to ceaselessly endeavor to seek out and meditate upon those things which make for edification."[6] He is willing to countenance the activity of angels and demons as Scripture revealed, but he is much less suspicious of their constant activity than is Luther. In part, this reaction was motivated by his deep criticism of the trajectory of angelology based on the mere words of Pseudo-Dionysius.

In the modern era, angelology became increasingly suspect in many theological systems.[7] Friedrich Schleiermacher (1768–1834) taught, for example, that the doctrine of the existence of angels can "have its place in Christian language without laying on us the duty of arriving at any conclusion regarding its

---

4. William Hazlitt, ed., *Martin Luther's Table Talk* (Great Britain: Christian Focus, 2003), 339.
5. Ibid., 340.
6. John Calvin, *Institutes of the Christian Religion*, trans. Ford Lewis Battles, LCC, vols. 20–21 (Philadelphia: Westminster Press, 1960), 1:14:4.
7. Or altogether absent. Many contemporary continental theologians omit a thorough discussion of angels almost entirely. An exception is Wolfhart Pannenberg, who discusses them as fields of force.

truth."[8] The major modern theologian who gave the most systematic treatment of angelology was Karl Barth (1886–1968) who devoted over 350 pages to the subject matter in his *Church Dogmatics*.[9] He considered angelology "the most remarkable and difficult of all" the dogmatic spheres of theology.[10] Nevertheless, he believed it necessary to treat the subject because the Bible talked with seriousness about angels and demons. His chief concern was to avoid the methodology of the past, which identified the angels with alien philosophical entities.

Regardless of the amount of sustained attention given to the subject, angelology remains an essential component of the doctrines of creation. Nevertheless, it is easy to see why a subject that has produced such speculations is often thought of as peripheral and unimportant.

Why Angelology?

Angelology can be significant and important in our theology without becoming the most important doctrine. We must resist the temptation to ignore the subject altogether or to be consumed with merely fabricating answers to our endless questions about spiritual matters. Indeed, we have good reason from Scripture to believe that we can (and must) say something positive about the angels because the Scriptures say something positive about the angels. Why is angelology important? Because the angels are regular participants in the story of the Bible both as active and background characters. To deny the existence of angels, or to withhold judgment, is just to set oneself against the bare claims of Scripture. No Christian account of the world can fail to account for angels (or angelology) without lacking seriously in content.[11] But, of course, insisting that something must be said leads to the theological concerns about what will be said.

Biblically, this concern is illegitimate. If Scripture says something about a topic, then our theology and philosophy must account for that something. Clearly, the Bible says something about angels. The basic word for angel in Hebrew (*mal'akh*) and Greek (*angelos*) appears around three hundred times in the Bible. The angels are regular, active figures in Scripture who play important historical and literary roles.

---

8. Friedrich Schleiermacher, H. R. Mackintosh, and James Stuart Stewart, *The Christian Faith* (Edinburgh: T&T Clark, 1928), 156. I see this as an enlargement and distortion of Calvin's principle of modesty. However, Schleiermacher protests too much and silences claims that are rooted in the biblical witness. Karl Barth memorably refers to this approach as "the angelology of the weary shrug of the shoulders" (*Church Dogmatics*, vol. 3.3 [New York: T&T Clark, 2010], 413).

9. Karl Barth, *Church Dogmatics*, vol. 3.3:169–531.

10. Ibid., 369.

11. Louis Berkhof says it well, "No one who bows before the authority of the Word of God can doubt the existence of angels" (*Systematic Theology* [Grand Rapids: Eerdmans, 1996], 2:143).

If we are to have a biblical theology, then angelology is a necessity, however delicate its claims may be. In fact, most dogmatic claims about the angels in Christian history have been quite modest. Philosophers and theologians have discussed and speculated about the nature of angels—but we must not confuse that with biblical doctrine. We need to take care to distinguish between what exegesis leads us to conclude about the angels and what seems reasonable to us in light of gaps in the biblical witness and our experience. In fact, the desire for more concrete answers about the angels sometimes leads us to read into the Bible information that is not there. So, we have to navigate between ignoring angelology and enlarging angelology. In the process, we will be able to discover what God has revealed about the celestial messengers.

Summary
Angelology is important because the Bible talks about angels and demons. If we are to have a theology based on biblical truth, then we must faithfully exposit what Scripture says about all matters on which it speaks. Such exposition is for our good. Furthermore, a proper angelology can help us critically evaluate the reports we hear (1 John 4:1) and prevents the excesses of popular imagination that will "fill in the gaps" in our doctrine with cute pictures of angels or wicked horned devils. Likewise, angelology is important because a biblical account of spiritual beings will help us ward off unbiblical accounts, such as those offered by the occult, spiritism, false religions, and popular culture. Speculation about such matters can be held in check by a firmer grasp on what the Bible teaches about these matters.

REFLECTION QUESTIONS

1. How have historical theologians regarded angelology?

2. What factor is crucial in having a healthy angelology?

3. Why is angelology important?

4. How does a biblical angelology prevent occult speculation?

5. Should we expect angelology to be a major part of our theology?

What Does the Bible Say about Angels?

The basic word for "angel" is used numerous times in the Bible. In the Old Testament, it appears more than 190 times, and in the New Testament more than 170 times. From the information that the Bible provides, we can draw several general conclusions about angels. These conclusions give rise to the fundamental scope of our angelology. There is not, however, a sustained treatment of these issues in Scripture. Consequently, angelology is a more cursory and piecemeal enterprise than other major heads of doctrine in Christian theology. To speak of a biblical angelology, then, is to speak in the first place of a catalog of facts about the angels that are attested in Scripture. Any constructive work will be based on implications or inferences drawn from this set. In addition to these considerations, less attention has been given to the literary significance of the angelic figures than seems warranted by their place in the canon.

"Angel" Describes a Vocation

There are as many as sixteen Hebrew words that are sometimes thought to refer to angels and are translated as "angels" in some English translations. The most common word is *mal'akh*, which has the basic meaning of "messenger." In fact, in more than half of the instances in which *mal'akh* or one of its forms appears, the word unambiguously refers to a human messenger. In the New Testament, there are fewer words used for angels, but the basic word *angelos* means simply "messenger" and is often used to refer to a human messenger. So, the language of the Bible stresses the function of the angels more than their nature. Clues from the context allow translators to make the decision whether the messenger in question is human or angelic.

The biblical authors sometimes use the ambiguity of the word to great effect. For example, in Genesis 19, two angels visit the home of Lot and report back to God that the city is indeed wicked and worthy of destruction. In verses 1 and 15, these two figures are referred to as *mal'akhim* (the plural of *maľakh*). English translations are univocal in translating this word as angel. However, the figures are referred to as men seven times in the surrounding passage (Gen. 18:2; 19:5, 7, 10, 12, 16). The tension between the perspective of the narrator and the perspective of the characters in the story shows us that these angels are mysterious creatures who are capable of appearing indistinguishable from men. At first, Abraham and Lot do not recognize them as angels. But, in Genesis 18:1, Moses identifies the three figures as representatives of the Lord, and, in Genesis 19:1, he identifies the two figures as angels. Yet, these angels who appear as humans to the people of the city are able to pull Lot away from the hands of the men of city and to strike them with blindness (Gen. 19:10–11). These appear to be more than men! The misidentification of angels with men is not limited to only this passage (cf. Judges 13).

Unlike men, angels are not created with bodies and are not properly ordered to the development of bodies. Like men, angels are intelligent and capable of making choices for which they bear moral responsibility. In the book of Hebrews, the proof-text for their incorporeality is 1:14: "Are they not all ministering spirits . . . ?" The implied answer to the question is, "Yes, they are ministering spirits," and that the word "spirits" (*pneumata*) in this case refers to their incorporeal nature (Luke 24:39). It is also true, however, that at various times certain angels have appeared to men as bodily creatures, to which the book of Hebrews also attests (Heb. 13:2).

There is a gap in the biblical witness in this regard, because there is no explanation for how angels take on or "assume" a body. What can be clearly observed from the biblical witness, however, is that it is in special circumstances (e.g., when God wishes to communicate a message) that angels take on a body. In some cases, they are merely visible in dreams or by special empowering (2 Kings 6:17; Luke 2:31).

Divine Messengers

In terms of their interaction with humans, the main function of the angels is what their name implies: to deliver messages. In particular, the angels are associated with important announcements, as well as words of judgment and prophecies.

The most famous good news brought to man by the angels is the announcement to the shepherds that Christ had been born. Luke tells us that

> an angel of the Lord appeared to them, and the glory of the
> Lord shone around them, and they were filled with great fear.
> And the angel said to them, "Fear not, for behold, I bring
> you good news of great joy that will be for all people. For
> unto you is born this day in the city of David a Savior, who
> is Christ the Lord. And this will be a sign for you: you will
> find a baby wrapped in swaddling cloths and lying a man-

ger." And suddenly there was with the angel a multitude of the heavenly host praising God and saying, "Glory to God in the highest, and on earth peace among those with who he is pleased!" (Luke 2:9–14)

We sing the words of the angels at Christmas when we remember the birth of our Savior. Relatedly, angels are often depicted as announcing the birth of significant personages, whether John the Baptist (Luke 1:11–22), Samson (Judges 3:3–7), or even Ishmael (Gen. 16:10–11).

Sometimes, the message of the angels is a message of judgment. A good example of such a message can be found in Genesis 19:13, in which the two angels say to Lot, "we are about to destroy this place, because the outcry against its people has become great before the LORD, and the LORD has sent us to destroy it." After the angels leave the scene, fire from heaven destroys the city. Perhaps we should infer from this that the angels returned to heaven before carrying out the judgment that God had spoken against the cities.

In other cases, the angels act upon the words of judgment that God has spoken. For example, John tells us in Revelation 16:1 that he "heard a loud voice from the temple telling the seven angels, 'Go and pour out on the earth the seven bowls of wrath.'" The rest of the chapter is a description of the bowls that the angels pour out. The angels declare that the judgments that they are carrying out by God's direction are just: "Just are you, O Holy One, who is and who was, for you brought these judgments" (Rev. 16:5). Not only are these angels the means of the judgment, they are also involved in communicating the message of judgment to John (Rev. 17:1). As messengers, angels both participate in God's acts and deliver his messages.

In Deuteronomy 33:2, when Moses reflects on receiving the law from God at Sinai, he notes: "The LORD came from Sinai and dawned from Seir upon us; he shone forth from Mount Paran; he came from the ten thousands of holy ones," which indicates that the angels were present when Moses received the law from God.[1] There is an awareness of this tradition that is sometimes quite elaborate in the literature of the Second Temple. However, the New Testament also provides the correct details on this event in several texts. For example, when Stephen is rebuking the people for their persecutions, his speech ends with the accusation that the Jews had "received the law as delivered by angels and did not keep it" (Acts 7:53). Likewise, Paul writes to the Galatians that the law "was put in place through angels by an intermediary" (Gal. 3:19). The author of the book of Hebrews likewise warns against ignoring the gospel, given that the "message declared by angels proved to be reliable" (Heb. 2:2). So, it seems that God involved the angels in the giving of the law to his people Israel.

---

1. John R. Gilhooly. "Angels: Reconsidering the Septuagint Reading of Deuteronomy 33:2," *Journal of Septuagint and Cognate Studies* 50 (2017).

Angels are also the deliverers of prophetic messages. Sometimes, these are manifest in words of judgment or of glad tidings as mentioned above. In other cases, these prophetic words are more extensive. Daniel 10 records the arrival of an angelic messenger who recounts to Daniel the future history of the nations.

Ministers

Provision and Protection of God's People

Angels also have the duty of ministering to Christians. Hebrews 1:14 says, "Are they not all ministering spirits sent out to serve for the sake of those who are to inherit salvation?" In other words, the angels fulfill their ministerial duties (such as delivering the messages of God) for the sake of Christians. The Greek word for ministering is *leiturgos*, which is used in other contexts to refer to the roles that human beings play in the administration in the church (Rom. 15:16) or in the world (Rom. 13:6). There is not a tremendous amount of detail about how specifically angels minister on a regular basis, but in the Old Testament we have some specific examples of angels ministering to individuals. In 1 Kings 19:5–7, there is an account of Elijah the prophet hiding from Jezebel, in which an angel feeds him. We are told in Daniel 6:22 that "My God has sent his angel and shut the lions' mouths," and that the angels ministered to Daniel by protecting him because he was "blameless" before God. Angels protected the apostles as well by freeing them from prison (Acts 5:17; 12:5). They also directed the apostles where to go (Acts 8:26) and, on at least one occasion, directed a devout Gentile to the apostles so that he might hear the gospel (Acts 10). It may even be that angels carry the dead in Christ to dwell with him in the intermediate heaven (Luke 16:22)!

Service to Christ

In addition to their duty of ministering to Christians, angels are said specifically to minister to the needs of the Son. For example, after Jesus is tempted in the wilderness, the angels come and minister to him (Matt. 4:11). In Gethsemane, Jesus is not supported in prayer by his disciples, who fall asleep while on watch with him. As he prays to the Father, an angel comes to provide him strength (Luke 22:43). Nor is this angelic ministry to the Son isolated to his adult life in moments of temptation or suffering. Even when he was a child, the Father sent angels to protect Jesus and to direct Mary and Joseph in caring for him. It is an angel who warns Joseph to flee Herod's wrath (Matt. 2:13). When Peter defends Christ by violence in the garden, the Lord rebukes him by saying, "Do you think that I cannot appeal to my Father, and he will at once send me more than twelve legions of angels?" (Matt. 26:53). Further, the messages of good tidings that the angels brought about the birth of Christ are in service to his worth and glory.

Worship of God

The angels in heaven are ministers of praise and worship of God on his throne. In Isaiah 6:3, Isaiah describes the seraphim calling to one another, "Holy, holy, holy is the LORD of hosts; the whole earth is full of his glory!" Another angelic praise is recorded by John in Revelation 4:8, where the "living creatures" around the throne of God ceaselessly confess, "Holy, holy, holy, is the Lord God Almighty, who was and is and is to come!" John also tells us of angels saying, "Worthy is the Lamb who was slain, to receive power and wealth and wisdom and might and honor and glory and blessing!" (Rev. 5:11–12). Sometimes, people describe these kinds of scenes as choirs of angels singing anthems to God, but Scripture does not generally use the verb "to sing" (Hebrew: *shir*; Greek: *psallo, hymnos*) in describing their activity.[2] Regardless of the timbre of these confessions, they are properly understood as confessions of praise to God.

Army of Heaven

Angels are described in both the Old and New Testaments as a heavenly army. Often, the angels are the reason that Israel is able to overcome its enemies in battle. In some cases, a single angel is described as leading the people, whereas at other times the whole army of heaven is depicted. In both cases, the duty of protection is in view.

Angel before You

A repeated formula in the Old Testament is God's promise to the people that he will send his "angel before" them. This duty of leadership, protection, and direction is seen to be an important function of the angels as a result. Abraham tells his servant in Genesis 24:7 that God "will send his angel before you." The Lord makes this promise himself to the Israelites in Exodus 23:20: "Behold, I send an angel before you, to guard you on the way and to bring you to the place that I have prepared." Already, Exodus 14:19–20 stated that "the angel of God who as going before the host of Israel moved and went behind them, and the pillar of cloud moved from before them and stood behind them, coming between the host of Egypt and the host of Israel." Angels serve as guardians for God's people.

Angelic Warriors

Angels sometimes fight on behalf of God's people in Scripture. A famous example of this duty is found in 2 Kings 6:16–20, when Elisha answered his

---

2. An exception might be Job 38:7: "when the morning stars sang (*be'ran*) together and all the sons of God shouted for joy?" The word comes from the root *ranan*, which is "to cry out." Many English translations render this word as "sang," but the textual basis for such a decision is weak.

servant, "'Do not be afraid, for those who are with us are more than those who are with them.' Then Elisha prayed and said, 'O LORD, please open his eyes that he may see.' So the LORD opened the eyes of the young man, and he saw, and behold, the mountain was full of horses and chariots of fire all around Elisha." These naturally invisible figures do not actually partake in the battle (in fact, there is no battle), but they give comfort to Elisha and his servant with their presence. Later, in 2 Kings, it is reported that "the angel of the LORD went out and struck down 185,000 in the camp of the Assyrians" (19:35; cf. 2 Chron. 32:20). At other times, the angels are sent against the people as a punishment (2 Sam. 24:16–17). The angels, then, are used sometimes as an expression of God's anger: "He let loose on them his burning anger, wrath, indignation, and distress, a company of destroying angels" (Ps. 78:49). John describes a vision of Michael and his angels fighting against Satan and the demons in a war in heaven (Rev. 12:7–8). The "legions of angels" stand ready to service Christ (Matt. 26:53). Such legions are organized in heaven (1 Kings 22:19)

Summary

Angels serve God as his messengers, but this duty expresses itself in a variety of ways. Angels deliver messages of hope, prophecy, law, and judgment. Chiefly, they now serve Christians according to Hebrews 1:14: "Are they not all ministering spirits sent forth to serve for the sake of those who are to obtain salvation?" This service probably manifests itself in certain divine protections and in the joy angels find in the salvation of the lost (Luke 15:10). Of course, because angels are spirits, they may frequently be serving God in ways that we do not even recognize.

REFLECTION QUESTIONS

1. What is the basic meaning of the word "angel"?

2. What are some various ways that angels serve as God's messengers?

3. How does the heavenly army relate to the angel's duties?

4. What role do angels play in divine judgment?

5. How might reflecting on the angels lead us to worship God?

Do Believers Have Guardian Angels?

M any religions hold that there are lesser celestial or angelic beings who keep watch over individual people. Indeed, a strain of this belief has been part of Christian theology since at least the third century. The biblical evidence for such beings is quite limited, however. The only text that may give ground for a belief in personal, guardian angels is found in Matthew's account of the gospel. In Matthew 18:10, Jesus says, "See that you do not despise one of these little ones. For I tell you that in heaven their angels [*angeloi*] always see the face of my Father who is in heaven." The fact Jesus speaks of their angels in heaven is thought to support the idea angels watch over individual people. Nevertheless, even if this text should be understood to support a belief in guardian angels, it tells us nothing about what these angels do.

Guardians and Tempters

The common folk idea that each person has an angel to guard them and a demon to tempt them is a literary fancy for which there is no biblical support.[1] There are some surprisingly early expositions of such doctrine in early nonbiblical Christian texts, however. For example, the Shepherd of Hermas (AD 150) teaches that each person has two angels, one good and one evil, and gives instruction on how to tell the difference between them. Both angels can "work in" a person. Evil desires are attributed to the working of the evil angel, and virtuous thoughts are attributed to the angel of righteousness.[2] Another early work, the Epistle to Barnabas, describes the angels as protectors of the way of light, and the angels of Satan as the guardians of the way

---

1. There are elliptical references to such beings in other religious texts (e.g., the Qur'an).
2. Michael W. Holmes, ed., *The Apostolic Fathers: Greek Texts and English Translations*, 3rd ed. (Grand Rapids: Baker Academic, 2007), 523–24.

of darkness.[3] In some cases, these references seem to be metaphorical ways of describing the "two ways," which seems to be primarily a reflection on the wide and narrow gates (Matt. 7:13–14). "Two Ways" discourse is common in the literature of the late-first- and early-second-century Christian writings, but the guardian-and-tempter idea is not. However, the idea of an angelic guide is somewhat common. For example, Origen writes in his First Principles that "every human soul is put in subjection to some angel."[4] Similar ideas are found in later nonbiblical Jewish literature, as well as in other religions.

Matthew 18:10

As we have seen, speculation about guardian angels abounds, but most of the speculation greatly outpaces what could be shown from Scripture. In fact, Matthew 18:10 is the only text that might give ground for a belief in personal angels, but it is a difficult text that does not go into any details.[5]

First, there is not another text in Scripture that could reasonably be used to support a belief in guardian angels. There are certainly texts that suggest that a particular angel has looked out for a particular person at a particular time. For an example, an angel protects Daniel in the lions' den (Dan. 6:22); and another angel protects Shadrach, Meshach, and Abednego in the fiery furnace (Dan. 3:28). But, only in Matthew 18 do we have a statement that might imply that all believers have a guardian angel. Some commentators hold that "these little ones" refers not to the disciples but to children. Their reasoning is that Jesus had just invited a child into the midst of the disciples (Matt. 18:2). It seems better to understand the referent as the disciples of Jesus for several reasons. First, the phrase "these little ones" requires a plural referent, but the text is explicit that Jesus has invited a child (singular) into their midst. Second, the word that Jesus uses (*mikroi*) is different than the earlier word that he uses for children (*paideia*). Third, Jesus' comments here come in the midst of his teaching about the church, and it is common for Jesus and his apostles to refer to Christians as "little ones" or as "children," especially if they are recent converts (Matt. 10:42; 1 John 2). Fourth, the disciples of the Messiah are referred to as "little ones" by Zechariah (13:7). So, "little ones" probably refers to disciples of Jesus in this text.[6]

---

3. Ibid., 433–34.
4. Origen, *Peri Archon* I.5.4.
5. There is one other text that is occasionally cited, Acts 12:15. However, this text merely records a response of some disciples to the incredulous story that Rhoda tells them. Because there is not a narrational endorsement of the idea, there is no ground for building a doctrine from it.
6. "The little ones of 18.10 are not literal children but believers" (W. C. Davies and D. C. Allison, *Matthew 8–18*, International Critical Commentary [London: Bloomsbury, 2004], 771).

If that is right, we still might wonder who "their angels" are? We are not given much detail. Many commentaries note Jewish belief in the notion of guardian angels, but these ideas are relatively late (later than the writing of Matthew, in most cases). Even in such supposedly cognate texts, there is no clear doctrine about the activity of these angels. It seems better to understand the reference that Jesus makes here in terms of the overall purpose of his teaching, which is that the disciples matter greatly to the Father. The reference to the angels is meant to accomplish this rhetorical purpose. An important text to keep in mind in that regard is Hebrews 1:14, which notes that the angels are "ministering spirits sent out to serve for the sake of those who are to inherit salvation." The later speculations about how the angels operate and how they "guard" believers find no basis in either of these texts. However, the fact that God cares for his children is manifest in that the angels rejoice in salvation (Luke 15:10), carry the faithful departed to heaven (Luke 16:22), and desire to watch the gospel unfold (1 Peter 1:12).

We cannot infer from these events, however, that all believers have an angel nearby to guard them, or that each has his or her own personal angel.

Some Christians have taken great comfort in the idea that an angel was close by to guide them or protect them from harm. Many Christian books record stories about angelic guardians. Certainly, the accounts are amazing. However, it is a mistake to overlook the promises that God has given us about his own presence to comfort and guide Christians. Since such promises are explicit and repeated in Scripture, we should spend less time speculating about guardian angels and more time reflecting on God's promises. Christ himself has said, "I am with you always" (Matt. 28:20). He is all the guardian one needs.

Summary

Matthew 18:10 is the only textual evidence that might promote the belief in guardian angels. However, it is not the point of the text to teach us about guardian angels; so, even if it implies that some angels are assigned as guardians, it tells us nothing about them. Attempts to infer from specific instances of angelic protection in the narratives of Scripture are likewise no basis for concluding either that we have guardian angels or that we do not. Given such weak textual witness, the focus on guardian angels should be considered interesting from a historical standpoint but should not receive significant emphasis in our teaching or Christian walk.

REFLECTION QUESTIONS

1. Why do people seem to desire guardian angels?

2. How would you evaluate a story you read about guardian angels?

3. Does the fact that God has sent angels to protect some people give us reason to think that all believers have a guardian angel?

4. Why should we be careful about theological ideas that are richly developed in tradition but limited in biblical warrant?

5. Is it surprising that Matthew 18 is the only biblical proof-text for guardian angels?

Who Is the Angel of the Lord?

Some scholars hold that there is a mysterious figure called the "angel of the Lord" in the Old Testament who appears and reappears in its pages. Furthermore, these scholars disagree about who he is. Some argue that he is God; others argue that he is the Word or preincarnate Christ; and others argue that he is simply an angel. One challenge for all of these positions is that they all assume that there is just one individual known by the title "the Angel of the Lord," and this assumption is mistaken.[1]

A bit of Hebrew grammar is necessary to see the error clearly. In Hebrew, there is a common grammatical construction called a "construct phrase." In a construct phrase, two nouns are set side by side and have a possessive relationship. For example, the Hebrew phrase *mal'akh Yahweh* consists of the two nouns *mal'akh*, which means messenger or angel, and *Yahweh* which is God's name. The construct phrase is translated "the angel of the Lord." Translators need to add some words that do not appear in the Hebrew text because Hebrew and English have different grammatical rules. In particular, in English, we add the definite article "the" to the phrase. Unfortunately, this addition can give the impression that the phrase "the angel of the Lord" serves as someone's name or title. The "the" in the phrase really just means "the one in question at this time." In other words, it is not correct to assume that "the angel of the Lord" always refers to the same person.

Consider a different construct phrase in Hebrew, *ebed Yahweh*. *Ebed* means "servant," so this phrase translates to "the servant of the Lord." This is a description that is used of both Moses (Deut. 34:5) and Joshua (Judg. 2:8).

---

1. There is a long tradition of scholars asserting without argument that each instance of the phrase refers to the same unique personage; for example, Daniel Finestone, in "Is the Angel of Jehovah in the Old Testament the Lord Jesus Christ?" *Bibliotheca Sacra* 95, no. 379 (1938): 373. He writes, "Other designations of the Angel of Jehovah are found in the names 'The Angel of His Presence,' 'Mine Angel,' 'The Angel of God,' all *doubtless* referring to the same Divine Being" (emphasis added).

Now, no one concludes that Moses is Joshua. They are two different people, yet both are *ebed Yahweh*, "the servant of the Lord." Likewise, more than one figure is called *mal'akh Yahweh*, "the angel of the Lord."

In fact, in Haggai 1:13, Haggai is referred to as *mal'akh Yahweh* in the Hebrew text, but English translations inadvertently disguise this fact. Because the word *mal'akh* can mean messenger or angel, the translator has to decide the appropriate choice whenever translating the word. Because Haggai is clearly not an angel, the phrase *mal'akh Yahweh* in Haggai 1:13 comes into our English translations as "the messenger of the Lord." Now, no one concludes from this that Haggai is the only messenger of the Lord. Rather, we understand that he is the messenger that the text is talking about at that moment. If *mal'akh Yahweh* served as a title for one specific individual, then we would have to conclude that Haggai was the Angel of the Lord. Just as it would be wrong to conclude that Haggai was an angel, so we are wrong to conclude that the phrase *mal'akh Yahweh* always refers to the same person.

What these two examples show is that determining whom the phrase "the angel of the Lord" refers to must be determined on a case-by-case basis. In fact, we should not assume that there is any one particular person who is "the Angel of the Lord." However, it could well be that the phrase often refers to the same figure. After all, *ebed Yahweh* most often refers to Moses even though it does not exclusively refer to him. Likewise, *mal'akh Yahweh* may sometimes refer to the same entity. With this important corrective in mind, we can examine the main positions that scholars hold in response to the question, "Who is the angel of the Lord?"

Major Interpretive Theories

There are three main theories:[2]

1. *Identification Theory:* The Angel of the Lord is a phenomenon through which God appears in the Old Testament (theophany).[3]

---

2. A fourth theory holds that *mal'akh Yahweh* was added to texts that originally just had the word *Yahweh* as Jewish theology became more abstract. See Marie-Joseph Lagrange, "L'ange De Iahve," *Revue Biblique* 12 (1903): 212–25. I will not consider this theory below because it seems unduly suspicious about the theological sensibilities of the authors of Scripture. Some scholars hold that the "insertion" of *mal'akh* is not an interpolation but rather a euphemism. Stephen L. White, "Angel of the Lord: Messenger or Euphemism?" *Tyndale Bulletin* 50, no. 2 (1999): 299–305.
3. Andrew S. Malone, "Distinguishing the Angel of the Lord," *Bulletin for Biblical Research* 21, no. 3 (2011): 297–314, defends this view.

2. *Logos Theory:* The Angel of the Lord is the Second Person of the Trinity. This view is sometimes called the preincarnate Christ view.[4] This view agrees with the Identification Theory that the figure in question is divine, but specifies that the Angel of the Lord is the appearance of the Son in the Old Testament.

3. *Representation Theory:* The angel of the Lord is an angelic legate of God. In other words, he is just one of God's angels.[5]

All this debate is summarized in James Moyer's conclusion that "there is no consensus" on the correct identification among biblical scholars.[6]

Identification Theory

This theory holds that the angel of the Lord is God himself. The arguments in favor of this interpretation are based on texts in which the angel of the Lord says things that only God could say while using first-person pronouns (like, "I" or "me") without introducing the discourse with a prophetic formula (e.g., "thus says the Lord"). For example, in Exodus 3:2–6, we read:

> And the angel of the LORD appeared to him in a flame of fire out of the midst of a bush. He looked, and behold, the bush was burning, yet it was not consumed. And Moses said, "I will turn aside to see this great sight, why the bush is not burned." When the Lord saw that he turned aside to see, God called to him out of the bush, "Moses, Moses!" And he said, "Here I am." Then he said, "Do not come near; take your sandals off your feet, for the place on which you are standing is holy ground." And he said, "I am the God of your father, the God of Abraham, the God of Isaac, and the God of Jacob." And Moses hid his face, for he was afraid to look at God.[7]

---

4. See, for example, James A. Borland, *Christ in the Old Testament* (Chicago: Moody, 1978). I will refrain from the preincarnate Christ language. See note 10.

5. René López, "Identifying the 'Angel of the Lord' in the Book of Judges: A Model for Reconsidering the Referent in the Other Old Testament Loci," *Bulletin for Biblical Research* 20, no. 1 (2010): 1–18.

6. James C. Moyer, *Evangelical Dictionary of Theology*, ed. Walter A. Elwell (Grand Rapids: Baker, 1984), 1087.

7. Though this text is often used to support the identification theory, it seems strange that Moses (the author) would introduce *mal'akh Yahweh* if he intended to communicate that Yahweh was present (physically? spiritually? by legate?) in the bush. Of course, strangeness is hardly a determinative objection.

In this text, *mal'akh Yahweh* appears to Moses in the bush, and then God calls to Moses out of the bush. Furthermore, Moses reacts as if he is in danger of seeing God. These two observations reinforce the idea that the angel of the Lord is God. The idea here is that the angel of the Lord could not speak as if he was God unless he was actually God.

One reason that theologians reject the Identification Theory is that the Old Testament teaches that no one will see God and live (Exod. 33:11). This objection to the Identification Theory is not decisive, as the angel of the Lord could be an attenuated vision of God, which is consistent with visions of the divine in the Old Testament (Exod. 24:11; Isa. 6:1–6).[8] A much stronger objection is that there are numerous instances in the Old Testament in which someone speaks as if he was God without using an introductory formula (e.g., "thus says the Lord").[9] So, the fact that the angel speaks as if he is God is not enough to prove that he is God. Furthermore, what this means is that most instances of the phrase *mal'akh Yahweh* that would support the Identification Theory would support the Representation Theory just as well. Furthermore, the truly decisive objection is that Stephen the martyr understands Exodus 3 to be the appearance of an angel (Acts 7:30).

Another difficulty for the Identification Theory is Zechariah 1:12: "Then, the angel of the LORD (*mal'akh Yahweh*) said, 'O LORD of hosts (*yahweh tsabaoth*), how long will you have no mercy on Jerusalem and the cities of Judah, against which you have been angry these seventy years?'" In this text, the angel of the Lord and the Lord of hosts are clearly distinguished from each other, because the angel of the Lord speaks to the Lord of hosts. Therefore, the argument is that the angel of the Lord cannot be God because the angel of the Lord speaks to God in Zechariah. Although the Identification Theory remains popular, there are some substantial objections to it.

Logos Theory

Another popular theory holds that the angel of the Lord is the Word of God.[10] This theory has two main advantages. First, this theory explains how one can see God and live (because one can see Christ and live).[11] As a result, it avoids the first

---

8. As Andrew Malone rightly argues in "Distinguishing the Angel of the Lord," *Bulletin for Biblical Research* 21, no. 3 (2011): 309–10.

9. For example, see 2 Kings 20:35 (the unintroduced message of the prophets is identified with the voice of the Lord); 1 Samuel 10:1–8 (Samuel's anointing of Saul is equated with the Lord's anointing); or Deuteronomy 29:2–6 (Moses freely transitions from third- to first-person speech about the Lord). Furthermore, a *mal'akh Yahweh* sometimes introduces divine discourse *with* a messenger or prophetic formula (Zech. 3:6–7).

10. Referring to this theory as the Logos Theory is preferable to the terminology usually put forward in the phrase "preincarnate Christ." This phrase could easily be misunderstood to ascribe humanity to the Son prior to his conception in Mary. See Duane Garrett's helpful caution on this point in *Angels and the New Spirituality* (Nashville: B&H, 1995), 22.

11. See John 1:18; 14:9.

objection against the Identification Theory noted above. Second, the argument goes, this theory helps explain Zechariah 1:12. If the angel of the Lord is the Son, then he can speak as God while still speaking to God (the Father). Hence, this theory arguably avoids two major objections to the Identification Theory.

Nevertheless, as noted above, the Old Testament authors are comfortable discussing visions and apprehensions (aural and visual) of God. Therefore, the objection from Exodus 33:11 is not persuasive against the Identification Theory. Hence, the fact that the Logos Theory avoids this objection is weak support for subscribing to the Logos Theory. With respect to the second advantage, the fact that the Son can address the Father is hardly reason to construe the angel of the Lord in Zechariah 1:12 as the Son. In fact, such an identification seems little more than an ad hoc attempt to rescue the Identification Theory from the problems that Zechariah 1:12 creates for it. Unless we had strong reasons to believe that there was one self-same figure "the Angel of the Lord" who was divine, we would have no reason to construe Zechariah 1:12 as the divine Son addressing the Father. Since we have already seen that Hebrew grammar does not support the belief that there is one self-same figure called "the Angel of the Lord," this reading of Zechariah 1:12 is untenable. In fact, it introduces difficulties into the text because it requires that the angel mentioned in verses 13 and 14 be a different figure from the angel of the Lord. However, that means that in verse 12 the angel of the Lord asks the Lord a question, and that the Lord answers a different figure. It is simpler to understand the angel of the Lord in this text to be one of God's many angels. The Logos Theory might be persuasive because we have a desire to find Jesus in the Old Testament, but such desire should not cause us to believe that the eternal Son of God appeared as an angel prior to his Incarnation. We would need some textual evidence for this view, which is lacking.

Another major plank in the Logos Theory is the claim that the angel of the Lord does not appear in the New Testament.[12] In other words, there is no *mal'akh Yahweh* in the New Testament. According to the Logos Theory, his absence is explained by the fact that the eternal Son has now come in the flesh as the definitive revelation of God. The problem with this claim is that it is simply false. Again, the main evidence is grammatical. In English, we frequently find references in the New Testament to "an angel of the Lord." This phrase is the translation of the Greek phrase *angelos kuriou*. Under normal circumstances, this phrase would only be translated into English as "the angel of the Lord" if there were some additional words in Greek. Unlike Hebrew, Greek does not make use of the construct phrase, so the same rules do not apply that affected the translation of *mal'akh Yahweh*. However, it is well attested by grammarians that the phrase *angelos kuriou* is a Septuagintism. In other words, it reflects the Greek used in the Greek translation of the Old

---

12. See James A. Borland, *Christ in the Old Testament* (Chicago: Moody, 1978).

Testament Hebrew. In the Septuagint, the translators render the Hebrew construct phrase *malakh Yahweh* (the angel of the Lord) as the Greek phrase *angelos kuriou*. So, if—as the Logos proponents believe—*malakh Yahweh* is a title, then consistency requires that *angelos kuriou* be rendered definite ("the angel of the Lord") because the Greek phrase is a translation of the Hebrew usage.[13] If the Greek just is a translation of the Hebrew, then we should translate them either as definite or indefinite consistently. Hence, "the" angel of the Lord appears frequently in the New Testament after all.[14]

Of course, as we saw, it is misguided to translate *malakh Yahweh* as "the angel of the Lord" in every instance of the Old Testament. Neither does the Old Testament teach that there is one self-same figure known by that title. What the Septuagintal Greek usage shows us is that, even if the phrase always referred to the same entity, the Logos theory would still be mistaken. The angel of the Lord cannot be the "preincarnate" Word of God because it is *angelos kuriou* (i.e., *malakh Yahweh*) who rescues Peter from prison (Acts 12:7). By the time of the event described in Acts, Christ had already ascended, and it would clearly be inaccurate to refer to Jesus as an angel. Furthermore, the angel that speaks to the women at the tomb is *angelos kuriou* (Matt. 28:2)! Surely, the Logos did not return to open the tomb of the dead and risen Christ to deliver the message, "Do not be afraid, for I know that you seek Jesus who was crucified" (Matt. 28:5). Consider also that it is *angelos kuriou* who tells Joseph not to be afraid to marry Mary (Matt. 1:20). Are we really to think that the preincarnate Word spoke to Joseph about the incarnate Word then growing within Mary's womb?

The textual evidence simply does not support the *Logos* Theory. If we accept the view that there is one self-same figure entitled the angel of the Lord in the Old Testament, such acceptance weakens the argument for the *Logos* Theory tremendously.[15]

---

13. W. D. Davies and D. C. Allison concur, writing: "The absence of the articles is a Septuagintism reflecting the Hebrew construct state" (*A Critical and Exegetical Commentary on the Gospel According to Saint Matthew*, 3 vols., International Critical Commentary [London: T&T Clark, 2004], 1:206).

14. "One of the many theologically significant constructions is *angelos kuriou* (cf. Matt 1:20; 28:2; Luke 2:9; Acts 12:7; Gal 4:14 [*angelos kuriou*]). In the LXX this is the normal phrase used to translate *malakh Yahweh* ('the angel of the Lord'). The NT exhibits the same phenomenon, prompting Nigel Turner to suggest that '*angelos kuriou* is not an angel but the angel [of the Lord].' Indeed, although most scholars treat *angelos kuriou* in the NT as 'an angel of the Lord,' there is no linguistic basis for doing so. Apart from theological argument, it is most probable that *angelos kuriou* is the angel of the Lord in the NT and is to be identified with the angel of the Lord of the OT" (Daniel B. Wallace, *Greek Grammar Beyond the Basics: An Exegetical Syntax of the New Testament* [Grand Rapids: Zondervan, 1996], 252). The reference to "Turner" is to Nigel Turner, *Syntax*, vol. 3, *A Grammar of New Testament Greek* (Edinburgh: T&T Clark, 1906), 180. Notice that Wallace seems to grant that there is just one figure "*the* Angel of the Lord" in the Old Testament.

15. For forceful presentations of theological arguments against this view, see W. G. MacDonald, "Christology and 'The Angel of the Lord,'" in *Current Issues in Biblical and Patristic*

Representation Theory

As a result, the Representation Theory is the strongest view. It holds that there is, as far as we know, no particular figure known by the title "the Angel of the Lord," and that this phrase generally refers to one of God's angels. This position has the advantage of not arguing beyond what exegesis can demonstrate in instances of the phrase *mal'akh Yahweh* in terms of Hebrew grammar and usage in the Old Testament. There may be instances in which something more is going on, but we would need to evaluate those arguments on a case-by-case basis. It is best to conclude that the angel of the Lord refers to one of God's many angels.

Summary

There are three primary theories among evangelicals about who the angel of the Lord is: (1) Yahweh, (2) the *Logos*, and (3) an angelical legate. The most likely theory is that *mal'akh Yahweh* is merely an angel who represents God. Of course, the best approach to this question would be a careful consideration of each instance of this figure in the Old Testament. Our question should not be "Who is the Angel of the Lord?" so much as, "to whom does the phrase *mal'akh Yahweh* refer in this particular text?"

REFLECTION QUESTIONS

1. How does understanding the original languages help illuminate this discussion?

2. Why is it significant that we interpret these texts rightly?

3. How might a desire to see Jesus in Old Testament texts influence one's interpretation?

4. What surprised you most about the discussion in this chapter?

5. Why is an awareness of translation issues helpful in interpreting the Bible well?

Interpretation: Studies in Honor of Merrill C. Tenney Presented by His Former Students (Grand Rapids: Eerdmans, 1975). If the angel of the Lord is the Son of God, it is curious that none of the New Testament texts that make mention of the eternality of the Son make mention of his appearing under such a guise.

Who Are the "Sons of God" in Genesis 6?

A tradition of late Jewish interpretation teaches that the "sons of God" mentioned in Genesis 6 are angels who are subsequently punished for producing offspring with the daughters of men. Some early Christian writers borrowed from this tradition in their explanation of the passage as well, so that it is common to identify the sons of God in the passage with angels even today. However, another Christian tradition holds that the sons of God are kings or descendants of the line of Seth. In this chapter, I will discuss the arguments for these various interpretations.

Genesis 6:1–4

The text of Genesis 6 in question is brief and sparse in detail. It reads:

> When man began to multiply on the face of the land and daughters were born to them, the sons of God saw that the daughters of man were attractive. And they took as their wives any they chose. Then the Lord said, "My Spirit will not abide in man forever, for he is flesh: his days shall be 120 years." The Nephilim were on the earth in those days, and also afterward, when the sons of God came in to the daughters of man and they bore children to them. These were the mighty men who were of old, the men of renown. (vv. 1–4)

One of the larger questions about this text is who the "sons of God" are. Because the phrase "sons of God" is used elsewhere in Hebrew to refer to angelic or heavenly beings, some interpreters understand the sons of God to be angels. Hence, this text is describing a situation in which angels found human women (daughters of man) attractive, came down from heaven, married, and had offspring with them. Usually, on this interpretation, the Nephilim are the offspring of these angelic/human pairings. The largest problem with this interpretation is that, while later Jewish retellings of Genesis 6 link the Nephilim with the offspring of the angelic/human liaisons, there is no grammatical or semantic connection in Genesis 6 that would allow that conclusion. Furthermore, the "sons of God" and even "gods" can also refer to human beings, in particular those in Israel (Deut. 32:8; Hos. 1:10). If we take the brief comment in Genesis 6 to be a continuance of the tragic genealogy of Genesis 5, then the intermarrying between faithful men and unfaithful women becomes the explanation for the widespread depravity of man prior to the flood (Gen. 6:5).

Book of Enoch

The Jewish tradition represented by the book of Enoch elaborates this story for thirty-six chapters, which is referred to as the Book of the Watchers. The Book of the Watchers recounts that the angels saw the human daughters of the men whom God had created and "lusted after them, and said one to another: 'Come, let us choose us wives from among the children of men and beget us children'" (1 Enoch 6:2). A consequence of these illicit unions was the birth of giants (Nephilim) who eventually turned on their human parents and fought against them. Actually, it is in consequence of these unions and the bloodshed that follows that God declares that he will destroy the world by flood, and he sends his holy angels to bind all the angels that took human wives. Most scholars see this section of the book of Enoch as a late interpretation and expansion of Genesis 6, which calls these fallen angels "Watchers" (cf. Dan. 4:17) and considers them to be the origin of demons. There are several versions of these stories in other Second Temple literature that resemble Greek myths as well.

The most obvious problem with the interpretation given by Enoch is that it is not an interpretation of Genesis 6. Rather, it is an imaginative elaboration whose purpose is to provide an account of the origin of evil in the world. Other Second Temple literature is similarly interested in questions of theodicy. Even if it is correct to identify the sons of God with angels, there is actually nothing in the Genesis text that suggests that the Nephilim are the children of the unions between the angels and the daughters of men. Rather than taking our cue from a later Jewish tradition, we should focus attention on the text of Genesis 6:1–4. At best, 1 Enoch gives us a later attempt to deal with a difficult and cryptic passage of the Bible, but there is no reason to suppose that the Enochic interpretation is valid.

New Testament Use of Enochic Tradition

Some see this kind of dismissal of Enoch as too hasty; many scholars argue that the tradition represented in the book of Enoch was recognized and accepted by New Testament authors. In particular, two New Testament texts are often cited in support of these claims: 2 Peter 2:4 and Jude 6.

To see the line of reasoning, we can begin with Jude verses 14–15: "It was also about these that Enoch, the seventh from Adam, prophesied, saying, 'Behold, the Lord comes with ten thousands of his holy ones, to execute judgment on all and to convict all the ungodly of all their deeds of ungodliness that they have committed in such an ungodly way, and of all the harsh things that ungodly sinners have spoken against him.'"

These verses establish some relationship between the Enochic tradition and Jude's writings because 1 Enoch contains a very similar prophesy in 1:9. The "citation" from Jude is not verifiably verbatim (since the textual witness of Enoch is particularly complicated—existing in various forms and fragments in three languages with dates of composition ranging over hundreds of years) but the fact that Jude seemingly refers to the same prophecy as 1 Enoch has been a source of consternation toward the book of Jude since the second century. For the purpose of understanding the argument here, we need only to see that the similarity between Jude 14–15 and 1 Enoch 1:9 is sufficient to conclude that Jude is aware of the tradition represented by Enoch.

On this basis, the tradition represented in Enoch is understood to be the background for the event that Jude references in verse 6 ("And the angels who did not stay within their own position of authority, but left their proper dwelling . . ."). In other words, Jude is referring here to the event in which the angels left heaven to pursue sexual relations with human women. The context of verse 7 supposedly supports this interpretation because the phrase "in like manner" in verse 7 is interpreted to mean that the sin of Sodom and Gomorrah (sexual immorality) is the same type of sin committed by the angels. This would be consistent with the theme of the Enochic elaboration of Genesis 6.

In the context of Peter's warning about the condemnation of false teachers, he references God's pattern of judgment in a way similar to Jude. One of the examples that he refers to is God's not sparing of the angels when they sinned. He writes: "God did not spare the angels when they sinned, but cast them into hell and committed them to chains of gloomy darkness to be kept until judgment" (2 Peter 2:4). This is followed by references to the judgment during the time of Noah, and the judgment of Sodom and Gomorrah. The argument is that this first, surprising reference to angels is a reference to the judgment of angels that took place before the flood. Hence, the argument is that Peter is referring to the Enochic tradition in which the angels who sinned with the daughters of men were punished at that time and are now awaiting final judgment. Since 2 Peter and Jude are thought to have a strong literary relationship, Jude's putative reference to the book of Enoch is sufficient to suggest that both Jude and Peter in some measure endorse the Enochic account of the fall of the angels (which is based on the book of Enoch's elaboration of Gen. 6:1–4). This argument has been persuasive to many commentators.

However, there are several reasons to be suspicious about the elaborate interpretation of 2 Peter 2:4 and Jude 6 given above. First, the citation (paraphrase would be a better word) of 1 Enoch 1:9 in Jude 14–15 is not an endorsement of the total content of the book of Enoch any more than Paul's citation of Epimenides is an endorsement of all that poet wrote (notice that Paul calls the man a "prophet," Titus 1:12). Furthermore, Jude makes no reference to the book of Enoch in his reference to the angelic sin (Jude 6). Finally, neither 2 Peter nor Jude mention anything about the nature of the trespass committed by the angels. Second Peter reads merely that they "sinned," whereas Jude mentions that they "did not keep" their dwelling (cf. John 8:44). The nature of the sin is not relevant to their literary purpose. Even if it was, the Book of the Watchers in 1 Enoch would remain a late elaboration of Genesis 6:1–4 that contradicts the account of other such elaborations in the Jewish tradition (cf. Jubilees 4:15–22). Since a nonbiblical book should not be the primary exegetical guide for Genesis, we should focus our attempt to identify the "sons of God" on the biblical text itself. It is sufficient to note that "sons of God" often refers to angels in the Hebrew Bible and that this fact is sufficient to give rise to a multitude of later Jewish stories about Genesis 6. What is more challenging for this view, finally, is that Genesis 6 reads that sons of God "took wives," which is foreign to angels (Matt. 22:30).

Second Peter 2 and Jude merely commit us to the view that in the past the angels sinned and will be judged finally in the last day for their rebellion. The fact that they refer to stock examples of divine judgment that are also registered in Jewish traditions is not itself sufficient reason to believe that 2 Peter 2 and Jude accepted the full content of those nonbiblical books.

Sons of God

It is also true, however, that "sons of God" also refers to men in the Hebrew Bible, in particular kings (Ps. 82) and judges or Israel (Deut. 32:5, 8; Hos. 1:10). Hence, another interpretation of "sons of God" holds that it refers to a particular group of men descended from Seth, who called on the name of the Lord (Gen. 4:26). Traditions dating to a similar period of the first "angelic" translations understand the figures to be human royalty (*Targum Onkelos*). So, the angelic language is not considered determinative by the earliest interpreters. Furthermore, while associating a putative angelic sexual sin with the flood is common in Second Temple writings, it is not obvious in the Genesis text. In fact, the intermarrying of the godly with the ungodly seems merely to be a recapitulation of sin consistent with the picture of Genesis 5. Hence, the picture here is humans reproducing until the time of the flood (Matt. 24:38–39). The connection to 2 Peter and Jude is clear here: The judgment of God is guaranteed and falls swiftly on the wicked, but the righteous are delivered. Perhaps, some of these men (the "sons of God") acted under the compulsion or authority of angels (see Luke 22:3; John 13:27), but Moses does not say.

Summary

Though historically popular because of the book of Enoch, the identification of the "sons of God" with angels is not a convincing reading of the Genesis text. Although it is true that "sons of God" often refers to angels in Hebrew, it does not always. The immediate context of the passage, especially Genesis 5, together with the mention made of this period of history in Matthew 24, make it more likely that the "sons of God" is a reference to the "righteous" Sethite line.

REFLECTION QUESTIONS

1. What are the main reasons for holding the "sons of God" to be angels?

2. How is the book of Enoch related to this interpretation?

3. Does Jude's citation of a book mean that he endorsed all of its teachings?

4. How does Matthew 22 inform our understanding of sons of God taking wives?

5. How does Matthew 24 inform our understanding of Genesis 6:1–4?

Questions Related to Demons

Should We Study Demonology?

In a word, "yes." In three, "yes, but carefully." Demons are real, and they are hateful and want to destroy mankind and disrupt God's purposes. As such, we need to recognize these facts so that we can withstand them. On the other hand, intensive study or focus on demons and their activities places an undue priority on them and their power. As such, we need to proceed carefully in investigating this part of theology.

Types of Demonology

It is important to distinguish between different types of demonology. In the first place, there is the type of demonology that belongs to angelology and thereby to Christian theology. The source material for study of this type of demonology is the Bible and what it says about the dark powers. The data given is quite limited. Another type of demonology belongs to occult practices, speculations, and witchcrafts of various kinds. The source material for study of this type comes from a mixture of folk beliefs, syncretic religious ideologies, demonic inspiration, and anecdote. The second type of demonology should not be studied by Christians (or anyone), whereas the first type is a necessary part of a whole-Bible theology. A third type of demonology is historical or sociological study about what people believe about demons, spirit beings, magic, rituals, and so on. This type of study is a significant part of cultural analysis and is important for historians, sociologists, missionaries, and evangelists.

Bible-Based Demonology

At first glance, it may seem that we ought as well leave demonology alone. After all, demons are wicked and scary. Wouldn't it be better to just not think of them at all and focus on better things? There is some wisdom in this caution. Certainly, we should not expect demonology to be a substantial portion of our theology or to arrest our attention for too long. Curiosity can lead to fascination, which often leads to investigation of the issue according to the occult-based demonology. However, the Bible speaks about the demons, so our theology must reflect what it says. Paul tells Timothy that "All Scripture is breathed out by God and profitable for teaching, for reproof, for correction, and for training in righteousness" (2 Tim. 3:16). Our theology should embrace that teaching and develop according to its logic.

The main caution that we receive about demons in Scripture requires that we know something about them. We are told to avoid the schemes of the Devil (2 Cor. 2:11; Eph. 6:11). Paul could not say this unless we knew what his schemes were. Of course, the biblical authors provide examples of the nature and type of schemes that the Devil and his angels use: temptation (Gen. 3:1–7; Matt. 4:1–11), in particular to lust (1 Cor. 7:5), pride (James 3:15), and deception (Acts 5:3); false teachers (2 Cor. 11:13–15; 1 Tim. 4:1); and false religions and beliefs (1 Cor. 10:20; Rev. 9:20). His main scheme is lying and deception (John 8:44; Rev. 12:9).

Part of a healthy approach to a Bible-based demonology, however, is the recognition that the Bible does not tell us much about demons or occult practice. The biblical authors focus on what is true and not primarily on what is false. No biblical author commands us to seek knowledge about demons specifically; to attempt to learn their names, locations, or occupations; to seek opportunities to encounter them; to learn rituals to cast them out or bind them; or to otherwise involve ourselves in occult speculation. In fact, God regularly forbids his people from occult activity (Lev. 19:31; 20:6, 27). The Chronicler notes that the sign of Saul's lack of faith in God is that he consulted an occultist (1 Chron. 10:13). While is it true that the disciples of Jesus are sometimes empowered to cast out demons (Luke 10:17), Luke makes it clear that Jesus' emphasis to his disciples was never on engaging hostile spirit beings (Luke 10:20). Furthermore, we are told nothing about how or in what sense the demons were made subject to Jesus' disciples.

Occult-Based Demonology

Occult-based demonology is not always pursued intentionally. When someone embraces anecdotal encounter with a demon, he runs the risk of being drawn into believing or accepting occult doctrines. Sometimes, we believe reports without considering what assumptions must be true if the reports are true. The Bible affirms that there are demons and that they are active in our world. The Bible affirms that witchcraft is a real phenomenon. Because these things are true, people are sometimes uncritical in their acceptance of reports about strange events involving demons, magic, or the occult.

When I say "uncritical," I do not mean to suggest that we ought always to be critical in the sense of angrily dismissing what others tell us. I mean "critical" in the sense of discerning—and we are commanded to be discerning in these ways. John says, "Beloved, do not believe every spirit, but test the spirits to see whether they are from God, for many false prophets have gone out into the world" (1 John 4:1), and "If we receive the testimony of men, the testimony of God is greater" (1 John 5:9). We should test everything against the Word of God, especially reports of spiritual activity as well as teachers on this topic.

If someone reports that he has spoken with a demon who has told him something about the demonic realm, how are we to respond? We cannot say that it is impossible that he spoke to a demon. After all, demons are real. But, there is not any reason to trust the report of a demon either. Say, for example, that it is true that a demon spoke to him and told him things about the demonic realm. Why should someone think that the demon told the truth? The Devil is a liar (John 8:44). Also, why should someone think it was a demon speaking? Why does our friend think so? How much does our friend know about demons? Where did he get the information? These questions are not always asked or they are considered to be unfairly suspicious of the informant. When we are dealing with potential demonic activity, however, being cautious is wise. The fact that the Bible does not provide a robust and detailed demonology does not mean that we should fill in the details with the doctrines of pagan religions, especially because false religions are one of the schemes of the Devil.

Historical or Sociological Demonology

Nevertheless, Christians should be comfortable studying the religious beliefs and practices of other cultures. In part, this task is important for engaging those cultures with the gospel because we need to achieve a certain level of understanding with a cultural group in order to be able to communicate with them well. Historical and sociological studies of folk beliefs, whether about demons or not, do not presuppose that any of the beliefs are true. In fact, secular historians and sociologists often shy away from making any particular evaluative claims about the beliefs and practices that they encounter at least in their capacity as historians or sociologists. Christians know, however, that some of the doctrines regarding demons and supernatural might have some truth to them, even in the guise of false gods in the midst of false religions. However, since the tactic of the enemy is deception, these beliefs could as well be totally false and they would be no less harmful. In any event, we need to know what people think and believe, so that we can present them with the truth of the gospel of Jesus Christ.

Summary

The study of demonology is important for a complete Christian theology, and for its ability to help us in mission and evangelism. However, demonology can also be studied from the perspective of the occult. Occult-based demonology should not be practiced by Christians. Instead, Christians should faithfully interpret what the Scriptures teach about the demons, and seek to understand the religions of those with whom we will share the gospel.

REFLECTION QUESTIONS

1. Why is fascination with demonology dangerous?

2. What are the different ways in which someone could study demonology?

3. How should we respond to reports about demonic activity?

4. What comfort can we draw from 1 John 3:8 about demonology?

5. Why is it important to remember that the Bible does not give much detail on demonology?

What Does the Bible Say about Demons?

Demons are the fallen angels: those spiritual beings who sinned after their creation, following the Devil in his rebellion, and now war against God and his holy angels. With respect to their nature, they are angelic beings, but they oppose the angels in moral character. In other words, as the angels are good, the demons are evil. Unlike angels, there are not clear references to the demons in the Old Testament. Furthermore, most presentations of demons occur within the gospel accounts in the New Testament. In fact, the Bible says relatively little about the demons. Chiefly, the important points are that they exist and that they intend to destroy God's people.

Old Testament

In reading the Bible in order to find references to angels and demons, one must be careful to distinguish between what the text reports and what the text affirms. In some cases, the Bible describes what some figure says without endorsing his or her words. In other cases, the Bible describes and endorses what is said. This distinction is important, because there are cases in which the Bible accurately reports what some person in the narrative believed without disclosing whether what that person believed was correct. It could be, for example, that a person makes a report about a spiritual being that is simply not true—even though the Bible truthfully records what that person reported. The trouble with Old Testament demonology is particularly involved in these distinctions. There are instances in which figures in the Old Testament worship what they understand to be gods. It could be that these gods are really what the New Testament would refer to as demons or wicked angelic beings of various kinds. It could also be that the gods are simply figments of vain imagining on the part of the worshipers. From case to case, it is sometimes difficult to tell.

One difficulty in studying these matters is that there is not as clear a distinction between "gods" and "demons" as might be indicated by English usage in the biblical languages. There are instances in which the Old Testament makes use of the words *el* or *elohim* (typically rendered "god") in a neutral way to refer to formidable spiritual realities. In fact, sometimes the terms are used in a way that simply suggests "grand," with no particular reference to celestial or infernal connotations. For example, in Jonah 3:3, Nineveh is described as a "very great" city, where "very great" is the English translation of the adjectival form of *elohim*. The context prohibits the translation a "godly city." So, in some cases, angels and demons are called "gods" in the loose sense of being celestial beings. Likewise, some human kings and judges are referred to with celestial or divine language, either ironically or because of their great authority.[1] The divisions of the supra-human realm are thus not as clear-cut in the Old Testament as sometimes assumed. In particular, there is not a word for "demon" as such in biblical Hebrew.

Nevertheless, there are some Hebrew terms that are normally understood to refer to demons or evil spirits: *sa'iyr* and *shed*. *Sa'iyr* means "goat" or "hairy one." Because goats were sometimes *worshiped* by pagan peoples as gods or as images of gods, some English translations render this word as "demons" or "goat demons" in Leviticus 17:7 and 2 Chronicles 11:15.[2] The suggestion seems to be that the Israelites were involved (or potentially involved) in pagan rites that associated goat-like figures with false deities (who are, in fact, demons).[3] In the background of this translation choice is 1 Corinthians 10:20. Paul writes in 1 Corinthians 10:20 that pagan sacrifices are made to demons and not merely to crafted idols. The word he uses is *daimoniois*, which means demons.[4] It could be that there is a terminological difference, such that the Old Testament refers to false gods (strictly speaking) as an accommodation but not an endorsement of pagan people's views. In fact, the false gods are

---

1. Psalm 82 is an example of this usage in which human judges are referred to ironically as *elohim*. Some have read this psalm as a divine council scene (with Yahweh addressing the angels), but this understanding does not do justice to the repetition of the word *shafat* in the psalm, nor to the interpretation of the psalm given by Jesus beginning in John 10:34. Further, it seems evident that those who receive God's word are sometimes present in the divine council. For a discussion of the roles of prophets in the divine council, see Samuel A. Meier, *Themes and Transformations in Old Testament Prophecy* (Downers Grove, IL: IVP Academic, 2009), 19–27, esp. 21. Other examples in which *elohim* is used for a human judge can be found in the Old Testament (e.g., Exod. 21:6; 22:8–9) as well.
2. The word *sa'iyr* appears also in Isaiah 13:21 and 34:14. Some hold that in these texts it should be understood as a reference to demons as opposed to "wild goats." This conclusion is generally based on reading Revelation 18:2 as an allusion to these texts in Isaiah. Revelation 18:2 mentions demons (*daimonion*) in desolate places.
3. In the way that Satan is often figured as a goat-like figure or satyr in popular culture and occult practice. See Question 14.
4. Making a clear distinction between false gods and demons is probably unwarranted. The word *daimon* is employed in the New Testament occasionally to mean something more akin to the Hebrew *elohim*—great or mighty beings.

demons. Reference to the New Testament allows us to make this conclusion. The terminology of the Old Testament is ambiguous in this respect.

The same is true of the word *shed*. This word only occurs twice in the Old Testament (Deut. 32:17; Ps. 106:37).[5] In Deuteronomy, English translations differ. In some cases, the word is translated "demon," and in other cases as "false god." Verse 16 reads that the people made God jealous with "strange gods," which makes "false god" more likely in immediate literary context. The Old Testament typically ascribes false worship to pagan gods, so that "demon" could be a misleading translation. However, again, there is some equivalence between demons and false gods (although some false gods seem to be mere figments of imagination rather than actual malevolent beings).

In addition to these two possibilities, there are some words that appear in poetic passages that have sometimes been interpreted as references to pagan deities. The deities in question are Lilith (Isa. 34:14; LXX = *onokentauros* = satyr; Vulg. = *lamia* = witch), Resheph (e.g., Hab. 3:5), Rahab (e.g., Ps. 89:9 or Isa. 30:7), or even Nergal (Job 18:14; *melek balahot* = king of terrors). It is debatable whether these usages are references to specific characters in pagan pantheons, so it also unlikely that we can draw metaphysical import from these allusions to the existence of specific, named demons. After all, there are only two angels known by name in Scripture. It would be surprising if we knew the names of many demons. Even if these are direct references to pagan deities, the literary usage of these terms is not itself any indication that these specific figures exist. However, it seems clear that the pagan peoples are in some cases worshiping some demonic being. At a practical level, who exactly these beings are is somewhat irrelevant. The Old Testament seems content to forbid the pursuit or worship of all beings save Yahweh, which is probably why there are not further elaborations on demonic beings and false gods.

New Testament

The New Testament contains more information about demonic activity than the Old Testament, but, aside from specific episodes in the gospel accounts, the information is still limited. Names of specific demons are relatively absent in the New Testament as well.[6] However, there is a wider of range of terminology for spiritual beings: demon (*daimon* or *daimonion*);[7] spirits (*pneumata*), both unclean (*akatharton*) and evil (*poneron*); and simply angels

---

5. Later Hebrew usage provides a better context for the interpretation of the word as "demon," but the difference in context is surely related to a difference in usage (see 4QShir[a]). In fact, Revelation 18:12 seems more parallel to the usage in Qumran.
6. Satan is called Belial (2 Cor. 6:15) and Beelzebub (Matt. 10:25). Another demon (or perhaps a group of demons) refers to itself as "Legion" (Luke 8:30).
7. The basic word *daimonion* meant either a divine or semidivine being in classical Greek, which roughly agrees with some usages of *elohim*. It comes to be used specifically for wicked spiritual beings in the New Testament.

(*angelos*). The text describes demonic activity primarily in terms of oppression of individuals and orchestrated effort against the church.

Demonization

Although English words used to describe these phenomena vary, the New Testament refers to demonic activity with regard to individuals as demonization (*daimonizomenos*). Early English translations of the Bible render this word as "possession," which is the paradigmatic example of this activity. In Matthew 15:22, we read of a mother who reports that her daughter is *kakos daimonizetai* or "severely demonized." The context does not make it clear how the phrase should be interpreted, except to say that Jesus is able to heal the girl. However, in other instances of persons "with" unclean spirits (Mark 1:23) or who "have" unclean spirits (Acts 8:7), their healing is described as "casting out" (*ekballo*), which suggests that the demon was inhabiting the person in question.[8] It also seems that the effect of demonic activity can be greater or less, ranging from causing illness (e.g., loss of speech: Matt. 9:32–33; blindness: Matt. 12:22; or, bodily deformity: Luke 13:11) to usurping control of the body entirely (e.g., Matt. 17:15–18, or Luke 8:27–29).

Assaults on the Church

The demons also make concentrated efforts to oppose the church. Paul tells of a generic struggle against spiritual forces (Eph. 6:12) as well as some specific ways that the demons oppose the church. Paul warns Timothy, for example, that false teachers are sometimes driven by demons. He says that, "the Spirit expressly says that in later times some will depart from the faith by devoting themselves to deceitful spirits and teaching of demons" (1 Tim. 4:1). These teachers will promote false doctrines and require ascetical practices (i.e., their false piety may be misleading). In fact, he counsels Timothy later that some who oppose the truth that Timothy preaches are ensnared by the Devil and taken captive by him (2 Tim. 2:25–26). The wisdom of false teachers may be earthly, sensual, or demonic (James 3:15). Likewise, John tells us that we should not "believe every spirit" but should "test the spirits to see whether they are from God, for many false prophets have gone out into the world" (1 John 4:1). He too associates false teaching with false spirits. Therefore, this testing is not a unique supernatural empowering. Rather, it is reflection on what is being said or taught in light of God's word.

Popular fascination with demons tends to focus on possession and demonic attacks on individual persons, probably because of the way demons are characterized in popular literature and films. But, the rampant demonic activity presented in the gospel accounts falls increasingly into the background in the remainder of the New Testament, with the exception of the activity

---

8. See Question 13 for further discussion.

of the demons in eschatological texts. Instead, the focus is increasingly on the opposition of spiritual forces to the progress of the church. Though the disciples were known by the authority that they had been given to cast out demons, their comfort was to be in Christ and not the authority granted them (Luke 10:20).

Summary

The Bible does not say much about demons, aside from a few important points of caution. The Bible teaches that Satan and demons are real beings who oppose the people of God. They promote false doctrines, are active in false religions, and seek to prevent the advance of the gospel. Therefore, Christians should stand ready to withstand the spiritual powers of darkness.

REFLECTION QUESTIONS

1. What does the Bible affirm about demons?

2. How should the limited information about demons in the Bible affect our discussions and thinking about them?

3. Should we be careful in studying false religions because of what Scripture reports about demons?

4. How does 1 John 3:8 bring comfort in understanding demonology?

5. How does the final judgment of the Devil and his angels glorify God?

Do Judaism or Islam Believe in Angels and Demons?

Both Judaism and Islam have teachings about the angels. One difficulty in outlining them stems from the fact that folk religious beliefs (the beliefs of those who self-identify as having a particular religion) vary widely. However, to the extent that we discuss certain texts as contributing either to the "official" religious teaching (e.g., the *Qur'an* for Islam) or the cultural folklore (e.g., Second Temple texts for Judaism), we can see how some religious ideas are codified over time. Besides these two major "Abrahamic" religions, other religions (e.g., Hinduism) or classes of religions (e.g., animism) have beliefs in spirit beings (both good and evil), but they increasingly differ from the picture of "angels" and "demons" to the extent that it is unhelpful to discuss them in the same context. For example, some might consider the devas of Hinduism to be angelic because they are celestial beings; however, they function as lesser gods and, as such, are merely a lower class of divine being and not created spiritual creatures as the angels and demons are and are thought of in Christianity, Judaism, and Islam. In what follows, I discuss some representative beliefs of Judaism and Islam on the angels and demons.

Judaism

Historically, Judaism developed a robust conception of angels and spiritual beings, with the majority of the growth in such ideas found in the literature from the Second Temple period (roughly, sixth century BC to first century AD). Both as a consequence of syncretism and religious imagination, many religious documents, in particular the pseudepigrapha,[1] develop ideas

---

1. Pseudepigrapha is a term that refers to Jewish and Christian writings that are falsely attributed to certain authors and were written during the period between the second century BC and first century AD. For example, the book of Enoch suggests that its author is the

about angels, many of which are contradictory one with another. It seems to be a chief delight of scholars of this literature to speculate about the relationships between these nonbiblical texts and their effects or literary relationships to the canonical text of the Bible.

One of the most significant documents in this regard is the Book of the Watchers, which comprises the first thirty-six chapters of 1 Enoch. The complete text of the work is only available to us in Geʿez or Ethiopic; but Aramaic fragments of the text were discovered at Qumran. The Book of the Watchers recounts that the angels saw the human daughters of the men that God had created and "lusted after them, and said one to another: 'Come, let us choose us wives from among the children of men and beget us children'" (1 Enoch 6:2). A consequence of these illicit unions was the birth of giants who eventually turned on their human parents and fought against them. Actually, it is in consequence of these unions and the bloodshed that follows that God declares that he will destroy the world by flood, and he sends his holy angels to bind all the angels who took human wives. Most scholars see this section of the book of Enoch as a late interpretation and expansion of Genesis 6, which calls these fallen angels "Watchers" (cf. Dan. 4:17) and considers them to be the origin of demons.[2] Much critical elaboration and revision of this tradition is found in Second Temple writings, and some early Christian writers accepted this story as the etiology of demons (that is, a story of where they came from) although nothing so elaborate could possibly be discovered in the Bible. The syncretic nature of these texts and beliefs is clear in the borrowing of "apotropaic" prayers from neighboring religious traditions (esp. remnants of Mesopotamian religious cults). Apotropaic prayers are prayers for blessing and protection against spirits or ill fortune. These are blended with Old Testament passages and interpretation. In fact, some relatively early Jewish texts (e.g., Genesis Apocryphon) make very free use of canonical accounts, such that it is difficult to classify them as either midrash or targumic.[3] In 1 Enoch, for example, a major concern seems to be to explain the origin of evil, which is attributed to the Watchers' illicit unions with human women. However, supposing 1 Enoch could be considered an interpretation

---

Enoch from Genesis 5. For more information, see Loren T. Stuckenbruck, "Apocrypha and Pseudepigrapha," in *The Eerdmans Dictionary of Early Judaism*, eds. John J. Collins and Daniel C. Harlow (Grand Rapids: Eerdmans, 2010), 143–62. For a collection of pseudepigrapha, see James H. Charlesworth, ed., *The Old Testament Pseudepigrapha*, vols. 1–2 (New York: Doubleday, 1983, 1985).

2. Scholars debate about the literary relation between various Jewish texts that mention the "Watchers." The only mention of beings called by that name in Scripture is in Daniel, and the context precludes our identifying them with the beings mentioned in pseudepigrapha.

3. See the discussion in Joseph A. Fitzmyer, *The Genesis Apocryphon of Qumran Cave I: A Commentary*, 2nd (rev.) ed. (Rome: Biblical Institute Press, 1971), 6–9. "Midrash" refers to a method of Jewish commentary on and interpretation of the Hebrew Bible. "Targums" are Aramaic paraphrases of the Hebrew Bible given for people who could not read Hebrew.

of Genesis 6, the sin of Adam in Eden precedes the union of the sons of God and the daughters of men, which makes Enoch's account a significant revision of the canonical understanding of how sin entered the world.

Another text that has received significant scholarly attention is the book of Jubilees, which is actually a "rewriting" of the Bible from Genesis to the middle of Exodus. This text, like Enoch, comes to us complete only in Ge'ez. The role of angelic activity is significantly more pronounced than in the Bible: for example, the main narrator of the work is an angel. It seems that by incorporating extended quotations of the Bible into this new composition, the author(s) hoped to grant their work some authority. However, the act of "rewriting" the Bible in this way actually undermines the authority of the biblical authors by removing their compositional and literary decisions and replacing them with emphases, concerns, or fantasies of some later author. In the case of Jubilees, some parts of the text seem to be attempts at interpretation; others seem to be attempts to elaborate on terse passages of the original. It holds that Satan is at work in the binding of Isaac and that demons are the descendants of the Watchers. It also holds that most of the demons were imprisoned for their rebellion against God except for a select few, who were made heads over the nations (i.e., became "territorial spirits" or local gods). This was done at the request of the Devil. The book also contains a rehearsal of the Watchers myth with some emendations. Unfortunately, much Christian spiritual-warfare writing borrows from these late Jewish, nonbiblical ideologies.

The angelology of the time period gave rise to a mix of beliefs about different types of spiritual beings, with the question of their origins (particularly of the evil beings) coming strongly into the forefront. That there were angels who mediated the giving of the Law and were active in ruling nations and patrolling the earth is well established in the Judaism of this period. Nevertheless, the nature of demonic and angelic beings in Judaism remained relatively fluid and imprecise. In most contemporary Jewish thought, the angels are understood as metaphors for psychological tendencies, and hence belief in angels is not a robust part of all modern Judaism.

Islam

Belief in angels is a fundamental part of Islam. According to Islam, the *Qu'ran* was delivered to Mohammed by the angel Gabriel. Hence, to disbelieve in angels would be to disbelieve in the messenger who delivered their holy book to the founder of the religion. The *Qu'ran* notes that: "Whoever is an enemy of Gabriel (who has by God's grace revealed to you the *Qu'ran* as a guide for joyful tidings for the faithful, confirming previous scriptures), whoever is an enemy of God, his angels, or his apostles, or of Gabriel or Michael, will surely find that God is the enemy of the unbelievers" (2:97). Failing to believe in angels is therefore failure to believe, period. In fact, Islam obligates one to believe in two angels in particular.

Beyond this requirement for Muslims, Islam has a more elaborate set of teachings about angels and demons than does the Bible. For example, the *Qu'ran* describes the fall of Satan as a consequence of his refusal to bow down to Adam (likewise, a tradition in some Jewish writings and sometimes uncritically articulated by contemporary Christian writers). It also notes a guardian angel for each soul explicitly. Islam also incorporates angels mentioned in the Hebrew Bible (Gabriel and Michael) as well as numerous others from a variety of sources. How angels look or what they do varies depending on the hadith one reads, but the majority of the angels are thought to be holding up Allah's throne (40:7). Only a minority serve as messengers. Unlike Christian theology, Islam does not consider the angels to be pure spiritual creatures but to have been made out of light. Another type of creature, the jinn, is said to be made from fire, and man from the clay. Apparently, the jinn inhabited the world before Allah made man, but refused to obey his commands. Like men, they are mortal and can eat and drink. They are normally invisible but can also be called upon in magic rituals. In many cases, they are suspected of possession. Like Judaism, the beliefs are relatively fluid in their content.

Summary

All of the so-called "Abrahamic religions" have beliefs in angels and spirit beings. In some cases, these beliefs seem remarkably similar, probably because certain claims about them derive from the Bible. The Old Testament is considered holy writing for Judaism and the whole Bible is considered holy writing for Islam. Hence, there will be some shared beliefs about its teachings regarding a variety of matters. But, the differences in the religions' accounts of angelic activity is larger than what they hold in common.

REFLECTION QUESTIONS

1. How are Jewish and Christian beliefs about angels similar and different?

2. How are Muslim and Christian beliefs about angels similar and different?

3. Can we learn anything about angels from other religions?

4. Is it surprising that Judaism and Islam contain so much more speculation about angels than Christianity?

5. Why should we be content with the biblical witness regarding angels?

Are There Territorial Spirits?

Many animist and polytheistic belief systems hold that there are regional deities—divine or semidivine beings who hold dominion over particular geographical areas, nations, or people. Of course, Christians recognize that if there is some aspect of truth to these religious beliefs, then these "gods" (the ones that actually exist, anyway) are really demonic entities. Some believe that the Bible implicitly affirms that there are powerful spirits (either angels or demons) who have dominion over different regions of the earth. In fact, certain models of spiritual warfare are largely predicated on a strong belief in the significance of territorial spirits (see Question 26).

There are a handful a key biblical texts that provide evidence that there are territorial spirits. In particular, Daniel 10 and Deuteronomy 32:8 stand out for special emphasis.

Daniel 10

The figures in Daniel 10 who are thought to be high-ranking angels and demons are the "princes" who are mentioned in verses 13, 20, and 21. Some scholars have made much of these passages. For example, James Montgomery goes so far as to say that "the bk. of Daniel presents a full-fledged doctrine of the Princes of the nations, i.e., their celestial patrons."[1] I find it hard to share his enthusiasm; it seems to me that three oblique references in one chapter do not constitute even a fledgling doctrine. However, the idea has seemed suggestive to many, especially pseudepigraphical authors of Jewish antiquity.

In Daniel 10, Daniel encounters a "man clothed in linen," who appears in a "vision." Based on his description, most scholars understand this "man" to be an angel. Given that the figure is an angel, it is surprising to discover that "the prince of the kingdom of Persia" is able to "withstand" him for twenty-one

---

1. James A. Montgomery, *The Book of Daniel*, International Critical Commentary (Edinburgh: T&T Clark, 1927), 419.

days.[2] The reader wonders how a human prince could withstand an angel. The angel, then, says that Michael, "one of the chief princes," came to help him (Dan. 10:13). The text goes on to describe Michael as "your prince" and "the great prince who has charge over your people" (Dan. 10:21; 12:1). Michael is identified in the New Testament as an archangel (Jude 9) and as a leader of the holy angels in the war against the Devil (Rev. 12:7). If Michael, an archangel, is called a "prince," then, so the argument goes, the "prince of the kingdom of Persia" is a spiritual being similar to Michael. Because the prince of the Persian kingdom withstood an angel, he must be a powerful and wicked spirit, i.e., a demon, although he is not as powerful as an archangel like Michael.

From this text then, some conclude that there are spiritual powers who are assigned to specific peoples or nations or have taken charge of them. The information is terse, more so than we might like it to be about matters that pique our curiosity, but there is enough data to piece together to suggest that in some cases angels (or demons) have charge over specific nations. Certainly we know that God assigns his angels to specific tasks at specific times. However, we have to be cautious about this line of interpretation, or—better—we have to be cautious about what we do with such an interpretation.

The identity of this figure—the prince of the Persian kingdom—is not clear. It is not central to Daniel's vision, and we do not get much information about him. It is also not clear what it means that this prince "withstood" the angel who came to Daniel. It involves a struggle or fight of some kind (Dan. 10:20), but the author does not divulge any details. It seems to me reasonable to conclude that this short section of Daniel is revealing that there is a larger unseen realm of conflict behind the human conflicts than we see daily. That would be consistent with Paul's warning about spiritual powers that are more than merely flesh and blood (Eph. 6:10–20). It even seems clear that Michael was assigned to Daniel's people in some capacity, or else one would have difficulty explaining the possessive pronouns used to describe him (Dan. 10:21, note the plural possessive). However, the fact that there are unseen struggles among spiritual powers and that Michael is assigned to Israel does not endorse a robust view of territorial spirits.

"Territorial"?

The case for "territorial spirits" is often enlarged in light of these clues in Daniel by citing other oblique texts of the Old Testament. Broadly speaking, there was a consistent strain of ancient Near Eastern religious belief that the power of authority of the gods was related to specific locations. The Bible places this belief in the mouth of servants of the king of Syria, "Their gods are gods of the hills, and so they were stronger than we. But let us fight against them in the plain, and surely we shall be stronger than they" (1 Kings 20:23). Because they thought that

---

2. The word translated "prince" in these passages is *sar*, and could be translated "captain" to distinguish the word from *nasi* (= "prince"), which is also used in Daniel (e.g., 8:25; 9:26).

this was true of God, they were defeated (1 Kings 20:28). Of course, the argument for territorial spirits from Daniel does *not* support the claim that the angels and demons have been appointed to certain regions. Michael, for example, is said to have charge over a people, *not* a region. In fact, the people over whom Michael has charge are in exile and, hence, do not even occupy their own region. Further, we are not informed of any particular hierarchy of angels and demons in this text. Theological speculation from the cursory comments in Daniel may lead us to make more out of this doctrine than there is to make.

Although this topic will be discussed more fully in the chapter on strategic-level spiritual warfare, it is important to note that, *even if* we believe that a case for angels of the nations can be made from Daniel 10, the proclamation of Jesus and the apostles described by the New Testament never involves binding, naming, or rebuking territorial spirits. In fact, there is no mention of territorial spirits at all. Since this is the case, we should reject the idea that acknowledging or being able to name territorial spirits is an important part of our evangelistic outreach. In other words, even if there are such things, the Bible never provides any guidelines for encountering them.

Deuteronomy 32:8

The other major text that is cited in support of the belief in territorial spirits is Deuteronomy 32:8. The Masoretic text and the Septuagint read the end of the verse differently. In the Masoretic text (the major Hebrew tradition), the final phrase is rendered "according to the sons of Israel," whereas most Greek texts have "according to the angels of God." Textual critics disagree about which ending of the verse should be preferred. If the first reading is preferred, then obviously this text would have nothing to say about territorial spirits at all. If the second reading is preferred, however, there is some evidence that the people groups or nations of the world were divided according to how many angels there were. From this idea, some infer that each of these angels has charge over a particular group of people, which is what the belief in territorial spirits usually holds.

There was a Hebrew text discovered at Qumran that has the reading *bene elohim* (= "sons of God"). This is considered to be the original reading. Both the Hebrew and Greek traditions can be understood as interpretations of this same text. The Masoretic text might have understood the sons of God to be a reference to the Israelites because of the text in verse 9, whereas the Greek translators seem to have taken the translation more atomistically. Also, the Greek translators of the Septuagint have an interest in angelology that affected their translational choices. Consequently, it is more likely that "according to the sons of God" is the correct text. But the question still remains as to how one should interpret the reference in the text: either to the Israelites or to the angels.

Both interpretations have difficulties. It is important to recognize that *even if* the "angels" translation were preferable, we would still not have anything like a robust doctrine of territorial spirits. In other words, the fact the original nations were divided according to the number of angels does not tell us about whether those angels currently have control over the nations or what it means that they have control over the nations or what they do as rulers of the nations, etc. There simply is not enough information in this text to build any sort of doctrine. We might conclude that there was some relationship between the territories allotted to the nations and the angels. We know from elsewhere that idolatry (worship of false gods or demons) is a common sin in the surrounding peoples (Deut. 4:19). But beyond that, we have nothing but speculation.

Summary

There is some limited evidence that the angels and demons play some role in the governance of the world and that (at least at certain times) major people groups or nations have been under the influence of demonic powers. It seems reasonable to believe that these principalities and powers are active in the world and are working to undermine God's purposes in the gospel. Furthermore, we should be aware that these struggles are real and dangerous (Eph. 6:10–13). However, many books about territorial spirits are not content with the limited amount of information given in the Bible about these matters. Hence, they fill in details with anecdotes or speculations based on the doctrines of false religions. We can admit that there are territorial spirits without making them central to our endeavors, or succumbing to speculation about them. We should not give the enemy more credit or attention than he is due.

REFLECTION QUESTIONS

1. Why should we be cautious about making much out of the doctrine of territorial spirits?

2. Is the identity of the prince of the Persian kingdom significant in interpreting the message of Daniel 10?

3. Why is it important for Christians that the New Testament makes no mention of territorial spirits?

4. Should we attempt to develop doctrines solely from difficult texts (e.g., Deut. 32:8)?

5. Why is Colossians 1:16 ("For by him all things were created, in heaven and on earth, visible and invisible, whether thrones or dominions or rulers or authorities—all things were created through him and for him") important to remember when discussing spirits and powers?

Can Christians Be Demon-Possessed?

This question is one of the most frequent in books on spiritual warfare or encounters with spiritual beings, and it is a question that has caused scholars some difficulty. The main reason for the difficulty is that many missionaries report that they have known of a Christian who was possessed by a demon. In fact, such reports famously caused Merrill Unger to reverse his position on this question. In his 1952 book, *Biblical Demonology*, he argued strongly for the view that Christians cannot be possessed by demons. He states, "the very nature of the believer's salvation, as embracing the regenerating, sealing, indwelling, and filling ministry of the Holy Spirit, placing him 'in Christ,' eternally and unforfeitably, is sufficient explanation why he is not liable to demon inhabitation."[1] After receiving "numbers of letters and reports of cases of demon invasion of believers . . . from missionaries in various parts of the world," he came to argue for the opposite view in his 1971 book, *Demons in the World Today,* and in his 1977 book, *What Demons Can Do to Saints.*[2] Part of the answer to this question turns on what one means by "possessed." Below, I will define this terminology in light of the biblical witness, and then discuss the responses to this question. I do not believe that Christians can be demon-possessed, because there is no biblical evidence that they can be, and because it is not fitting with what the Bible teaches about the status of the believer. Arguments from experience are not self-interpreting, no matter how sincere, but need to be interpreted in light of what Scripture claims. One of the greatest challenges in this area of study is how easy it is to allow anecdotes to be the controlling material of our thinking about our doctrines.

---

1. Merrill F. Unger, *Biblical Demonology* (Wheaton, IL: Scripture Press, 1952), 100.
2. Merrill F. Unger, *What Demons Can Do to Saints* (Chicago: Moody, 1977), 59. See also Unger, *Demons in the World Today* (Carol Stream, IL: Tyndale House, 1971), 116–17.

What Is Possession?

Of course, any such argument depends on carefully identifying what is meant by "possession." In English Bibles, the term is often used as the translation for the Greek term *daimonizomai*. Many times this will be translated as "demon-possessed" or even "possessed with demons." The reason for this choice in translation seems to be that the Greek word came into the Latin Vulgate as *possessio,* which informed the choices of early English translators. In Latin, *possessio* refers to having occupancy or control, so by "possession," we typically understand that a demon is inhabiting a person and either controlling them entirely or taking control from time-to-time. However, the Greek word *daimonizomai* is not the only way in which the New Testament authors describe a person afflicted by a demon.[3]

In some cases, they are demonized (*daimonizomai*) but in others they are said to have a demon (*echo + daimonion*),[4] or to have a demon with them (*en*),[5] or to be afflicted by a demon (*ochleomai*).[6] It is not clear that these terms should be rigidly distinguished. In other words, they are not technical terms with scientifically precise meanings. In fact, in the story of the Gadarene demoniacs (Matt. 8:28–34; Mark 5:1–20; Luke 8:26–39), Matthew uses the term demonized (8:28), Mark uses the term with an unclean spirit (5:2) and demonized (5:16); and Luke says demonized (8:36) as well as having demons (8:27). So, there is clearly significant overlap in these phrases, and we should not reduce them to technical terms. Nevertheless, it is clear that the demonized are often inhabited by the demon.

The word often used to describe the removal of a demon's influence in a person's life is *ekballo*, usually translated "cast out." The idea here is that the demon is being removed from within the person in some sense. The man among the tombs in Mark 5 is described as a man "with an unclean spirit," yet the demons are still commanded to come out of him (Mark 5:2, 8).

Fred Dickason's Position

There is no biblical evidence that believers can be inhabited by a demon. Neither are there any indications that someone could be saved and still have a demon that had to be separately exorcised. At best, proponents of the view that Christians can be demonized have an argument from silence when it comes to the witness of the inspired authors of the Bible. The entire case for possessed believers rests on anecdotal evidence. This is problematic, because it denies that we are equipped by Scripture for every good work (2 Tim. 3:16–17).

---

3. *Daimonizomai* is the second-most-often occurring word (Matt. 4:24; 8:16, 28, 33; 9:32; 12:22; 15:22; Mark 1:32; 5:15, 16, 18; Luke 8:36; John 10:21).
4. Matthew 11:18; Mark 3:30; 5:15; 7:25; 9:17; Luke 4:33; 7:33; 8:27; John 7:20; 8:48, 49, 52; 10:20; Acts 8:7; 16:16; 19:13.
5. Mark 1:23; 5:2.
6. Luke 6:18; Acts 5:16.

Typically, those who argue that Christians can be possessed by demons begin their arguments by stating that Scripture does not unequivocally state that believers *cannot* be inhabited by demons.[7] The most significant work defending the view that believers can be inhabited by demons is C. Fred Dickason's *Demon Possession and the Christian Life*.[8] One of his main tasks in reviewing the biblical material is to show that the Bible does not conclusively answer the question whether believers can have demons either way. He writes, "None of the passages we have studied can with any fair treatment be construed to eliminate the possibility of a genuine believer's being inhabited by wicked spirits."[9] He also writes, however, that "we cannot conclusively say that the Bible clearly presents evidence that believers may be demonized."[10] His point is that, ultimately, some other evidence will have to decide the question. He dismisses theological arguments against possession of believers as inconclusive. Therefore, "clinical" considerations become the cornerstone of his defense. In other words, what he (and others who share his view) believe settles the issue is the information provided by "clients and counselors who have been involved in handling demonic oppression."[11]

He goes on to reason in principle that believers could be inhabited by wicked spirits for the same reasons that believers could have cancer. His idea is that, by examining the biblical and clinical evidence related to the question, "Can Christians have cancer?" we are able to come to a reasoned conclusion. Likewise, by examining the biblical and clinical evidence related to the question, "Can Christians be demon-possessed?" we should be able to come to a similarly reasoned conclusion.

Dickason responds to what he believes might be three objections to his analogy. First, he says that someone might object that this method elevates experience to the level of biblical truth. He responds that since the Bible does not settle the question, there is nothing wrong with taking our experience into consideration. Second, he says that someone might object that the analogy takes a common occurrence (cancer) and compares it to something rare (demonic possession). He responds that demonization is common (without argument). His point is that we cannot dismiss the analogy without investigating the evidence. The final objection he considers is the reliability of the

---

7. They often also point out that "possession" is too strong a word for the condition that believers have when they are demonized. See Charles H. Kraft, *Defeating Dark Angels: Breaking Demonic Oppression in the Believer's Life* (Ann Arbor, MI: Servant, 1992), 35. Unfortunately, for his argument, Kraft does not notice that the terms he cites from Scripture are often used interchangeably by the biblical authors.
8. C. Fred Dickason, *Demon Possession and the Christian Life: A New Perspective* (Westchester, IL: Crossway, 1990).
9. Ibid., 99.
10. Ibid., 127.
11. Ibid., 149.

research. He thinks this is an unfair objection. He writes: "it is amazing how Christians accept without question 'the assured findings of modern science' or the testimony of Christians regarding the Lord's interventions and supernatural occurrences, and yet will not accept what appears as genuine evidence from clinical observation by reliable and qualified persons that Christians can be demonized."[12] In fact, he goes on to say that the burden of empirical proof is on the opponent, who must "search all parts of the world to determine that no Christian in all the world, present or past, has even been demonized."[13]

Response to Dickason

Dickason does not address the most significant argument against his analogy or his position. First, the issue is not that evidence from experience is used to shape our understanding of the world. Of course, in medicine, for example, the Bible says relatively little and we use our best judgment based on our observation and study. But, in that case, the things that we are studying are things that we can actually look at and touch. That is not the case for demons. Hence, the problem with the analogy is not that cancer is common and demonic oppression is not. Rather, the problem is that we can look at cancer cells, measure them, count them, and fight them by using our senses, whereas we cannot similarly evaluate the spiritual realm.

Furthermore, cancer and disease do not come about through idolatry, whereas proponents of possession of believers are quick to attach moral and spiritual significance to demonic oppression; namely, that the possession is based on some past occult activity or idolatry or ritual, etc. In fact, many go on to chart the types of sins over which specific demons have authority and which provide opportunity for demons to enter a person. For example, Charles Kraft claims that: "demons cannot live in a person unless two conditions exist: (1) they must have discovered an 'entry point,' an emotional or spiritual weakness through which they can enter, and (2) they must have a 'legal right,' a right that accords with the laws of the spiritual universe, allowing them to be there."[14] Where did Kraft discover "the laws of the spiritual universe"? Since the Bible does not discuss the issues (as admitted by the foremost apologist for this view), they must have been learned solely from clinical experience. Thus, this methodology does raise experience to the level of biblical truth in areas of spiritual and moral significance. The issue is that this analogy supposes that there are acute spiritual conditions about which the Bible provides no instruction. Hence, implicitly, the view does not affirm the sufficiency of Scripture. Yet, the Bible does claim such sufficiency for itself.

---

12. Ibid., 160.
13. Ibid.
14. Kraft, *Defeating*, 121.

Even if that is not right, there is a problem with the type of evidence adduced from clinical experience. None of it is testable or repeatable, and it is based on the subjective responses and diagnoses of the people involved. Hence, many of these books dealing with demons contain solely anecdotal examples of power encounters for how believers should deal with the demonized (whether believer or not). Information about the demons and how to deal with them usually comes (according to the reports) from the demons themselves! For example, one frequently reads accounts that contain insights like this: "we found out from the demons behind Jennifer's voices that they had entered her before she made a commitment to Christ."[15] Furthermore, either the incidents are generally known only to the authors, the names of people are changed, or the accounts are utterly anonymous. So, we must question in what sense these persons are qualified to make pronouncements on such matters.

In fact, all the evidence for discerning whether a person has a demon is ultimately subjective. Since experience is not self-interpreting, we cannot merely trust reports because they are sincere. Frankly, some of the reports may not even be sincere. It is especially unhelpful that so many of the books written on this subject are filled with anecdotes that are presented as unimpeachable and which could not possibly be investigated.

Can Christians Be Inhabited?

I think the answer is no. There are no instances in anecdotal reports about demon-possession of Christians that cannot be explained just as well by psychological abnormality, the power of suggestion, or the fact that the person is not a genuine believer. There are no tests of demon-possession given in the Bible. Neither is there a gift for exorcism. Neither is exorcism ever commanded or mentioned in the letters to the churches. As Alex Konya notes, "this is a silence that roars!"[16]

If we do encounter an instance of demonic possession, we should expect it to resemble the descriptions of demoniacs in Scripture. Even so, cultural and historical studies make it clear that possession-behaviors vary by culture and can be learned. In fact, in early modern Europe, the behaviors of supposed demoniacs are different between Catholics and Protestants, even though they do mirror the biblical narratives.

Finally, the theological argument is the strongest. Christians are inhabited by the Holy Spirit of God. How could a demon take possession of such a person? Some will argue that this argument is based on poor semantics.[17] The

---

15. Ibid., 65. In other cases, previous occult activity is the source of information. C. Peter Wagner, "Territorial Spirits," in *Wrestling with Dark Angels*, eds. C. Peter Wagner and F. Douglas Pennoyer (Venture, CA: Regal, 1990), 80.

16. Alex Konya, *Demons: A Biblically Based Perspective* (Schaumburg, IL: Regular Baptist Press, 1990). This is one of the best books on the subject.

17. Dickason, *Demon Possession*, 130.

idea is that "possessed" means ownership or control but that *daimonizomai* in the Bible means something else. However, the ability of the demon to assert violent control over the person is the evidence that they have a demon. So, the theological argument cannot be avoided by claiming that something is lost in translation here.

Finally, the clinicians who claim to have these experiences flatly contradict one another. For example, Dickason says that a demon "does not have the legal right to reside in a Christian,"[18] which is completely the opposite of Kraft's claims. For all the language about the care of investigation, there are no guidelines for how one sets out to pursue these matters in Scripture, and hence we are left to fill in the outlines with human opinions or the supposed claims of demons and occult religions.

Summary

Can demons oppress and fight against believers? Absolutely. The Bible is clear on this point (Eph. 6:10–14; 1 Peter 5:8). However, the Bible is also clear that this attack is typically through deception, false teachers, and false doctrines. It is curious then that so many counselors who affirm that Christians can be possessed seem to rely on the reports of the demons of those they encounter. Possession never comes up as a concern for Christians in the New Testament. Sin does. We should focus our warfare accordingly.

REFLECTION QUESTIONS

1. Does the Bible use the word "possession" in the strict sense in which we use the term in movies and popular culture?

2. Do the biblical authors ever command Christians to deal with possession?

3. How is focus on possession a distraction from the typical ways that demons threaten Christians?

4. Why is it concerning that books teaching on the nature of possession draw lessons solely from their experience in conversing with demons?

5. What is the ultimate cure for every spiritual weakness?

---

18. Ibid., 134.

Questions Related to the Devil

Who Is the Devil, or Satan?

The Devil, or Satan, is the chief of the fallen angels. Though the Bible contains no explicit comments regarding his creation or subsequent fall, we can infer much about Satan's character and attributes. At present, his goal is to disrupt God's purposes, a goal to which—although ultimately fruitless—he is wholly committed together with his angels, the demons. There are many demons—but there is only one Devil.

Names of Satan

There is some ambiguity regarding the word "Satan," with respect to whether it should be understood as a title or as a name. In Hebrew, he is known by a phrase, *hasatan,* which literally means "the adversary" (the *ha* is the definite article "the" in Hebrew). Most English translations render the Hebrew phrase *hasatan* as the single capitalized name, Satan, with our English word simply transliterating the Hebrew. The Hebrew phrase appears only a handful of times in the Old Testament, primarily in Job.[1] In the Old Testament, the phrase is clearly titular and not a proper name. In Hebrew, proper names do not take the article whereas *satan* always does. Hence, the translation "the adversary" would be much more appropriate than the translation "Satan."

In the New Testament, we find the word *satanas*, which is a Greek transliteration of the Hebrew. In general, the word appears with the definite article, just as it does in Hebrew. Whether this usage should lead us to conclude that the word functions as a title as opposed to a proper name is difficult to say, because Greek frequently makes use of the article with proper names.[2] In

---

1. Job 1:6, 7, 8, 9, 12; 2:1, 2, 3, 4, 6, 7; and Zechariah 3:1, 2.
2. See the discussion of this use of the article in Daniel B. Wallace, *Greek Grammar: Beyond the Basics* (Grand Rapids: Zondervan, 1996), 245. Wallace notes: "we are unable to articulate clear and consistent principles as to why the article is used in a given instance."

critical editions of the Greek text, editors typically capitalize the first letter of the word to identify it as a proper name. Paul usually uses the article with this loan word.[3] When the word appears without the definite article, it is typically because someone is being addressed directly. For example, Jesus speaking to Peter in Matthew 16:23 says, "Get behind me, Satan (*Satana*)!"[4] Speaking directly to the Devil at his temptation, Matthew 4:10 records the same usage: "Be gone, Satan (*Satana*)!" However, in Matthew 12:26, Jesus' reference to the Devil uses the article again, "And if Satan (*ho Satanas*) casts out Satan (*tov Satanan*). . . ." It seems that we could translate these instances as "adversary" instead of as Satan (e.g., "Be gone, adversary!"). Nevertheless, it could be that the Hebrew title began to function as a proper name. Reference to the Devil as an adversary does not always make use of the borrowed term *satanas*. For example, Peter uses the word *antidikos* ("adversary") in 1 Peter 5:8 (along with *diabolos*, "devil"). This word is a legal term for the opposition. Therefore, it seems clear that Satan is as much a description of the character of this being as it is his name.

Even if it is best to understand "Satan" as a proper name, most of the terms used to identify the Devil in the New Testament seem to be titular or descriptive. The most common term is *ho diabolos* or "the Devil." *Diabolos* almost always takes the article, which is probably best understood as monadic, which means "the Devil" should be understood as "the one and only Devil." In two cases, the word appears in the plural.[5] In both cases, the word refers to human women and is normally translated "slanderers." The similarity to "adversary" is apparent. The "monadic" usage of the article indicates that there is

---

3. There is one exception in 2 Corinthians 12:7: "So to keep me from becoming conceited because of the surpassing greatness of the revelations, a thorn was given me in the flesh, a messenger of Satan (*angelos Satanas*) to harass me, to keep me from becoming conceited." In this case, *Satanas* appears in a genitive construction. Curiously, *Satanas* is modifying *angelos,* typically translated as messenger but which is the New Testament's basic word for angel. If understood as "an angel of Satan," then a demon was sent to harass Paul. See Simon J. Kistemaker, *Exposition of the Second Epistle to the Corinthians*, New Testament Commentary (Grand Rapids: Baker, 1997). He says, "Paul writes that his physical affliction is a messenger of Satan, namely, one of Satan's evil angels" (416). Likewise, Murray J. Harris comments, "there must be some sense in which the thorn was Satan's own agent or deputy, whether we translate the phrase as 'an angel of Satan' or 'a messenger of Satan'" (*The Second Epistle to the Corinthians*, New International Greek Testament Commentary [Grand Rapids: Eerdmans, 2005], 855). There are many opinions on this text, however. After listing four classes of interpretive options, Kruse concludes, "the plain fact is that there is insufficient data to decide the matter" (Colin G. Kruse, *2 Corinthians*, rev. ed., Tyndale New Testament Commentaries, vol. 8. [Downers Grove: IVP Academic, 2015], 266).
4. Likewise, in the parallel account (Mark 8:33).
5. 1 Timothy 3:11 and Titus 2:3.

just one Devil, although there are many demons.[6] The other references to the Devil are similarly monadic.

The Devil is also referred to as "the tempter" (Matt. 4:3), "the deceiver" (Rev. 12:9), "your adversary" (1 Peter 5:8), and "the enemy" (Matt. 13:39). John frequently calls him "the evil one" (1 John 2:13; 3:12; 5:18), as does Matthew (13:19, 38). He is described as the father of lies and a murderer (John 8:44). His position as the chief of the demons is discovered from the name Beelzebub and Belial (Matt. 12:24; 2 Cor. 6:15).[7] Furthermore, Paul calls him "the prince of the power of the air" (Eph. 2:2) and "the god of this world" (2 Cor. 4:4). It is clear that the Devil is understood to be great in power, even though he is morally decrepit. In addition, he is described in Revelation as the great dragon, and together with his angels he wages war against Michael and the angels of heaven (Rev. 12:3). These names indicate that he is altogether wicked and deceitful and is driven by his desire to tempt and lead astray. He is almost always described according to his misdeeds and not by a name.

Popular Depictions of Satan

In terms of popular conceptions of his appearance, Satan is typically depicted as a kind of satyr, a humanoid figure with cloven feet, horns, and a tail. Of course, Scripture does not describe Satan's physical appearance, so these depictions are largely artistic fancy. It is possible that the textual antecedent for such a depiction comes from the Hebrew word *sa'iyr*, which means "goat." In a few instances, however, the word is used to refer to the idols of pagan gods that are forbidden in the Levitical code. For example, in Leviticus 17:7, we read, "They shall no more sacrifice their sacrifices to goat demons (*sa'iyrim*), after whom they whore." Likewise, Jeroboam replaces the Levitical priests for his own priests for "the high places and for the goat idols (*sa'iyrim*) and for the calves that he had made."[8] The KJV renders the word as "satyr" in Isaiah 34:14 and 13:12. No text indicates that the Devil himself was depicted in these pagan rituals as a goat, but certainly demonic

---

6. The word *diabolos* does appear in the singular and without the article in John 6:70: "Jesus answered them, 'Did I not choose you, the twelve? And yet one of you is a devil (*diabolos*).'" Most translations render this as "a devil"; however, given the absence of the article it seems better to render the phrase a slanderer or accuser, particularly because the following verse reads, "He spoke of Judas the son of Simon Iscariot, for he, one of the twelve, was going to betray him." The association of Judas and the Devil is undeniable because John says "the devil had put in his heart to betray" Jesus and, more forcefully, "Satan (*ho Satanas*) entered into him [Judas]."

7. Beelzebub occurs also in 1 Kings 1:2, in which he is called the god of the Ekronites. Later Jewish thought came to associate him with the Devil (e.g., 11QMelchizedek)

8. It seems plausible that false gods are in fact demonic forces, but the words in these passages just mean "goats"—so the decision to render the phrase "goat demons" is an interpretation. In the instance of the worship of the golden calf, for example, the idol was described as the god who led the people from Egypt, not as some pagan god.

false gods were at times represented by such images. Perhaps this pagan idol, then, is the antecedent of later depictions of Satan in artwork. Satanic cults continue to make use of this imagery.

In fact, the only animal that the Bible identifies the Devil with is the serpent (or the dragon). In Genesis 3, we read that the serpent was the subtlest of the beasts of the field, who uses his craftiness to deceive Eve and Adam. The Bible does not say why Satan chose to inhabit or appear as a snake in order to tempt our first parents. However, later Scripture associates this figure with the Devil (Rev. 12:9). It is clear that Satan disguises himself and adopts different forms. Paul asserts that "Satan (*ho Satanas*) disguises himself as an angel [messenger?] of light" (2 Cor. 11:14). The goal of such deceptions is our downfall, to the extent that sinners are often referred to as his offspring (1 John 3:10). Peter warns us that "the devil prowls around like a roaring lion seeking someone to devour" (1 Peter 5:8).

Summary

Satan is known by many titles in Scripture, but they all indicate that he is evil and that he is set against God's people. Although popular depictions of the Devil display him with horns and a forked tail, there are no such descriptions in the Scriptures. Instead, he is described as one of God's angels. He is active in deception and temptation today, but he can be resisted by the power of the Holy Spirit because Jesus "appeared to destroy the works of the devil" (1 John 3:8).

REFLECTION QUESTIONS

1. Why is it important to believe in a personal Devil?

2. Why is it important not to worry about a personal Devil?

3. How should we regard popular depictions of the Devil?

4. What does the Bible say about the Devil's deceptions?

5. How can we both caution and encourage one another about the Devil?

Why Did God Create the Devil?

This is a tough question, and, frankly, I do not know the answer. Not everything in theology is black and white. Some of our questions are speculative, and certainly this is one of them. Now, with any theological or philosophical question, especially the speculative kind, we have to get clear on what we are really after. And, with this question, we are wondering what *reason* God had for creating the Devil. It's a question that will have occurred to most of us in the course of our Bible reading. And, as it stands, it seems merely to be a question of curiosity. It certainly is not an exegetical question because the biblical authors don't ask it—and incidentally, they don't answer it either.[1]

But, anyone educated in Christianity knows about the Fall—knows that our father Adam succumbed to temptation, failed to protect his wife, to obey God, ate of the fruit, deformed his own soul, and distorted the nature of his progeny. And, we can read for ourselves how the serpent, who is Satan, prompted Adam's wife in the garden, and bewitched her with his craftiness so that she defied the commands of God. So perhaps, in light of such a story, and certainly in light of its residual implications for the whole world, we find ourselves wondering why God would allow such a thing to happen. Why would he make a creature like a tempter, an accuser, an evil one? It is precisely because Moses does not tell us that we find ourselves curious. Yet, curiosity doesn't just kill cats. Some questions are dangerous, because they disguise themselves as children of curiosity when they are really offspring of unbelief.

---

1. This is a shortened version of a chapel talk at Cedarville University on 4/4/2017. The talk is available at: https://www.cedarville.edu/Chapel/Archive.

Special Form of the Problem of Evil[2]

The question about the reason that God made the Devil is usually a special form of the problem of evil. The problem of evil is a philosophical problem that attempts to show that belief in God is irrational. There are two broad versions of this problem: (1) the logical problem and (2) the evidential problem. The logical problem says that the existence of God and the existence of evil are logically contradictory. In other words, the existence of evil disproves the existence of God. Amongst philosophers of religion, this argument is generally considered now to have only historical interest because no one has been able to show that the existence of God and the existence of evil are logically incompatible—that is, that some formal contradiction exists between them. The evidential problem, by contrast, merely says that the amount and kind of evil present in our world makes it very difficult to believe that God exists. The main reason for thinking so is that some evils seem to be unjustifiable, i.e., there seems to be no good reason that they had to happen. It just cannot be, the argument goes, that God would allow unjustifiably bad things to happen. Yet, because such things seem to happen, God probably does not exist. If a being like God does exist, he lacks some property or ability that Christian theism says that he has. All that is left for the evidentialist to do to make his case is to suggest some examples of unjustifiable or "pointless" evils. These range from the innocuous to the severely tragic.

For example, there does not seem to be any reason that it had to happen that I stubbed my toe on the way into the office this morning. It seems that God could have made the world in such a way that everything else was the same (or basically the same) and I did not stub my toe. That way of making the world, it seems, is better than the way things actually happened. Nothing was improved by my toe-stubbing. No evils were prevented. So, my stubbing my toe was pointless, and, if God existed, pointless evils would not happen.

Likewise, a world without the Devil seems to be better than a world with him. He is, after all, altogether wicked and hateful and intends to uproot the good plans of God and destroy mankind. It seems like God should just snuff him out of existence or should have refrained from making him in the first place. Why would a good God make such a creature? We are really asking, "What is the point of such a creature? He isn't good, so what good was it to make him?" Hence, the question, "Why did God create the Devil?" is a version of the evidential problem of evil. The questioner is looking for the justifying reason that God created the Devil—an act that may seem on the face of it to be pointless and cruel.

Notice how deeply pernicious it is to question God's justice in this way. In effect, this question can be antagonistic because it questions whether God made the right decision in creating the Devil. This question points to a broader

---

. See Benjamin H. Arbour and John R. Gilhooly, eds., *Evil and a Selection of its Theological Problems* (Newcastle upon Tyne: Cambridge Scholars, 2016), 96–113.

one by implication, namely, "Does God really know what he is doing?" or—even—"Is God really good?" It may appear that a man is within his rights to ask why God did something, but it may be that curiosity is merely a façade for unbelief. And, temptations to question God come from the Devil himself. How sad that the Devil can use a question about his own wickedness as a temptation to question God's goodness!

Divine Creation

Furthermore, this particular question leads to a much broader inquiry than might at first be recognized. Here is how this inquiry develops: In response to the initial question, "Why did God make the Devil?" the first response should be, simply, he didn't. Now, at first glance, that is a puzzling response. After all, didn't God make everything? Surely, he did. But, when God made the angel now known as Satan, he made him good. This has been the general conclusion of Christian theologians throughout history. The angel then sinned through his own fault and became the Devil—the adversary, the accuser, and the evil one. Some might be satisfied by this response because if the Devil sinned through his own fault, then it was not up to God whether the Devil went wrong.

Since the existence of evil seems to present a problem for Christian theology, some theologians claimed that God is not responsible for the evils of the world because they are not up to him (he lacks some power to prevent them) or because he did not know that they would happen (he lacks knowledge of the future). Notice in both cases God has been made something less than omnipotent (all-powerful) and omniscient (all-knowing) in the classical understanding of those terms. Certainly, he is no longer sovereign over all things. If we recall that the Bible teaches us that God is sovereign over all things, then the response that God did not make the Devil will not satisfy the tenacious questioner. He will go on to ask a more penetrating question, "Why did God make an angel if God knew that the angel would sin?" In other words, if God knew that Satan would turn out like he has in fact turned out, why would he make him anyway?

The nature of the inquiry has now changed. God also knew that Adam would sin, yet he made him. In posing the question of this chapter, are we not also asking, "Why did God make Adam?" Furthermore, God also made all of us knowing that we would sin. Are we not also asking, "Why did God make me?" The reason that we do not associate the question, "Why did God make the Devil?" with the question, "Why did God make me?" is primarily because we do not think that we are rebels against God with exactly the same intensity as the Devil. We think the Devil is wicked and makes the world worse than it would otherwise be simply by existing, but that *we* do not make the world worse than it would be. We think that God is obviously within his rights to make us but has probably made a mistake in making the Devil. So, what sounds at first like a question about why God made one nasty creature turns out to lead to the question, "Why did God make anything?" beneath which is the assertion that it would have been better for him not to create at all.

Let's start with an easy answer and a rebuke: We do not know the reason that God made the Devil, because God does not say. This is important. We are hardly in a position to say that God did not have a good reason for doing something simply because we do not know what his reason was, especially because we have so much evidence that he is faithful and that we can trust him. A worry is that behind the question "Why did God create the Devil?" is not merely curiosity but instead a subtle irreverence. When we place our moral intuitions against God, what we might be saying is, "My judgment is better than God's" or "I would have done it better." But, that is not so. If that is really what is behind our question, then we should repent.

Purpose of the Devil

On the other hand, we might really be asking, "What purpose does the Devil play in God's plan?" In this case, our question is really one of curiosity and not mere suspicion. As it turns out, there are many things we can learn from the fact that there is a Devil. First, the Devil shows how powerful and pernicious sin is. The Devil shows that even an angel made in the sight of God can sin against him. Second, the Devil shows that God alone is holy. No created being is above sinning against God, apart from God's grace. Third, the Devil shows that God is just. God will ultimately judge the enemy and cast him into hell forever (Rev. 20:10). Likewise, the Devil shows that God is sovereign for the same reason. Although for now the Devil is the god of this world, God will cast him down at the time of his choosing. Each of these lessons points us toward a broader truth about God, which is that he is altogether holy, righteous, transcendent, mighty, sovereign, and glorious. The mightiest and most powerful of his enemies—*the* enemy—is pitifully small and wicked and weak in comparison to God. How glorious is our King!

Summary

We really do not know why God made the Devil specifically, but it makes sense that (1) God had some good reason to make him and (2) that we will attribute to God the glory requisite to his decisions when at last we see him face to face.

REFLECTION QUESTIONS

1. Why is it significant that the biblical authors do not ask or answer this question?

2. In what ways does this question relate to broader questions about evil and suffering?

3. Why should we be cautious about the source of such questions (whether curiosity or suspicion)?

4. What does it take to trust that God acted rightly in this area?

5. Is it comforting to know that the Devil is just one of God's creatures and not his equal?

Why and When Did the Devil Fall from Heaven?

Among theologians, the term "the Fall" generally refers to Adam's sin in the garden of Eden (Gen. 3:1–17). However, theologians also refer to a "moral fall" of the Devil, which is the term used to describe the incidence of his initial rebellion against God. In addition, the Bible mentions a literal fall of the Devil from heaven (Luke 10:18; Rev. 12:7–9). Theologians disagree about whether the moral fall corresponds to the literal fall, as well as about when the literal fall took or will take place. Some hold that in the remote past, after creation but before Adam's sin, the Devil sinned and was cast from heaven. Others hold that the Devil will be cast from heaven during the end times. On the question of why the Devil fell, Christian theology largely agrees that the Devil's rebellion was based on pride.

Nature of the Question

The biblical authors are not overly concerned with these types of questions since it is not significant to their message about the Messiah. However, many people of various religions grapple with similar questions. People really want to know how evil entered into the world. Since the Devil is the arch-enemy of God, his fall becomes a method that people use to get the answer to that question. As a consequence, many cultures and religions tell stories about the defeat of an evil one (sometimes even personified as a dragon). In most cases, these other religious accounts are not distracting for Christian theology because of the many other differences between the religions. However, Jewish and Muslim accounts of the fall of Satan are more problematic because those religions believe in one Creator God and an evil angel called Satan. Furthermore, both of those religions testify to the authority of the Old Testament. And, late Jewish nonbiblical writings as well as the *Qur'an* do tell a story about the fall of the Devil. In fact, the Jewish tradition has more than one. One common thread in some of these accounts is that the rebellion of the Devil came when God required that he serve Adam, the first man. There is no such event described in the Bible. The Bible describes the Devil as wicked from his first appearance in the Garden of Eden. As a result, we have to presume that his moral fall occurred prior to the events described in Genesis 3.

The church fathers had debates about which day of the creation week the Devil fell. A common conclusion was Day Four, on the supposition that the angels have some relation to the heavenly bodies. The difficulty for that discussion is that Moses does not tell us when God made the angels, since in his description of God's creation week he only mentions the creation of the physical world and the preparation of the land for Adam.

By the medieval period, the discussion had changed. Whichever day of the week the angels had been made, the question was now, how soon after their creation did the angels sin? One group held that the sin occurred in the first instantaneous moment of their creation. However, another group argued that it was not instantaneous, since that view runs the risk of it appearing that some of the angels had been created evil. So, they argued for the second instantaneous instant of creation instead. As is the case with much angelology, the debates are speculative and something other than the importance of the answer is usually driving the conversation. In the ancient case, the goal was primarily to fill out the details of God's creation of all things, invisible and visible (Col. 1:16). In the medieval case, the goal was to articulate more clearly the relationship between the intellect and the will. Angels became a test case for this debate, because they lacked bodily passions and did not require physical senses to know and act. Although such debates might be interesting, the question about what the Bible says about these matters can be answered fairly simply because there are not many details given in Scripture. In all historical cases, theologians agree that the Devil was made good (Gen. 1:31; John 8:44) and sinned through his own fault. In some cases, the language that describes the downfall of kings in the prophets is applied to the Devil (Isa. 14:12–15; Ezek. 28:12–15) as an additional proof that he was originally good, although neither of those texts is about the Devil.

Luke 10:18

Commentators are somewhat divided on the precise meaning of this passage. An older view was that in this verse Jesus describes a vision of the primordial fall of Satan from heaven. Very few commentators still hold this position.[1]

---

1. It had broad Patristic support: for example, Origen, *De Principiis* I.5.4–5. A new edition in English is available in Henri De Lubac, *Origen on First Principles*, trans. G. W. Butterworth (New York: Christian Classics, 2013). One of the only (perhaps the only) modern commentator to take this position is Kittel who writes, "Jesus spoke of His pre-existence [as the Word] either by open reference or by hint" (Gerhard Kittel, ed. *Theological Dictionary of the New Testament*, trans. Geoffrey W. Bromiley [Grand Rapids: Eerdmans, 1967], 4:130). In a footnote (#220), he cites Luke 10:18 as an example, as well as the reference to Origen's

First, such an interpretation does not make good sense of the fact that Jesus' comment occurs in the middle of a conversation with his disciples (Luke 10:17–20). Second, there is no record of a fall of Satan from heaven in Scripture except for this text and Revelation 12:7–9. A second view is that Jesus saw Satan fall while the disciples were on their assignment. The trouble with this interpretation is that Satan is described as active in the remainder of Luke-Acts. Furthermore, Paul's later warnings to the church about spiritual warfare refers to spiritual forces of darkness "in the heavenly places" (Eph. 6:12). A final view is that Jesus is speaking prophetically about the future casting out of Satan from heaven. When the disciples heal and cast out demons in Jesus name, it is prefiguring the eventual casting out of Satan that precedes his future judgment.[2] A related view holds that Jesus is describing the effect of the disciples' actions: Seeing their success in their task is like seeing the fall of Satan from heaven. The reason for thinking that the event must be understood as future is usually that Satan is not fully defeated at this point. For example, he continues to play a role in the Lukan narrative (Luke 22:3; Acts 5:3). Hence, the last two views seem the most plausible given the context.[3]

Revelation 12:7–9

In this passage, Satan and his angels are cast from heaven during a battle with Michael and his angels. Some commentators see this as a primordial fall, perhaps reflecting the vision of Jesus in Luke 10:18. This view is usually based on the Jewish tradition related to Enochic interpretations of Genesis 6.[4] However, none of those traditions are based on the Bible. Rather, they are based on late Jewish midrash or retellings of terse portions of the canonical Scripture. It is true that the Old Testament contains references to defeats of serpents or dragons, but these are best understood in their immediate contexts.[5] In any case, none of these mention heaven or a fall from heaven. In the

---

interpretation. In the note, he writes, "the very general modern rejection of reference to a pre-historical event (cf. esp. Zn. Lk., *ad loc.*) demands serious investigation."

2. For example, see John Nolland who writes, "in vision he [Jesus] sees the coming triumph of the Kingdom of God over the rule of Satan and has identified this triumph as his own task . . . . This vision is becoming reality" (*Luke 9:21–18:34*, Word Biblical Commentary, vol. 35B [Dallas: Word, 1993], 564). See also Joel B. Green, *The Gospel of Luke*, New International Commentary on the New Testament (Grand Rapids: Eerdmans, 1997), 419.

3. As an example, see Robert H. Stein, *Luke*, New American Commentary, vol. 24 (Nashville: Broadman, 1992), 309. For a recent discussion of interpretive options, see Simon Gathercole, "Jesus' Eschatological Vision of the Fall of Satan: Luke 10,18 Reconsidered," *Zeitschrift für die neutestamentliche Wissenschaft und die Kunde der* älteren *Kirche* 94 (2003): 142–63.

4. Grant R. Osborne, *Revelation*, BECNT (Grand Rapids: Baker Academic, 2002), 468–73.

5. It is important to realize that the prophets also contain an eschatological outlook, which means that the patterns exemplified in historical accounts become examples of God's ultimate judgment.

casting out described in Revelation 12:7–9, the text reads that "there was no longer any place" for Satan and his angels in heaven. However, Satan appears in heaven (Job 1:6) long after he had become the deceiver and adversary. The Bible presumes a moral fall of the Devil, since he is wicked from his first appearances to us (John 8:44), but it is never described in the Bible. The literal fall depicted here (actually, a casting out) is better understood as a future event, consistent with the plan laid out by John (Rev. 4:1). Furthermore, in the following verses (10–12), the rejoicing makes no sense if the Fall described is primordial. Finally, the appearance of the Beast is Revelation 13 establishes a continuity with Satan's casting out in the previous chapter.[6] So, both mentions of a literal fall from heaven (Luke 10:18; Rev. 12:7–9) are eschatological.

Primordial Fall

On the issue of his moral fall, the Scriptures are silent. There is no description of what exactly precipitated Satan's initial sin, what the logistics of his temptations were, or any other details about the event. However, the Christian tradition has largely agreed that his sin was pride. Granted, part of the reasoning for this conclusion comes from what seem to be mistaken interpretations of Isaiah 14 and Ezekiel 28 (see Questions 17 and 18). However, 1 Timothy also points to the same conclusion. When Paul is instructing Timothy on the qualities to look for when appointing elders, he mentions that recent converts should not be appointed because it could lead them to arrogance. He writes: "He must not be a recent convert, or he may become puffed up with conceit and fall into the condemnation of the devil" (1 Tim. 3:6). The phrase, "the condemnation of the devil" could mean that the Devil would condemn the recent convert, but that seems unlikely as the interpretation. First, the Devil is happy to lead men astray (1 Peter 5:8). Second, the Devil has no authority to condemn a believer. Another way to understand the phrase is to read it as "the devil's condemnation," meaning the same condemnation that the Devil fell into. On that understanding, being puffed up with conceit (pride) would put one at risk for condemnation (1 Cor. 10:12), and this the same condemnation as the Devil. Hence, the primary sin of the Devil is conceit or pride. An inkling of this pride is apparent in his temptation of Eve. He persuades her that eating the forbidden fruit will make her like God, which is desirous to him and, tragically, to Adam and Eve (and all their children).

Summary

The Devil rebelled against God and fell morally even before he tempted Adam and Eve in the Garden. When exactly this took place is not revealed in Scripture. It does seem likely that his sin was a sin of pride. In the end times,

---

6. Robert L. Thomas, *Revelation: An Exegetical Commentary* (Chicago: Moody Press, 1995), 128–29.

the Devil will be cast out of heaven and will fall to the earth in anticipation of the return of Christ to judge the living and the dead. His ruin is sure, but he has not been completely subdued by the Lord at this time.

REFLECTION QUESTIONS

1. Is it significant that the biblical authors do not say when the Devil sinned?

2. What reasons might lead us to think his sin was pride?

3. What surprised you most about the history of this question?

4. How is it helpful to separate the question of the Devil's moral fall from his being cast out of heaven?

5. Why is it important to know that the Devil can prowl around now, but that his ruin is sure?

Does Isaiah 14 Describe the Fall of the Devil?

There is a long tradition among Christians of interpreting Isaiah 14 and Ezekiel 28 as referring to the primordial fall of Satan. Certainly, there is a consistency to the fall of persons in positions of great power and authority, and the Bible tells us clearly that "pride goes before destruction" (Prov. 16:18). However, the arguments given since Origen that these two texts are about the Devil are weak, and they only have persuasive effect because they have been repeated for such a long time. It seems clear that, considered in context, both Isaiah 14 and Ezekiel 28 (see Question 18) are prophetic speeches about particular human kings consistent with the overall messages of the books of Isaiah and Ezekiel. If someone wanted to speculate that behind the authority of these kings was a supernatural occult power, that would be fine so far as it goes. However, the text does not say as much, neither is it significant for what the authors intend to accomplish. A plain reading of these texts shows that it is self-aggrandizement and abuse of power and authority that causes these human kings to be cast down from their positions of power. In Isaiah 14, because the King of Babylon characterizes himself as a god, he is graphically reminded by Isaiah that there is only one God. Hence, this text is about (as the text explicitly states) the King of Babylon.

It is also true that the prophetic texts in general have an eschatological character.[1] In other words, the prophets often describe specific historical

---

1. See, for example, the discussion in Odil Hannes Steck, *The Prophetic Books and their Theological Witness*, trans. James D. Nogalski (St. Louis: Chalice Press, 2000), 137–52; Christopher R. Seitz, *Prophecy and Hermeneutics: Toward a New Introduction to the Prophets* (Grand Rapids: Baker Academic, 2007), 248–52; and John H. Sailhamer, who writes, "The early Jewish readers of the Old Testament understood the whole of the Old Testament to be a prophecy of, and for, their own future" (*Biblical Prophecy* [Grand Rapids: Zondervan, 1998], 44).

accounts as portrayals of the way God judges in general, and thus they establish a pattern for his future judgment as well. Hence, it would be consistent with the prophetic authors' goals to think of this text as pointing forward to the day when all false kings and gods (the Devil included) are cast down; but it is not correct to see a primordial fall of the Devil in either Isaiah 14 or Ezekiel 28. Could the Devil be partially behind the activity of the King of Babylon at this point in history? Absolutely. But, there is no need to postulate an identity between the two in order to understand this text.

Isaiah 14

Verses 12–15 of this chapter have been thought by some to reference the Devil:

> How you are fallen from heaven, O Day Star, son of Dawn! How you are cut down to the ground, you who laid the nations low! You said in your heart, "I will ascend to heaven; above the stars of God I will set my throne on high; I will sit on the mount of assembly in the far reaches of the north; I will ascend above the heights of the clouds; I will make myself like the Most High." But you are brought down to Sheol, to the far reaches of the pit.

Origen says of this passage: "How can we possibly suppose that what is said in many places by Scripture, especially in Isaiah, about Nebuchadnezzar is said about a human being? For no human being is said to 'have fallen from heaven' or to have been 'Lucifer' or the one who 'arose every morning.'"[2] He also says that, "most evidently by these words is he shown to have fallen from heaven who formerly was Lucifer, and who used to arise in the morning. Nay, even, the Savior Himself teaches us, saying of the Devil, 'Behold, I see Satan fallen from heaven like lightning.'"[3] This viewpoint was later also adopted by Augustine.[4] The basic argument is that there is no way that this person could

---

2. Origen, *De Principiis* 4.3.9. See Henri De Lubac, *Origen on First Principles*, trans. G. W. Butterworth (New York: Christian Classics, 2013). This work was written around AD 230.

3. Origen, *De Principiis* 1.5.

4. He makes reference to both Isaiah 14:12 and Ezekiel 28:13 in his discussion of how the Devil was not made with a sinful nature. "Take another of St. John's texts: 'The devil sins from the beginning.' The Manichaeans do not understand that, if the Devil is evil by nature, there can be no question of sin at all. They have no reply to the witness of the Prophets, for example, where Isaias, representing the Devil figuratively in the person of the Prince of Babylon, asks: 'How are thou fallen from Heaven, O Lucifer, who didst rise in the morning?' or where Ezekiel says: 'Thou wast in the pleasure of the paradise of God: every precious stone was they covering'" (*The City of God*, Books VIII–XVI, The Fathers of the Church, vol. 14, trans. Grace Monahan and Gerald G. Walsh [Washington, D.C.: Catholic University of America Press, 2008], 210–11).

be a human given his description, and that argument has been repeated in essentially the same form through the twentieth century. However, even among those who believe this passage references Satan, there is disagreement about whether the passage refers to the primordial fall or his future judgment.

We have seen that there are two basic assumptions underlying the arguments. The first is that the text refers to a "lucifer" and that this is a proper name of the Devil. The second is that the lofty descriptions of the figure in the text could not possibly refer to a human king. Both assumptions are false or highly questionable.

With respect to the second assumption, there is no *a priori* reason to think that a human being could not be referred to with such "lofty" descriptions, especially when it is recognized that the text in question is a satirical lament. In Isaiah 14:4, Isaiah tells us that he has been instructed to take up a "taunt against the king of Babylon." The first thing to notice is that the target of the taunt is the king of Babylon. Unless there is extremely compelling textual evidence to do otherwise, we should identify the figure in the text as the king of Babylon because that is what the text says (vv. 4, 22). It makes no mention of the Devil. The language of lament that follows this instruction is clearly satirical because the prophetic speech is intended to be taunting. So the grandiose descriptions applied to the king of Babylon fit the genre. Further, these grand statements are false statements that the king made about himself, and the prophet is now using the same terms to mock him. Whereas once the kings of the earth oppressed the nations (Isa. 14:5), God is now laying low such kings (of whom the king of Babylon is one). The dead in the grave will also mock the judged kings because they died just like all the mortal men, and they rot and decay just like other men. Isaiah 14:11 makes this explicit when it says, "Your pomp is brought down to Sheol, the sound of your harps; maggots are laid as a bed beneath you, and worms are your covers." Unless there is a completely unannounced change of topic in verses 12–15, those verses are addressing the same figure who will be judged with death and decay from verses 4–11.

Notice also that in verse 13, the king of Babylon is one who is saying to himself that he will ascend to heaven and raise his throne about the stars of God. This is not unlike the bold claims of the men at the tower of Babel ("Come, let us build ourselves a city and a tower with its top in the heavens," Gen. 11:4).[5] The claims that the king of Babylon made about himself are false, and so Isaiah tells him that he will die like any other man (Isa. 14:16). In fact, his death will be worse than other kings who have tombs (Isa. 14:18) because he will not be buried (Isa. 14:20) but will lie dead on the battlefield (Isa. 14:19).

All the details of the text should lead us to conclude that the figure referred to is a human king, the king of Babylon, who will be judged for his

---

5. In fact, the word translated "Babel" in Genesis 11 is everywhere else translated "Babylon" in the Old Testament.

presumption and cruelty. This is in keeping with the judgment of the other kings in the prophets and especially in this section of Isaiah, which also described the judgment that will come to other foreign nations (Babylon in Isa. 13–14; Moab in 15–16; Damascus in 17; Cush in 18; Egypt in 19, etc.). So, the argument that this could not merely be a human king is simply not true.

The other assumption underlying these arguments is that "Lucifer" (KJV) or "Morning Star" (most modern English translations) is a proper name for the Devil. This can only be true *if* the referent of the text is the Devil (which cannot be decided in advance) and *if* "Lucifer" is the proper translation of the Hebrew text. In other words, we use the word "Lucifer" as a name for the Devil because of a particular interpretation of this text. However, I have argued above that such an interpretation is unduly speculative. We have already seen that there is no special reason to think that the taunt of Isaiah is directed against anyone other than the king of Babylon.

We should also investigate whether "lucifer" is a faithful translation of the Hebrew text. In fact, the term Lucifer comes to us from the Latin translation of the Bible. "Lucifer" simply means "light-bringer" and is not a proper name in Latin (except because it has become a word we use to refer to Satan). Typically, it is used to refer to the morning star (the planet Venus). It comes into our English Bibles through the King James Version where the translators simply borrowed from the Latin instead of translating the Hebrew text. So, the word "lucifer" simply does not appear in the original text. The word in the Hebrew text is *helel*, and *helel* does not mean "morning star" or "light-bringer." Both of those translations are interpretive and grammatically unlikely.

The trouble is that some early translators understood the word *helel* to derive from the root word, *halal*, which can mean "to shine." So, the word in Isaiah 14:12 is understood to mean "shining one." Because the next phrase is clearly "son of the morning," the "shining one" is interpreted to be the morning star and hence "Lucifer." So, to arrive at "Lucifer," several steps are taken in translation. First, the word *helel* is interpreted as a derivative of the root *halal* and understood therefore to mean "shining one." Then, the next phrase, "son of the morning," is used to help make sense of "shining one." This leads to the conclusion that the "shining one" is the star that appears in the morning. For this reason, the Greek translators chose to render the word *heosphoros* ("morning star"). A way to express the same idea in Latin is "lucifer." Even on this analysis, however, the word "lucifer" is not a proper name and is not treated as a proper name until much later.

The biggest problem with this analysis is that *helel* does not derive from the root *halal*. There are a few problems with assuming the root word *halal* for this text. First, the verb *halal* is quite rare with the meaning "to shine," although it is common with the meaning "to praise." Second, translators need to revocalize the Hebrew text in order to make *helel* a plausible derivative of *halal*. In other words with the vowels that appear in the Masoretic text, the word is undoubtedly a verb and not a noun. That means that this text would be the only place that the word occurs in this form. Given that there is another root word that commonly appears in this form in Hebrew, it makes much more sense to translate it from the other root word, which is *yalal*.

Yalal means "to wail" or "to howl," and this is actually the preferable translation because it is the literal reading of the Hebrew text. In fact, Jerome, the translator of the Latin Bible who bequeathed to us the translation "lucifer," claims as much in his commentary on Isaiah.[6] He writes that the Hebrew of verse 12 should be expressed as *ulula*, which is "howling" in Latin. The translation of the Latin Bible, he says, is given for the ease of understanding. Because Jerome was already convinced from his reading of Origen that this text referred to Satan, he provided a translation of the text that he admits is not a reading of the Hebrew! So, the introduction of the word "lucifer" into the text is admittedly interpretive, and the grammatical reading is admittedly "to howl" or "to wail."

Of course, this conclusion is strongly supported by evidence from the Hebrew Bible (as Jerome clearly knew). First, *yalal* in the form found in Isaiah 14:12 (the Hiphil imperative) is common.[7] The verb is also in this section of Isaiah (Isa. 15:2, 3; 16:7). All such usage is a common feature of judgment and lament. In fact, the word only occurs in the prophets and is frequently parallel to other Hebrew verbs for crying out in sorrow and distress (*za'aq* and *sapad*). Since this particular passage (Isaiah 14) contains admitted elements of lament, the natural translation for the term would be "Wail!" or "Howl!," not "light-bringer." Hence, the verse should be translated, "How you are fallen from heaven! Wail, son of the morning! How you are cut down to the earth who once weakened the nations." This translation is consistent with the prophets' usage of Hebrew and follows standard analysis of Hebrew verb forms. This language of judgment even appears in the New Testament (James 5:1). It is also the translation of the Hebrew suggested by the originator of the Latin Bible.

Why then do modern translations usually adopt a translation based on the root *halal*? The first reason is the influence of the King James translation, which uses the Latin and not the Hebrew as the guide for this word. The second reason is completely unrelated to this historical arc from Jerome to the present. There is a deity referenced in some Ugaritic texts (a language that is similar to Hebrew) called *Helel*, "son of the dawn." Some modern scholars believe that Isaiah is calling the king of Babylon by this name in order to mock him. There are two major problems with this interpretation. The first is that we know even less about Ugaritic than we do about biblical Hebrew, so taking our cue from another language is not the best first course of action. Secondly, we have a

---

6. See *Corpus Christianorum*, Series Latina (Turnhout, Belgium: Brepols, 1953), 73:168–69.
7. The Hiphil imperative of *yalal* is also found in Isaiah 13:6; 14:31; 23:1, 6, 14; Jeremiah 4:8; 25:34; 51:8; Ezekiel 21:12; 30:2; Joel 1:5, 11; Zephaniah 1:11; Zechariah 11:2.

perfectly viable translation from *yalal* that is consistent with usage in biblical Hebrew. Hence, there is no need to postulate a pagan mythological background in order to understand Isaiah's prophecy. However, even if the Ugaritic background does explain why the root of the verb is *halal*, there is still nothing in the text to provide us reason to think that it is about the fall of the Devil.

Summary

The argument that Isaiah 14 describes the primordial fall of the Devil is based on two faulty assumptions. First, it is not true that the figure referred to in the text is described in terms too lofty to be a man. Origen simply asserted as much without argument, and the assertion has been repeated. Second, there are good reasons to doubt that "Lucifer" is a sensible translation of the word *helel*. Even the originator of the translation "lucifer" admits that it is not a translation of the Hebrew. Even if it turns out (for a totally unrelated reason) that the root derives from Ugaritic, there is still nothing in the text (or anywhere else in the Bible) that connects that name to Satan.

Given that the prophetic works have an eschatological character, one could see in the specific historical judgment of the king of Babylon a motif in a pattern of divine judgment that repeats itself and will repeat itself finally in the judgment of the Devil and all his sons in the end time. However, there is a significant difference between recognizing a pattern in prophetic portrayals of judgment and holding that this specific text informs us about the moral fall of Satan. Our desire to fill in gaps in our theological stories should not cause us to read into the prophets what they do not intend to say.

REFLECTION QUESTIONS

1. What drives us to want details about the fall of the Devil?

2. Why are translation issues significant in interpreting texts?

3. Where does the name "Lucifer" enter the Christian tradition?

4. Should grammatical context or theological need drive our interpretation of the Bible?

5. How does reading all of Isaiah 14 in context cast doubt on the interpretation that it relates to the Devil?

Does Ezekiel 28 Describe the Fall of the Devil?

In the previous question, I noted that there was long a tradition of interpreting Isaiah 14 as referring to the primordial fall of the Devil. The same is true for Ezekiel 28, which is textually similar to the passage in Isaiah 14. Also like the Isaiah text, Ezekiel 28 does not refer to the Devil, except perhaps in the sense that it offers a prophetic portrayal of God's judgment against false self-righteous kings.

Ezekiel 28

The particular text in question is found in Ezekiel 28:11–19, a lamentation over the king of Tyre:

> Moreover, the word of the LORD came to me: "Son of man, raise a lamentation over the king of Tyre, and say to him, Thus says the LORD GOD: You were the signet of perfection, full of wisdom and perfect in beauty. You were in Eden, the garden of God; every precious stone was your covering, sardius, topaz, and diamond, beryl, onyx, and jasper, sapphire, emerald, and carbuncle; and crafter in gold were your settings and your engravings. On the day that you were created they were prepared. You were an anointed guardian cherub. I placed you; you were on the holy mountain of God; in the midst of the stones of fire you walked. You were blameless in your ways from the day you were created, til unrighteousness was found in you. In the abundance of your trade you were filled with violence in your midst, and you sinned; so I cast you as a profane thing from the mountain of God, and I destroyed you, O guardian cherub, from the midst of the stones of fire. Your

heart was proud because of your beauty; you corrupted your wisdom for the sake of your splendor. I cast you to the ground; I exposed you before kings, to feast their eyes on you. By the multitude of your iniquities, in the unrighteousness of your trade you profaned your sanctuaries; so I brought fire out from your midst; it consumed you, and I turned you to ashes on the earth in the sight of all who saw you. All who know you among the peoples are appalled at you; you have come to a dreadful end and shall be no more forever.

The arguments that identify the king of Tyre with the Devil are similar to the argument from the passage in Isaiah 14 (see Question 17). They are more compelling for this text than for Isaiah 14, because the king is referred to as a cherub and he is said to have been in Eden, the garden of God. Obviously, that suggests a connection to the presence of the Devil in the garden (Gen. 3). Furthermore, the Christian theological account of the Devil holds that he was created blameless and fell into sin before being judged. Since this description depicts this personage as a blameless angel in Eden who sinned after his creation, it fits the general pattern of the Christian account. Of course, the reason that it fits the account is because this is one of the texts that was used by early Christian theologians to work out the account in the first place. As I suggested earlier, John's witness is sufficient to confirm the theological account (see John 8:44). There is no need to contort Ezekiel's message to fill in the details.

As in the case of Isaiah 14, the principal reason to be suspicious of the claim that the oracle refers to the Devil is that the text explicitly identifies the target as a foreign king, as well as the sin that requires judgment.

You (Were) a Cherub

One of the key planks in the argument is that verse 14 refers to the Devil. Most English translations render this verse as "You were an anointed cherub." On the face of it, this is an obscure sentence—even in English. Yet, the text traditions are even more challenging.[1] One of the major challenges is with the first word of the phrase.

In Hebrew, it consists of only two consonants, and the word itself can be vocalized in several different ways. Traditionally, Hebrew was written without vowels. It was only later that a tradition of vocalizing (i.e., writing in the vowels) the consonants became established. The common Hebrew text, the Masoretic text, has a system of vowels, and it vocalizes the first word as a feminine singular. In English, the fact that the word appears as a feminine pronoun is obscured because the English word "you" is the same whether the person addressed is male or female. This is significant because the king

---

1. As the ESV and most modern English translations point out in their notes.

of Tyre is a masculine figure, and all the other related words in the oracle are masculine.

The only ancient text tradition that arguably presents us with a masculine pronoun is the Targum, which is written in Aramaic. Curiously, the Targum does not mention a cherub. Instead, it uses the word "king." In other words, it understands "cherub" to refer to the splendor of the king and takes it as a metaphorical claim and not an ontological one. The other major early translations, the Septuagint and Syriac, both understand the two-consonant Hebrew word to have a different vocalization. These translations do not understand it as a pronoun at all, but as the preposition "with." Hence, their translations read, "You were with the cherub." If those translations are correct, then the original Hebrew does not even arguably equate the king of Tyre with a cherub. So, the difficulty with this text—that the first word of the sentence can be understood in at least three different ways—is understated in the English translations and in arguments that identify the king of Tyre with the Devil.

Context of the Lament

Even granting that the reading should be "You were a cherub," it still does not follow automatically that the claim is ontological. The text is clear that this passage is a lament or dirge, and it is presented in the context of a series of judgment oracles against the nations (Ezek. 25–32). So, the context should lead us to see the address in Ezekiel 28 as an address against a foreign power. Given the grandiose claims that foreign kings make about themselves in general (Isa. 14) and in the local context of Ezekiel (28:1–10), it is appropriate to see this "lament" as a satire against the king of Tyre. For example, in the previous oracle of the same chapter, the prince of Tyre is said to be "wiser than Daniel" (Ezek. 28:3), but the context of the previous verse makes it clear that this is satirical. Both these men pretend to be gods, but they are not gods (Ezek. 28:2). Hence, the lofty language that the prophet uses to describe them is a mockery of their vanity. This is consistent with Ezekiel elsewhere (e.g., Ezek. 29:3 where Pharaoh is called "the great dragon that lies in the midst of his streams").

Furthermore, Ezekiel picks out the specific type of sin that the king is guilty of when he writes: "In the abundance of your trade you were filled with violence" (v. 16) and "in the unrighteousness of your trade you profaned your sanctuaries" (v. 18). Thus, the sin of the king of Tyre is his unrighteous commercial practices. That makes sense if the address is to the king of Tyre (as the text says) but is nonsensical if the address is actually directed to the Devil. Likewise, the judgment of the figure before other kings (v. 17) and the peoples (v. 18) is consistent with the judgment of other nations and human kings.

Summary

Some translations seem to initially support the idea that Ezekiel 28 is directed against the Devil, but a contextual reading of that chapter shows that the passage is directed to the king of Tyre. The text mocks him with lofty language in a way consistent with the prophets and identifies his sin as commerce and his judgment as before other kings. The Devil was not in Eden multiplying commerce to himself, nor was he ever actually cast from the mountain of God. To read this as a reflection of the primordial or future judgment of the Devil requires us to wrench the text from its context and ignore some significant features of the passage.

REFLECTION QUESTIONS

1. What drives us to want details about the fall of the Devil?

2. Why are translation issues significant in interpreting texts?

3. Should grammatical context or theological need drive our interpretation of the Bible?

4. How does the identification of the king's sin (commerce) cast doubt on the interpretation that this text relates to the Devil?

5. How does the broader context of Ezekiel's oracles against the nations help us understand this text?

What Is the Role of the Devil in Temptation?

The Bible clearly describes the Devil as a tempter. In the Garden, he tempts Adam and Eve under the guise of a serpent. He tempts Jesus in the wilderness. He "enters into" Judas on the night that Judas betrays the Lord. However, these are isolated and powerful incidents. Most temptation does not take place in these ways, and it seems unlikely that the Devil personally tempts each person. Having said that, the Devil is the god of this age and he has angels of his own, the demons. The world as we know it remains under his lingering shadow in anticipation of the return of the king. As such, his lies are present in false doctrines, beliefs, and thoughts; and it seems appropriate to speak of such things as of or from the Devil in a generic sense. His voice and its echoes can be discerned in our world. In fact, we can see this kind of language in the book of James. However, the Devil does not have authority over the believer, even if he can draw on our sinful desires which entice us to act wrongly.

James on Temptation

Although it is true that things outside of us can present to us occasions for temptation, temptations strictly speaking arise from within ourselves. This is the reason that Jesus can say, "What comes out of a person defiles him. For from within, out of the heart of man, come evil thoughts, sexual immortality, theft, murder, adultery, coveting, wickedness, deceit, sensuality, envy, slander, pride, foolishness. All these evil things come from within, and they defile a person" (Mark 7:20–23). James develops this teaching in the first chapter of his letter:

> Let no one say when he is tempted, "I am being tempted by God," for God cannot be tempted with evil, and he himself

tempts no one. But each person is tempted when he is lured and enticed by his own desire. Then desire when it has conceived gives birth to sin, and sin when it is fully grown brings forth death. (James 1:13–15)

The desire to sin is already present in men. Tempters merely draw on what is already present in order to fan the flame of our desires. It is important to recognize that when we are tempted, (1) God is not the tempter and (2) if the Devil is involved, he is working with what is already there. That is why James later writes: "Who is wise and understanding among you? By his good conduct let him show his works in the meekness of wisdom. But if you have bitter jealousy and selfish ambition in your hearts, do not boast and be false to the truth. This is not the wisdom that comes down from above, but is earthly, unspiritual, demonic" (James 3:13–15). The Devil can tempt us to celebrate what is good in us to the level of pride. He does this by drawing on our sinful desire for praise and recognition. But this type of wisdom is false, and James can say "demonic."

Sinful Desires

In most cases, the New Testament authors write about temptation in ways that focus on sinful desires and not on the activity of the Devil or demons. This tendency does not mean that the Devil is not active in tempting God's church, but it does mean that the primary attention of the biblical authors is on dealing with our own sinful desires and attitudes. Hence, combatting sin and temptation through the Word and Spirit should be the primary focus of spiritual warfare. The biblical authors want us to be aware that there is more to this battle than flesh-and-blood enemies, but they are quick to point out that it is our own brokenness that leads us to such trouble.

As a result, there are no clear biblical tests by which someone could decide whether a demon was involved in a particular temptation or not. Given what the biblical authors do tell us, however, we do not need such a test. The New Testament teaches that the world, the flesh, and the Devil cooperate, and provides instruction on resisting temptations in general. Hence, there is not a different method for combatting sin if the Devil, or the world, or the flesh brought on the temptation. In any case, the blame is placed on our sinful desires and not the antagonism of the enemy. No one can say, "The Devil made me do it!" (Gen. 3). We have to be comfortable with a certain level of ambiguity in this regard because the biblical authors simply do not tell us precisely how the Devil tempts us. Even in the Lord's Prayer, we can see this ambiguity. Jesus tells us to pray, "Lead us not into temptation, but deliver us from evil *tou ponerou*" (Matt. 6:13). In some cases, this is translated as "deliver us from evil," but the presence of the definite article (*tou* = the) as well as the article (*apo*, not *ek*) makes it clear that the translation should be "deliver us from the evil one," which is another title for the Devil.[1] To deliver us from evil is, in this setting, to deliver us from the one who is evil.

Persecution for the Faith

One of the often overlooked—but primary—ways that the Devil tempts us is through persecution and affliction because of the gospel. Overcoming the temptation of the Devil, therefore, requires perseverance (Mark 4:15). Paul expresses specific concern about the Devil's activity in 1 Thessalonians. In chapter 2 of the letter, Paul describes his earnest appeal to the Thessalonians and he is grieved for the afflictions that they face because they believed that Paul's message was the word of God. In light of those troubles, he writes: "I sent to learn about your faith, for fear that somehow the tempter had tempted you and our labor would be in vain" (1 Thess. 3:5). The important thing to notice for our purposes is that Paul does not specify how exactly the Devil might have tempted them away from the faith. The point is that the Devil is able to tempt them, and his attempts might have been disguised as outward persecutions (1 Thess. 2:14). When Paul is hindered from traveling to visit the church, he attributes the difficulty to Satan (1 Thess. 2:18). In the previous verse, he was describing how the countrymen of the Thessalonian church were preventing him from sharing the gospel. This discussion shows us that the Devil works through many means and that we might rightly attribute certain hardship to him even if he is not personally manifest in the situation. An analogy might be if a wicked king sends soldiers to block a road, it is acceptable to say that the king blocked our path even though he might be far away; "the whole world lies in the power of the evil one" (1 John 5:19). So, when circumstances hinder our faith or the gospel, we can rightly see these as devilish. But, praise God, "he who was born of God protects him, and the evil one does not touch him" (1 John 5:18). The Devil does not have authority to cause us to sin, and we can resist temptations to sin by the power of the Holy Spirit (Rom. 6:14; 1 Cor. 10:13).

Summary

The Devil is active in the world because it lies in his power. He is active in his pursuit of the unwary (1 Peter 5:8). He uses many different means to tempt us to despair and sin. In particular, he wants to cast doubt on God's goodness and his word (Gen. 3:1–4; Matt. 4:6). The root of temptations, however, is not solely the activity of the Devil. We sin through our own fault (James 1:14). Yet, because of the weakness of our flesh, the Devil can entice us to act out on our sinful desires (1 Cor. 7:5; Eph. 4:27). Yet, he has no authority over the believer

---

1. See the discussion of the usage of the prepositions in David Alan Black, *It's Still Greek to Me* (Grand Rapids: Baker Books, 1998), 87. Black notes that *apo* is used with persons, not with nonpersonal enemies.

(1 John 5:18)! We must resist him by prayer (Matt. 6:13) and by drawing near to God in Christ (James 4:8). If we resist him, he will flee from us (James 4:7).

REFLECTION QUESTIONS

1. Why is it important to recognize that sinful desires come from within?

2. Is it comforting to know that the Devil has no authority over the believer?

3. What are some practical ways that we "resist" the Devil?

4. How is there a sense in which something can be "devilish," even when the Devil is not directly involved?

5. Why is it important that we expect persecution because of the faith?

PART 3

QUESTIONS ABOUT
SPIRITUAL WARFARE

Questions Related to
Spiritual Warfare in History

What Does the Bible Say about Jesus and Spiritual Warfare?

A key verse relating to Jesus and spiritual warfare is found in John's first letter. He writes: "the reason the Son of God appeared was to destroy the works of the devil" (1 John 3:8). Make no mistake: God and the Devil are not equals. The Devil is God's creature, something that he made, as much as anything else that exists. Because of this, it is good news that God has not left us on our own to wrestle with principalities and powers. Instead, because of his love for us, God sent his Son to destroy the works of the Devil. In Christ, we have all we need for life and godliness (2 Peter 1:3) and that includes the equipping to wage spiritual warfare. The Bible tells us that the reason that victory in spiritual warfare is possible is because of the power and authority of Jesus. We can see this theme clearly in Jesus' temptations and in his authority over demons.

Temptations of Jesus

The Synoptic Gospels all contain a record that Jesus was tempted by the Devil himself (Matt. 4:1–11; Mark 1:12–13; Luke 4:1–13). While Matthew and Luke certainly present a historical account of how Jesus responded to the temptations of the Devil, the primary purpose of these texts is not to teach their readers how to ward off the Devil. The primary purpose is to reveal something about Jesus, in particular that he is the one able to resist the Devil and do the will of God. In fact, as a general rule, we should caution ourselves against a rush to application in reading the Bible. When we come to the text of Scripture intent on finding something to do—some concrete action to take—we run the risk of running roughshod over what the biblical authors are trying to tell us. The temptations of Jesus are a good example of this phenomenon. Frequently, discussions of these texts focus on how Jesus uses the Word of God to ward off the temptation of the Devil.[1] The application for our lives is then obvious: like Jesus, we can rely on Scripture to resist the temptation of the enemy. However, if we leap from what Jesus does to an implied command about what we should do, then we miss an opportunity to reflect on the fact that Jesus actually resists the temptation of the Devil by the power of the Holy Spirit *when it is the temptation of the Devil himself.* Before we think about how we should imitate Jesus, we should reflect on how amazing it is that Jesus can do what absolutely none of us could have done.

The lesson for spiritual warfare in these texts is this: Jesus has the power to defeat the Devil. Because he is our armor (Eph. 6:11–12), we can likewise resist the allure of the enemy (1 Cor. 10:13).

Casting Out Demons

In a similar way, the accounts of Jesus healing demoniacs are not intended to be how-to guides for exorcism and deliverance. They are instead demonstrations of his power and authority. These stories are part-and-parcel of the apostles' testimony that Jesus is the Messiah. Take Mark's account as an example. In Mark, there are records of three different encounters between Jesus and a demonized person (Mark 1:21–28; 5:1–20; 9:14–29) but casting out demons was a general feature of Jesus' ministry (Mark 1:34, 39). Often, in reading these accounts, we focus on the details of the encounter, but it would be better to turn our attention to the narrative comments that Mark makes, because the authors of Scripture often tell us how to interpret their stories.

The incident recorded in Mark 1:21–28 is a good example of this. Mark tells us that Jesus entered into the synagogue to teach and that the listeners were amazed because he spoke differently than the scribes. He spoke like one who had authority (v. 22). In verses 23–26, Jesus encounters the man with an unclean spirit and casts out the demon. Then, in verse 27, the people who had been amazed by the authority of his teaching are now also marveling at his authority over demons. The effect of this is that his fame increases in the region (v. 28). The point of describing this particular encounter is not so that we could cast out demons the way that Jesus did, but to demonstrate that Jesus has authority. In fact, ironically, the one to correctly identify the true identity of Jesus is the demon! This identification—that Jesus of Nazareth is the Holy One of God—is sandwiched by Mark between two different evidences of the authority of Jesus: his ability to teach and his ability to command

---

1. "What Jesus does is exemplary and representative. . . . Jesus shows the reader the path to faithful walk with God" (Darrell L. Bock. *Luke 1:1–9:50*, Baker Exegetical Commentary on the New Testament [Grand Rapids: Baker, 1994], 383–84). See also Robert Stein who notes, "Jesus' experience became a model of how Theophilus was to live out his life. . . . The passage's primary function, however, is to demonstrate to Luke's readers why Jesus was the kind of Messiah he was" (*Luke*, New American Commentary [Nashville: Broadman Press, 1992], 148–50).

unclean spirits. Why does Jesus have authority over the spirits? Because he is the Messiah. The demons know this and so they are commanded to be silent (Mark 1:34). So, the casting out demons is not an example for us to imitate. Rather, it is evidence that Jesus is who he says he is.[2]

In fact, that same theme is picked up by Mark in his chapter 3. Jesus has been gathering crowds by teaching, healing the sick, and casting out demons. We have already seen that he surpassed the scribes in doing this (Mark 1:22). The scribes accuse him of having authority of the demons, not because he is the Messiah, but because he "has" Beelzebub (the Devil) and uses Satan's power to cast out demons (3:22). Jesus uses the opportunity to rebuke them: He does not cast out demons by unclean spirits but by the Spirit of God (3:30). He can do this because he is the one able to bind the strong man (3:27). He has that power because he is the Son of God. This same theme is consistent in the book of Mark, because Mark wants his readers to see that Jesus is the Messiah.

Notice the repetition of this pattern in Mark 5. Jesus encounters a man with an unclean spirit who no one can "bind" because "no one had the strength to subdue him" (5:2). But, at the mere presence of Jesus, the man calls out similarly to the incident in Mark 1: "What have you to do with me, Jesus, Son of the Most High God?" (5:7). When the people see that Jesus had restored the man, they are afraid (5:15). The effect of the report of this story is that the people in the Decapolis "marvel" at Jesus (5:20). The point of these accounts is to show us that Jesus is the Messiah, with authority over all.

Even when Jesus sends the twelve out, there is no instruction given for how they will heal or cast out demons. The text reports merely that Jesus (who had the authority) "gave them authority over the unclean spirits" (6:7) and that, in fact, "they cast out many demons" (6:13). When Luke writes about the disciples casting out demons, they are joyous because "the demons are subject to us in your name" (10:17). But, Jesus tells them that the authority that he has given them is not the reason that they should rejoice. Rather, they should rejoice that their "names are written in heaven" (Luke 10:19). In fact, the limits of their authority are established in Mark 9 in which Mark notes that they were unable to cast out a spirit that made a boy mute and caused him to have seizures (9:18). Jesus is able to command the demon to leave the boy (9:25). When the disciples ask why they could not cast the demon out, Jesus tells them that "this kind cannot be driven out by anything but prayer" (9:29). Matthew tells us that the disciples lacked faith in Jesus

---

2. This is consistent in the gospel accounts. "What is decisive is not the exorcisms but the exorcist" (W. C. Davies and D. C. Allison, *Matthew 8–18*, International Critical Commentary [London: Bloomsbury, 2004], 341). "Remarkably, in spite of the attention Luke gives to Jesus' instructions to the seventy-two, he provides no account of the mission itself. Again, the narrator maintains a more narrow focus on Jesus" (Joel B. Green. *The Gospel of Luke*, New International Commentary on the New Testament [Grand Rapids: Eerdmans, 1997], 417).

and so could not complete the work (Matt. 17:20). And, Luke summarizes the conclusion of the whole matter: "And all were astonished at the majesty of God" (Luke 9:43).

Summary

The main teaching of the Bible about Jesus and spiritual warfare is that victory is possible in spiritual warfare because of the authority of Jesus Christ. Speaking on his own authority, Jesus is able to cast out demons. The gospel writers use testimonies of this power as evidence that Jesus is the Messiah. Our victory against spiritual powers of darkness comes from our having put on Christ. Our union with him means that we are able to resist the Devil and escape sin and temptations. The demons have no authority over the disciples of Jesus.

REFLECTION QUESTIONS

1. What does the example of Jesus in the temptation narrative teach us about Jesus and ourselves?

2. How do the authors of the Gospels use the exorcism accounts?

3. How might we help ourselves distinguish between descriptions (what happened) and prescriptions (what we should do) in the gospel accounts?

4. How can we encourage one another to be courageous because of the authority of Jesus over the enemy?

5. What are three important lessons about Jesus that help us understand spiritual warfare?

How Was Spiritual Warfare Understood in the Apostolic Church?

The majority of the record of the apostolic church is contained in Luke's narrative account in the book of Acts. Other details about the patterns of activity in churches in the first century can be inferred from the New Testament letters. Spiritual warfare is more or less a modern, twentieth-century concept, so it does not make appearance in these writings as a discrete subject, even though the idea of spiritual battle is biblical and a concern of the early church (see Question 22). However, topics dealing with spiritual development, angels, and demons are important features of these texts.

Acts

Luke organizes his second book around the prophetic and programmatic statement of Jesus found in Acts 1:8: "you will receive power when the Holy Spirit has come upon you, and you will be my witnesses in Jerusalem and in all Judea and Samaria, and to the end of the earth." Throughout the course of the story in Acts, Luke shows how the church grows and witnesses in ever-expanding circles. The growth of the witness is empowered by the Holy Spirit, and thus constitutes a kind of spiritual warfare. However, the principal enemy is not principalities and powers, but rather unbelief. Hence, the answer to a repeated question in the book ("What shall I do to be saved?") is: Repent, and be baptized. Baptism becomes the sign or proclamation of the new believer's faith, and this is sometimes attested by outward manifestation of the Spirit. The emphasis is on the power of the Spirit to affect real change in the lives of those who submit to Christ and his gospel. So, the centerpiece of spiritual warfare in the apostolic church is the gospel, which stands to reason as it is "the power of God for salvation to everyone who believes" (Rom. 1:16).

Angels in Acts

In Acts, Luke describes a handful of angelic encounters with key persons in the narrative. These incidents are conspicuous because they are rare and receive essentially no mention in the New Testament letters. Hence, they are not central to the apostolic church's conception of itself or its practices. Like elsewhere in Scripture, the angels appear to deliver messages, typically to one of the apostles (Acts 1:10; 5:19; 8:26; 12:7–9). Consistent with other appearances of the angels in Scripture, these appearances are not always understood clearly at first. For example, Peter does not know that the angel who frees him from prison is real because he thinks he is seeing a vision or dream (12:7–9). In one significant instance, an angel appears in a vision to someone who is not an apostle, the centurion Cornelius (10:3). This is an important moment in the book and in history because it inaugurates the preaching of the gospel to the Gentiles and shows that the gospel is for all peoples, as Peter explains (10:35; 11:15). This becomes central to Paul's mission in the second half of the book.

Demons in Acts

It is clear that apostles were able to do signs and wonders, including casting out unclean spirits (Acts 5:16). However, these gifts seem to be limited to the apostles (5:12), whether Peter (5:15) or Paul (16:18; 19:12), or their appointees, such as Philip (8:5–6). The Jewish exorcists who think that invoking the name of Jesus is a kind of magical rite are sorely mistaken (19:13–16). In fact, this story seems to highlight a significant difference between how Christians engage in spiritual warfare and how other religions engage with spirits. Furthermore, although exorcisms were part and parcel of the apostles' ministry, there are no admonitions in the New Testament letters for Christians to engage in spiritual warfare of that kind.

Spiritual Warfare in the New Testament Letters

"See to it that no one takes you captive by philosophy and empty deceit, according to human tradition, according to the elementary spirits of the world, and not according to Christ" (Col. 2:8). If we are to wage spiritual warfare, then it must be based on what God has revealed to us and not merely on our own forays in the world. In that regard, we should note that spiritual warfare is not a major theme in the New Testament letters, except insofar as they continue to proclaim the centrality of the gospel.

There are some specific references to spiritual forces that make it clear that the New Testament authors expected Christians to be aware of spiritual realities and to take their discipleship seriously. There are rulers and thrones (*kuriotetes, thronoi*; Col. 1:16), angels and powers (*angeloi, dunameis*; Rom. 8:38), elemental spirits (*stoicheia*; 2 Peter 3:10), and glorious ones (*doxas*; Jude 8). It is important to note that these Greek terms often refer to merely human leaders and authority structures, and that these terms are used in passing and in lists. It is simply wrong to conclude from the mention of these entities that the New Testament authors have any particular interest in engaging them in spiritual warfare through exorcisms, ritual cleansings, bindings, spiritual mapping, or other popular contemporary methods. Why? Because while the New Testament authors make passing mention of spiritual powers, they never prescribe any such practices. In fact, stooping to reliance on magic formulas actually implicates Christians in the pagan practices that Christ has defeated.

One might infer from the warfare metaphor (itself a theological construct) that we should fight the Devil in the way in which we would fight an enemy human army. In other words, we should study his tactics, find out where his strongholds are, and systematically attack them. We should try to convert his disciples to our side and mine them for information (as when someone relies on a former occultist's information about demons). But, all these insights, plausible as they are in light of the warfare metaphor, are not once recommended by Scripture. Notice that the passage that gave rise to the modern spiritual warfare idea (Eph. 6:10–20) involves only two simple commands: Stand, and pray. Stand in the truth of your identity in Christ with all the blessing and protection that entails, and pray for the perseverance of the saints and the bold proclamation of the gospel. In Ephesians 6, that is Paul's strategy for our wrestling with the cosmic powers. So, we see that as the church grows at the waning of the apostolic period, the apostles' teaching emphasize our identity in Christ and prayer as our means of spiritual warfare. The scriptural record indicates that the Devil and his angels are less interested in possession than deception. The attacks of the enemy are described as deception (Rev. 12:9; 20:10), temptation (see Question 19), false doctrines (1 Tim. 4:1; 1 John 2:22; 4:3) and denying Christ (John 6:70; 8:31, 44; 1 John 3:10). The antidote for his assaults is right teaching (2 Cor. 10:5).

Summary

The apostolic church believed and experienced the reality of angels and demons, and the apostles' teaching contains reference to their continued presence and activity in his history. However, "spiritual warfare," as it is usually understood and practiced today, is not a significant feature of church life as reflected in the New Testament letters. Although there was a continued ministry of miraculous healing and deliverance by the hands of the apostles (Acts 5:12), contemporary spiritual warfare practices such as spiritual mapping, exorcism, identification repentance, and deliverance ministry receive no endorsement (in fact, no mention) in the New Testament documents. There was, however, a development of beliefs in angels and demons toward the end of the first century that is reflected in the teaching of the ancient church.

REFLECTION QUESTIONS

1. What does the waning focus on angels and demons in Acts and the New Testament letters tell us about their centrality in contemporary Christian life?

2. Is it significant that we sometimes interpret theological metaphors in light of our cultural experience and not biblical usage?

3. Should we expect to share in the miraculous ministry of the apostles (Acts 5:12)?

4. What is the centerpiece of spiritual warfare in the apostolic church?

5. How can our prayer life reflect the attitude of the New Testament church toward spiritual powers (Eph. 6:10–20)?

How Was Spiritual Warfare Understood in the Ancient Church?

The ancient church took the assaults of the enemy and the threat of spiritual warfare seriously. In that sense, the ancient church struggled with understanding spiritual warfare in much the way the contemporary church does. These are difficult topics. In this chapter, I survey some major figures from the first several centuries regarding their belief about angels and demons.

Origen

In his writings on the spiritual life, Origen makes much of the idea of a conflict for the soul that takes place between the Devil and God. He rejects the idea that temptations are all from the Devil, which some Christians believed at that time. For example, he thinks it is strange that the Devil would care about certain areas in which we sin. He writes incredulously, "is one supposed to think that the Devil concerns himself with our eating and drinking?"[1] At the same time, he notes that "within you is a battle you are to fight."[2] Origen's idea is that sin provides an occasion for the enemy to become stronger. In other words, we afford him an opportunity to "get ahead" in the battle for our souls when we sin. This is true for all people. Once someone becomes a Christian, however, he should expect to be threatened by spirits of evil. He writes:

> Just as there are many orders under God, so too in the opposing camps there are not only powers but also "world rulers of this present darkness" and "spiritual hosts of wickedness in the heavenly places" (Eph. 6:12) and perhaps also principali-

---

1. Citations from Origen come from Hans Urs Von Balthasar, *Origen: Spirit and Fire*, trans. Robert J. Daly (Washington, DC: Catholic University of America Press, 1984), 223.
2. Ibid., 224.

ties. For I think that everything that is on God's side also has its corresponding opposite.[3]

Of course, that last statement is necessarily false if it implies that God also has an "opposite" power, since God has no equal in any respect.[4] But, Origen is really getting at the idea that there is some hierarchy to the spiritual realm, and that the forces of evil are organized. The head of them is the Devil who "as master of all this wicked warfare, makes war on the whole world."[5] He rightly notes, therefore, that the Christian life is a life of "warfare," but because it is Christ who calls us to follow him, "there is really nothing difficult, nothing arduous in it."[6]

Origen's philosophical understanding of the human person as a composite creature leads him to speculate that each person has both a good angel and a bad one. He is elaborating on a tradition here contained in the Shepherd of Hermas, an early nonbiblical Christian writing. The early church made much of Jesus teaching that there were two paths to walk, a wide path and a narrow path. In Origen, the governor of the narrow path is Christ and the governor of the wide is the enemy. The soul left to its own devices would commit all kinds of sin, but it is obvious according to Origen that evil spirits look for opportunity to move our souls down the wrong path. In particular, in the battle for the soul the enemy attempts to make us doubt the truth of the gospel. From this basis, he develops his doctrine of "spiritual sense," which is an elaborate metaphor for developing spiritual insight based on our physical sense. He regularly drifts between literal and allegorical interpretations of the Bible in ways that are often creative but ignore the historical sense. Nevertheless, Origen understands the centerpiece of spiritual warfare to be between the person and his own flesh. Left alone, people would seek after merely fleshly desires and lack spiritual insight, especially if tempted by the enemy. But, God is able to use temptations to show us the weakness of the flesh, even in areas that we did not know we harbored sin.

In sum, Origen develops an account of the battle for the soul that serves as an early attempt to articulate the Christian experience of temptation. While much of his speculative theology was rejected by the church, certain ideas and expressions from his writings continue to have an impact on Christian vocabulary.

---

3. Ibid.
4. As Athenagoras notes, "We do not mean that there is anything opposed to God in the way that Empedocles opposes strife to love and night to day in the phenomenal world. For even if anything did manage to set itself up against God, it would cease to exist. It would fall to pieces by the power and might of God" ("A Plea Regarding Christians by Athenagoras the Philosopher," in *Early Christian Fathers*, ed. Cyril C. Richardson [Louisville: Westminster John Knox Press, 1953], 326).
5. Von Balthasar, *Origen*, 225.
6. Ibid.

Augustine

Of course, the greatest theologian of the early church is Augustine, and he also had some significant contributions to the discussion of spiritual warfare. He speaks without hesitation of the role demons play in generating false religions and doctrines, and he notes in particular that believing superstitions is participating in the work of demons: "I refused sacrifice to demons on my behalf; yet by adherence to that superstition I sacrificed myself to them."[7] His references to the activity of the Devil are almost always in the context of false religions and deceptions.

The idea of spiritual battle (as seen in the context of Origen) is usually reserved for the understanding of the ascetical life, which denies the flesh its desires in order to draw closer to God. The common textual reference for this idea is 1 Corinthians 9:27, about the nature of self-discipline. The combat with the flesh is difficult because the enemy and his angels tempt us in accordance with our sinful desires. Another level of this battle (and an area of greater focus) is the battle for the mind. False thoughts and beliefs may arise from the enemy, and they have to be counteracted with the truth of the Bible. This struggle is fundamental for Augustine.

In fact, in one of his often neglected writings, *De Agone Christiano*, or "The Christian Struggle (or Combat)," he describes the war with temptation and the flesh. At the same time, the Devil is both a defeated foe and the prince of the forces opposed to God. Likewise, in his *City of God*, he characterizes a conflict between God and the god of this world in terms of the whole human race and not merely the individual person. Many of the discussions of spiritual warfare in the ancient church take place on these two levels.

With respect to the struggle of the Christian life, however, the battle is internal as Augustine sees it: "all who fear the fire prepared for the Devil and his angels should take means to overcome the Devil within themselves. For we win an interior victory over the adversaries who assail us from without by conquering the evil desires by which those adversaries hold sway over us."[8] Hence, he holds that Paul's teaching is focused on chastising the flesh in an effort to eliminate the means by which demonic temptation can take place. "If we would overcome the world," Augustine says, "we should chastise our body and bring it into subjection. For it is by sinful pleasures, by vanity, and baneful curiosity that the world can obtain the mastery over us. That is to say, these things of the world, by their deadly delight, enslave the lovers of things transitory, and compel them to serve the Devil and his angels."[9] So, it is by subjecting ourselves to the will of God that the temptations of the Devil will subside and that

---

7. Augustine, *Confessions*, trans. Henry Chadwick (Oxford: Oxford University Press, 1991), 54.
8. Augustine, "The Christian Combat," trans. Robert P. Russell in *Writings of Saint Augustine*, vol. 4, ed. Ludwig Schopp (New York: Cima, 1947), 317.
9. Ibid., 321–22. He restates his citation of 1 Corinthians 11:1 in the opening line.

Christians ultimately have victory over him. In particular, he emphasizes right doctrine (teaching) as a means of right belief about God and right action, which explains his extended treatment of basic Trinitatarism and Christology in this pamphlet. His book contains a constant refrain of "Let us not heed those who say . . ." followed by some false teaching that contradicts the witness of the apostles. In this way, he follows the admonition of John to be wary of false teachers who serve as antichrists (1 John 2:22; 4:3; 2 John 1:7).

In summary, Augustine teaches that there are only two doors or ways by which the enemy "obtains ascendancy over us": (1) covetousness of temporal things and (2) fear of losing temporal things.[10] The Devil "must be driven out; first by the fear of God, then by love. We ought, then, to long more eagerly for the clear and distinct knowledge of Truth, according as we see ourselves advancing in charity, having hearts made pure by its simplicity, for it is by the eye of the soul that Truth is perceived."[11]

Summary

Although some early Christian writings make reference to angels and demons in discussion of the Christian walk, later teachers focus more intently on the internal struggle against temptation. The fight against sin and for a right understanding of Jesus Christ is what constitutes the bulk of spiritual warfare in the mindset of the early church. That the power of the gospel could free people from the control or influence of the devil was never in any doubt. Being close to Jesus was the only security for the Christian against the wiles of the devil.

REFLECTION QUESTIONS

1. What are some differences between Origen and Augustine on spiritual warfare?

2. What are some major similarities in their theology?

3. Why does Augustine focus on right doctrine as crucial to spiritual warfare?

4. Why is it significant that both thinkers give most of their attention to internal struggles?

5. Who did you find yourself agreeing with more? Why?

---

10. Ibid., 352.
11. Ibid.

How Was Spiritual Warfare Understood in the Medieval Church?

The medieval church took the assaults of the enemy and the threat of spiritual warfare seriously, especially because some of the apophatic and mystical theology of the ancient church became increasingly prominent among certain schools of theology,[1] though this peaked at the time of the Reformation. The major scholastic theologians took the threat of the enemy seriously, but also applied a more rigorous philosophical analysis to traditional doctrines. Spiritual warfare *per se* is not a major emphasis in their writings, because it was not conceived of as a distinct branch of discussion (either as a part of pneumatology, missiology, or discipleship) in the way that it is now so considered. After all, the term "spiritual warfare" is an invention of the twentieth century. The medieval theologians were not in any sense materialists, however, and had a robust sense of the spiritual nature of the world.

Scholastic Theology

Angelic speculation is most often associated with the theology of the Middle Ages. In fact, some of the greatest theologians of the period are named after angels (Thomas Aquinas and Bonaventure, for example). However, their way of speaking and thinking about the angels is much different than what we find in most spiritual-warfare literature today. This has in part to do with the type of theological inquiry practiced by the great cathedral schools in the Middle Ages.

---

1. Apophatic or "negative" theology attempts to speak about God by saying what he is not. The idea behind this approach is that true knowledge of God's essence is beyond the reach of created beings. As an example, Cyril of Jerusalem says, "For of God we speak not all we ought (for that is known to Him only), but so much as the capacity of human nature has received, and so much as our weakness can bear. For we explain not what God is but candidly confess that we have not exact knowledge concerning Him." See Catechetical Lecture VI in Philip Schaff and Henry Wace, eds., *Nicene and Post-Nicene Fathers*, vol. 7 (Peabody, MA: Hendrickson, 1999), 33.

This type of theology came to be called "scholastic" theology, even by the six-teenth century. The term was originally an alternative way to refer to someone who was educated (like "scholar"), but came to represent a certain methodology for approaching the task of theology in which the subject matter was divided into specific topics that were taken up and examined one by one. For example, the medieval theologian would first ask whether God exists, considering arguments for and against. Next, he would discuss whether God's existence was self-evident, considering arguments for and against. In this way, the theologian would meticulously work through each topic of theology.

Of course, the term came to be a way to ridicule a system of learning and studying theology, in which questions about meaningless matters were piled up endlessly to no purpose. Hence, the question, "How many angels can dance on the head of a pin?" came to be a satirical example of the pointless speculation of the medieval scholastic theologians.[2] In fact, there is no evidence that any medieval theologian was particularly interested in that question—although they did ask a similar one: namely, whether several angels could be in one place at the same time. (Aquinas said no.)

Demonic Assaults

Thomas Aquinas taught that demons assailed human beings either to instigate them to sin or as a punishment by God. One of the more interesting questions on this score was whether demons could instigate wrongdoing by the appearance of miracles. Aquinas thinks that it is possible for demons to do acts that far exceed human power and thus appear "miraculous." He does want to reserve the term "miracle," however, for works of God. Nevertheless, he holds that it was, for example, by demonic power that the magicians of Pharaoh were able to imitate the miracles that God did by Moses' hand.

Medieval theologians held that the created order was organized according to the powers of various beings. Hence, angels and demons had a governing power over lower creatures (like men and animals and plants). Therefore, they often taught that it was possible for demons to manipulate the air in order to form the appearance of physical things. Following Augustine, this is, for example, how they believed that the Devil appeared as a serpent. This is also a common development of the idea that the Devil is the "prince of the power of the air" (Eph. 2:2).

Temptations

The medieval theologians held that the demons were responsible for some, but not all, temptations. The free choice of man (because of his sinful desires; James 1:14) was also responsible for most temptation. However, they also debated to what extent resisting temptation caused particular demons to be unable

---

2. This despite the fact that the scholastic tradition lived on in Protestant circles uninterrupted for nearly 250 years after the Reformation.

to continue to tempt. One major school of thought held that resisting temptation drove away the Devil from a person permanently (James 4:7), but others held that the demon would only leave for a certain period of time (Matt. 12:44).

Most medieval theologians held that God assisted Christians in fighting temptation in part by sending angels to help them (see Question 6). The frequent proof-text for this doctrine of guardian angels is flimsy (Ps. 91:11).[3] However, the understanding is not merely that the angels protect men, but that they in some way move them toward the right decisions. On the basis on Matthew 18:10, many held that each person had a guardian angel assigned to him (although they debated about when someone received the protection of the angel—whether baptism or some other time).[4]

The writings of a figure known to the medieval church as Dionysius loomed large in these discussions. The medieval church believed that the author of these writings was Dionysius from Acts 17:34. Because they believed this, they held his writings in high regard (having near apostolic status although no one ever considered them to rise to the level of Scripture). It turns out that the author of these documents was not Dionysius (see Question 4). This significantly undermines the authority of some of their positions on these matters.

Occult Matters

There was also a significant literature on occult topics, such as magic and divination of various kinds. In part, there was an attempt to understand the mechanics of magic. In other words, how does a particular ritual cause something to happen? This investigation even extended to the rudimentary medicine of the time. Theologians held, as a rule, that all occult activities were forbidden to Christians on the basis of the clear testimony of Scripture. Since they felt sure that such activities produced effects that were beyond the power of men, the only explanation was a compact with demons. This was the reason that they gave for the divine prohibition of sorcery and divination.

At the same time, one of the mechanisms of the church had been to embrace local cultural practices and religious beliefs and reinterpret them within a Christian context. The legends associated with pious Christian people continued to be a significant part of the life of the church, and the trade in relics of the saints (e.g., a fingerbone) were prized for their cultic power. Although procedures for canonization of saints did not develop until the early thirteenth century, from the first century there were records of saints and (often) fantastic stories about miracles that they performed both before and after

---

3. "For he will command his angels concerning you to guard you in all your ways."
4. See, for example, Thomas Aquinas, *Catena Aurea*, vol. 1: *Gospel of Matthew*, trans. J. G. F. and J. Rivington (London: J.G. F. & J. Rivington, 1842), 621–48. He provides the major Patristic citations that guided medieval discussion.

their deaths. Hence, objects associated with the saints were thought to have special significance and power in warding off demons (see Question 35).

By the late fourth century, there were attempts to systematize a theology of relics, which could explain their ability to enhance intercessory prayer. The earliest attempt comes from Victricius of Rouen, a fourth-century bishop, who composed a work, *De Laude Sanctorum* (= Praising the Saints) in which he goes so far as to say God is actually present in the relics, because the saints to which the bodies belong are in union with God (cf. 1 Kings 13:20).[5] However, this "theology" is simply an attempt to produce a "pious" magic to the extent that relics even became a source of currying political and ecclesiastical patronage. This trajectory continued throughout the Middle Ages, and was a critique for both Erasmus and Luther. Others held that the relics were simply a source of memorial of faithful Christian lives in the way that a good Christian biography might be utilized today.

Summary

Like every age, the Middle Ages saw a blend of superstition in areas of its religious consciousness, because of attempts to understand contrasting religions and to establish footholds for Christian witness. The belief in a personal Devil who was voracious in his attacks against mankind was widespread, as was the belief that the faithful had recourse to both guardian angels and the departed saints for protection. In many cases, fear of spiritual forces of darkness led to superstitious compromises with "pious" magic and mediators for God's favor, other than Christ.

REFLECTION QUESTIONS

1. What were two different accounts of the role of saints in the Middle Ages?

2. How was the scholastic approach to angels and demons different from folk piety?

3. What was the general position of the medieval church on guardian angels?

4. How can the robust concern about the Devil's temptations be a distraction from gospel living?

5. What is admirable about the seriousness with which the medieval church approached issues of spiritual warfare?

---

5. See Gillian Clark, "Vitricius of Rouen: Praising the Saints," *Journal of Early Christian Studies* 7, no. 3 (1999): 365–99 for a commentary and translation.

How Was Spiritual Warfare Understood in the Reformation Church?

He who will have, for his master and king, Jesus Christ, the son of the Virgin, who took upon himself our flesh and our blood, will have the devil for his enemy.

~Martin Luther, *Table Talk* 588

The Reformation Church had a robust view of spiritual activity and the role that angels and demons played in the lives of believers. In some of the reformers the emphasis on angelology and demonology was more pronounced than in others; nevertheless, there is a sustained interest in angelology as a distinct branch of theological studies until the late seventeenth century. Much of the commentary on the nature of spiritual beings and their interactions with mankind is found in the biblical commentaries of the early reformers. As such, the comments are somewhat cursory and piecemeal. However, in some compendiums or larger theological works, major reformers do devote significant attention to the nature of spiritual beings.

The Reformers do not teach on spiritual warfare as such, but they do have many opinions on the spiritual realm and its activities. That there was a war between the good and bad angels, in which men were inextricably bound up, was never in doubt for the Reformers. Particular strategies for engaging the spirit forces, however, do not constitute a major field of inquiry for them. Nevertheless, testimonies of angelic visitations and demonic assaults of various kinds are a consistent theme of the theological literature of the period. Likewise, witchcraft and sorcery, as well as folk magic of various kinds, was a significant cultural phenomenon during this time period. Consequently, the writings of the Reformers often indicate that they believe in the reality and danger of such practices.

To give a sense of the sweep of this history, to which I can hardly do justice in a short chapter, I summarize some of the major teachings of Luther and Calvin on angels and demons, before discussing more generally some major themes related to what we now call spiritual warfare. The treatment of these themes will be offered in broad strokes both because of the limitations of space and because of the fragmentary and cursory historical artifacts that exist from which to draw generalizations about popular religion in a historical period.

Martin Luther

For Luther, spiritual warfare was simply the activity of the Christian life, in which the Christian clung to God and resisted the Devil in the midst of his temptations and assaults. The activity of the spiritual world was palpable in the effects that it had on human living. Luther held that the Christian life was a constant struggle against the wiles of the Devil and his demons, and that the angels of God supported and protected the Christian. "An angel," says Luther, "is a spiritual creature created by God without a body, for the service of Christendom and of the church."[1] Part of the service is unseen works of ministry, which includes driving away the Devil when he assaults us. Angels are able to serve in this way because their "long arms" allow them to stand before the face of God and yet be "hard by and about us."[2] This protection is needful for us because "the devil is also near and about us, incessantly tracking our steps, in order to deprive us of our lives, our saving health, and salvation."[3] Luther does not speculate on how this battle takes place or how the angels protect Christians: "how or in what manner it is done, take no heed. God says it, therefore it is most sure and certain."[4] In fact, Luther thinks we might despair if we could see how many angels were round about us to protect us.

As to the assaults of the Devil and his demons, Luther asserts that they are responsible not merely for temptations and prejudices but also "hail, lightnings, and thunderings, and poison [in] the air, the pastures, and grounds" because evil spirits sometimes occupy black rain clouds.[5] He dismisses the attempts of philosophers and physicians to attribute such events to "natural" or planetary causes. Likewise, the Devil is the source of plague and fever, injustice in the courts, war and massacre, and the corruption of preachers. The Devil also leads people to suicide. Luther was also clear that magic and witchcraft were actually the work of demons or persons who had been in contact with demons.

---

1. William Hazlitt, ed., *Martin Luther's Table Talk* (Fearn, UK: Christian Focus, 2003), 339.
2. Ibid., 340.
3. Ibid.
4. Ibid.
5. Ibid., 341.

For example, he is inclined to believe stories about witchcraft and magic. In one notable example, Luther recounts that his own mother was plagued by a neighbor who was a witch, who could hex children so that they would cry with such force that they would die. In another case, a warlock ate an entire hay cart, including the driver. Martin Luther was convinced that the Devil was behind these pursuits, and that the Christian's only defense was the name of Christ.

John Calvin

Calvin was more reluctant than Luther to discuss instances of necromancy and witchcraft, and he was less apt to speculate on the nature of the spiritual realm and its activity. However, he also held that angels defended the Christian, and that the demons were assaulting humanity in often unseen ways. He agrees with Luther that "in discharging the office of our protectors, they war against the Devil and all our enemies, and execute vengeance upon those who afflict us."[6] At the same time, he emphasizes that not all of our blessings come by way of the angels. To that effect, he quotes the rebuke of the angel to John in Revelation 19:10. Calvin also elaborates on angelic (and demonic) activity as a substructure beneath God's activity. The angels and demons only act insofar as God has ordained for them to do so. Hence, the angels and demons should not be considered scarier or more awe-inspiring than God. At the same time, the assaults of the Devil and his demons are not for Calvin any mere metaphor: They are real wicked entities bent on our destruction, not mere carnal thoughts or delusions. The reason that the Bible warns us about the demons is so that we will be diligent in our pursuit of Christ:

> Being forewarned of the constant presence of an enemy the most daring, the most powerful, the most crafty, the most indefatigable, the most completely equipped with all the engines and the most expert in the science of war, let us not allow ourselves to be overtaken by sloth or cowardice, but, on the contrary, with minds aroused and ever on the alert, let us stand ready to resist.[7]

Notice that it is our own sins (sloth and cowardice) that the Devil can use to overtake us. Furthermore, Calvin denies that the Devil ever has ultimate victory over the believer. The trials of the Devil are common to all believers

---

6. John Calvin, *Institutes of the Christian Religion*, trans. Ford Lewis Battles, LCC, vol. 20–21 (Philadelphia: Westminster, 1960), I.14.6.
7. Ibid., I.14.13.

(Eph. 4:27; 1 Peter 5:8), but the promise of victory in the Son (Gen. 3:15) "applies alike to Christ and all his members."[8]

The Period in General

Divines continued to devote pages of their theological works to questions about the spiritual realm and spirit beings nearly without interruption until the late eighteenth century.[9] By the late seventeenth century, however, the increasingly mechanistic worldview began to displace a robust conception of spirits and spiritual activity among the educated classes, although the reality of angels and demons remained a commitment among the populace. For example, in 1680, Pierre Bayle published his treatise on comets which was intended to dispel the common notion that they were harbingers of some imminent doom.[10] Even writers who were committed to spiritual warfare disagreed significantly regarding practices like exorcism. In part, these differences had to do with the extent to which a commitment to a free and active spiritual realm was thought to impinge on God's sole authority, and the extent to which exorcism could be preserved as anything more than papal magic.

Summary

Like the periods of Christian history before, the Reformation church had a commitment to the existence of personal spirit beings, both good and evil, who were intimately involved in the daily life of human beings. Likewise, there continued to be significant discussions regarding what role these beings played in daily life. However, all the disputes about how angels or demons interact with men, or how men ought to interact with angels and demons, presupposed a few key agreements: First, such beings were real and were described with authority in the Bible. Second, angels and demons continued to play some role in history. Third, whatever role they played in life or spiritual warfare, the only defense against the wiles of the Devil was the power of Christ. In the midst of ongoing debates about spiritual warfare, these affirmations remain as important today as they were in the Reformation and post-Reformation church.

---

8. Ibid., I.14.18.
9. For an interesting discussion of angelology in the Protestant scholastics of the post-Reformation, see Andrew T. Sulavik, "Protestant Theological Writings on Angels in Post-Reformation Thought from 1565–1739," *Reformation and Renaissance Review* 8, no. 2 (2006): 210–23. Contrary to what is commonly thought, angelology remained a consistent feature of theological reflection during this period.
10. See Pierre Bayle, *Various Thoughts on the Occasion of a Comet*, trans. Robert C. Bartlett (Albany, NY: State University of New York Press, 2000). In some cases, such "rationalist" responses were intended to safeguard divine authority.

REFLECTION QUESTIONS

1. How did Luther and Calvin differ about spiritual warfare?

2. What were some major controversies of the period regarding spiritual entities?

3. Why is it significant that the church continued to assert a belief in the spiritual realm?

4. Did Luther or Calvin give too much credit to demonic forces for catastrophes?

5. Who do you agree with more about spiritual warfare?

Questions Related to Contemporary
Models of Spiritual Warfare

What Is the World-Systems Model of Spiritual Warfare?

The World-Systems model of spiritual warfare is commonly associated with the work of Walter Wink, who wrote a trilogy of books on the subject of the powers in the New Testament.[1] In Wink's view, the powers primarily refer to the "interiority" of structures of authority and influence rather than discrete agents (e.g., demons). His model thus emphasizes the importance of systematic changes to structures of governance and infrastructure as a way to eliminate oppression. However, he also argues that liberation theology has been mistaken precisely because it ignored the spiritual or mythical aspect of the powers. Hence, he seems to locate his view as a corrective both to an overemphasis on spirits and a neglect of the spiritual aspects of institutional power. In this chapter, I will outline his argument for this position and discuss what is helpful in his reflections. Ultimately, his view has to be rejected or substantially revised, because it holds that the Devil and his angels are a kind of psychological metaphor in the New Testament. One cannot be victorious in spiritual warfare if one denies the reality of the Devil.

The Language of Power in the New Testament

Wink's perspective on spiritual warfare is based on his word studies regarding the language of power in the New Testament.[2] The thrust of his

---

1. Walter Wink, *Naming the Powers: The Language of Power in the New Testament* (Philadelphia: Fortress Press, 1984); idem, *Unmasking the Powers: The Invisible Forces That Determine Human Existence* (Philadelphia: Fortress Press, 1986); idem, *Engaging the Powers: Discernment and Resistance in a World of Domination* (Philadelphia: Fortress Press, 1992). A more recent summary of his view is presented in James K. Beilby and Paul Rhodes Eddy, eds., *Understanding Spiritual Warfare: Four Views* (Grand Rapids: Baker Academic, 2012), 47–71.
2. His word studies often assume that usage of terms in nonbiblical texts is determinative for their meaning in biblical texts, which is dubious despite his claims that "every

argument is that traditional theology has focused incorrectly on the spiritual nature of the "powers," without recognizing that the terms in use (e.g., *dynamis, arches*) often extended beyond the spiritual realm and in many cases are simply mundane words for the power structures (nations, laws, rulers, etc.) in human affairs. In cases where the author does not specify, Wink suggests that the terms be read as referring to the broadest possible scope of meaning. In other words, if the author does not say that he is referring only to spiritual beings, then he isn't. Likewise, if the author does not say that he is referring only to political machinery, then he isn't.[3] In light of this rubric, he proceeds to analyze disputed passages and show that they variously refer to human or angelic powers or both.

Wink's proposal is to view the "spiritual Powers not as separate heavenly or ethereal entities but as *the inner aspect of material or tangible manifestations of power*."[4] A consequence of this view is that Wink argues that the metaphysical question of whether or not there are demons is uninteresting and overlooks more pressing matters.[5] Language about angelic and demonic entities is merely an attempt to express some archetypical truths: "Satan is the real interiority of a society that idolatrously pursues its own enhancement as the highest good. . . . We are not dealing here with the literal 'person' of popular Christian fantasy, who materializes in human form as seducer and fiend. The Satan of the Bible is more akin to an archetypal reality, a visionary or imaginal presence or event experienced within."[6] Notice he is not denying that there is something more than material in our world; he is merely arguing for a broader view of spiritual powers than that which associates them only with the work of discrete spiritual beings. Yet, to deny the importance of the metaphysical questions requires that

---

commentator qualified to judge has agreed that the biblical authors assume a content for these words which is familiar to the readers as a part of the background beliefs of the epoch, held almost universally by the age" (Wink, *Naming*, 15). While it is fair to say that the general usage of the terminology in texts of the period is helpful in establishing the semantic range of a particular term, it is hasty to think that the NT authors uncritically accepted the background beliefs of the epoch or that these background beliefs were shared across all speakers of the language. In fact, it seems obvious from Paul's writings than many of the background beliefs of the culture were being explicitly rejected in his theology. Simply borrowing the usage of a nonbiblical text and inferring that the biblical usage conforms to it is sloppy (e.g., when he argues that "thrones" of Colossians 1:16 is illuminated by the usage of the Ascension of Isaiah). Why would the intention of Paul be signaled by the (putative) intention of anonymous composite work available to history in a translation of a language different than Paul's? Setting aside such infelicities, he does establish a pervasive pattern of generic usage of the terms in the first century, which includes merely human and supra-human connotations, with the semantic range of the terms he discusses.

3. Wink, *Naming the Powers*, 39.
4. Ibid., 104 (emphasis original).
5. Wink, *Unmasking the Powers*, 26.
6. Ibid., 25.

he psychologize in ways that ignore (or even deny) the significance of the historical or ontological claims of the Bible. In part, he does so because he believes that one can reject a biblical worldview without rejecting some of its theological insights. That's true, but of course that requires rejecting a biblical worldview.

In the Epilogue to the second book in his trilogy, Wink writes that the place of Satan, angels and demons

> in the ancient and medieval cosmologies was consistent with the consciousness of their times, a consciousness that projected these Powers out onto the screen of the cosmos and granted them ontological status. For that age the devil really "existed" and could assume human shape; demons actually seized people from without and entered them; angels flew between heaven and earth as messengers, sat in the heavenly council representing their nations, or presided over congregations or cities or other corporate entities. . . . We cannot simply revive that ancient worldview without jettisoning much of what humanity has gained in the interval since. But we can reinterpret it. We can and must seek to recover in it the eternal truth revealed through its characteristic thought-forms, images, and presuppositions.[7]

Objections to This View

This final sentiment makes clear what is objectionable in his view, namely, that it conceives of the worldview of past Christians as basically primitive. But, there seems to be nothing about the rise of science or industrialism that would make the belief in spirits anything more than unpopular. The worldview that he describes as ancient is not merely invented by peoples who knew too little about the laws of nature to do anything other than deify them; it is a worldview promoted and developed with reference to the words of the Bible. The biblical authors say that the Devil exists (1 Peter 5:9), that demons possess and are excised (Mark 1:34), and that angels are messengers (Matt. 2:13). And, it was partly from passages of Scripture that the notions of heavenly council and territorial spirits emerged, the question of whether the exegesis was sound in all instances notwithstanding. That the pagan religions also believed in such entities is not proof that the beliefs were merely symptomatic of the age. Why not rather think that the disregard of such things in our age is the mistake?

The thought-forms of the biblical authors are available to us only in the words that they produced. On Wink's view, it seems that we can somehow

---

7. Ibid., 172.

excise the truth by freeing it from its primitive expression. But, how is such excision to be done? Should we simply disregard the plain meaning when it seems to us primitive? Likewise, Wink seems committed to elements of Jungian interpretation.[8] Should we think that the culture of that interpretive method is somehow preferable to the biblical authors? If one wants to argue that cruelty and oppression and warfare are great and terrible evils that Christians (and everyone) ought to strive against, so be it. But, one doesn't really need the Bible for such an argument. One can argue for increasing social justice without also arguing or believing that it is only by being born again that a man can be freed from the sinful nature that leads to injustices. Wink's model of spiritual warfare seems to confuse gospel implications with gospel realities, and it does this by denying ontological claims made by the biblical authors.

Redeeming the View

Of course, it is not necessary to confuse the gospel reality with its implication. If we recognize that pervasive social injustices are caused because sinful people following their sinful desires, then we are in a position to make good of some of Wink's emphases. Surely, there are world-systems that are inimical to God's plan. But, this is so because "the god of this world has blinded the minds of the unbelievers, to keep them from seeing the light of the gospel of the glory of Christ, who is the image of God" (2 Cor. 4:4). Spiritual warfare begins with the power and authority of Christ over his creation. Christians walked in such ways when they were dead in their sins in obedience to the ruler of the power of the air (Eph. 2:2). Christians escape this condition only because of the blood of Christ. Wink is right to say we must examine the interior condition of reality in order to discover its weaknesses, but there are no corporate bodies that are not populated by people—and it is people whose hearts must be changed. And, it is only by the blood of Christ and the regeneration of the Holy Spirit that they can be changed. Otherwise, the Devil—not an archetype but a concrete, personal being—will merely delight in our sins and destroy us. Spiritual warfare must start with the gospel, and concern with global injustices can then follow.

Wink is right to say that we need to concern ourselves in spiritual matters with more than whether there is such a being as the Devil. Further, spiritual warfare must be something other than attempting to find demons to bind them or cast them out. The strongest points of his method embrace the need to see beyond the mere figure of Satan to all the works that imply his presence. Consider the provoking question, for example:

---

8. This method of interpretation was especially popular in the 1980s. It takes its name from Carl Jung, a psychologist famous for his interpretations of archetypes.

> Why should Satan reveal himself more often in individual cases, when he can, from invisibility, preside over an entire global culture that spreads over the whole planet like a cancer: a civilization which systematically erodes traditional religions; that treats people who produce and serve as robots; that denies not only the spiritual but even the poetic, the artistic, and the inner; that propagates belief in the ultimate power of money; and that organizes an economic system exploitative of most of the peoples of the world and anchored in a permanent war economy?[9]

If we are merely concerned with Satan's local activity in our lives or the lives of our family, then we will neglect his activity elsewhere, perhaps even in corporate or government systems. It may be illuminating to think of our cultural engagement and political activity as authentic spiritual warfare. But, if this is so, it is only because "now many antichrists have come" (1 John 2:18). Because Wink has a tendency to conflate Satan and the world, his psychologizing has also eroded the traditional Christian religion. Certainly, we need pay attention to the world and our own sins in spiritual warfare, but an overemphasis on the schemes of the Devil that draws us away from attention to our own sinful desires (James 1:14) cannot be corrected by a pendulum swing that denies his reality or pretends it does not matter.

Summary

Although the World-Systems Model rightly emphasizes the pervasive nature of sin and spiritual conflict, it denies the existence of a personal Devil and thus departs from traditional Christian orthodoxy. Hence, while Wink reminds us to be cognizant of broader cultural and political systems that might be affected by the Devil's schemes, his method might lead us to diminish the important of personal evangelism and spiritual disciplines in favor of liberation and social pursuits.

REFLECTION QUESTIONS

1. Why is it important to know that the Devil and his angels are personal beings?

2. Why is the focus on institutional evils and suffering a helpful insight of the World-Systems model?

---

9. Walter Wink, "The World Systems Model," in *Understanding Spiritual Warfare: Four Views*, eds. James K. Beilby and Paul Rhodes Eddy (Grand Rapids: Baker Academic, 2012), 60.

3. What pressures cause us to move away from belief in literal spirits and occult powers?

4. What is foundational in spiritual warfare for addressing social ills?

5. Should we be interested in political changes to address injustice as part of spiritual warfare?

What Is the Strategic-Level Deliverance Model of Spiritual Warfare?

Proponents of the Strategic-Level Deliverance model define spiritual warfare as "an invisible battle in the spiritual realm involving a power confrontation between the kingdom of God and the kingdom of darkness."[1] The idea originates in the 1980s and 1990s in a series of symposia based on developments in Pentecostal and charismatic approaches to evangelism and world mission in particular. The model rests on a basic commitment to the existence of hostile territorial spirits (demons) who have a specific domain and control over different areas of the world (whether cities, localities, or nations). According to most proponents of this theory, there are multiple "levels" of conflict between Christians and demons, ranked by the scope of power of the hostile entity. The most basic is the encounter with a demon-oppressed or demon-possessed individual (low-level). However, in some cases, proponents of this view argue that the conflict is with one of the reigning principalities in a particular region (high-level or cosmic-level). Praying against the principalities is considered to serve as a catalyst for the advance of the gospel in a particular region. Strategic-level warfare proponents focus on these higher-level encounters.

This model of spiritual warfare significantly overstates the Scriptural evidence available for its practices, and hence commends practices and attitudes that distract from more helpful methods of spiritual engagement. In some cases, its practices are predicated on misunderstandings of Scriptural texts or borrowed beliefs from animistic or occult religions. Hence, the model is potentially dangerous and unhelpful.

---

1. C. Peter Wagner and Rebecca Greenwood, "The Strategic-Level Deliverance Model," in *Understanding Spiritual Warfare: Four Views*, eds. James K. Beilby and Paul Rhodes Eddy (Grand Rapids: Baker Academic, 2012), 178.

Engaging Territorial Spirits

Simply put, the Bible never commands its readers to engage territorial spirits (or spirits of any kind, for that matter). Leaving aside whether we have good evidence to believe that there are territorial spirits (see Question 12), there is no good biblical evidence that we are commanded to engage with them in direct confrontations. We are not told what their names are, where they reside, how they wield their influence, what their organizational structure is like, or that we should attempt to uncover any of this information. As it turns out, the source for such "information" is typically the reporting of former occultists, which is dubious at best, especially because sorcery is explicitly condemned in Scripture (Lev. 19:26–27; Gal. 5:20). Even Michael does not dispute with the Devil (Jude 9).

Arguments to the contrary are not convincing, but they paint a vivid picture often by ignoring textual details or by drawing speculative inferences. A recent example of these tendencies is found in the commentary of Rebecca Greenwood on the incident Luke records in Acts 16.[2] Greenwood argues that the story holds the "fairly inescapable conclusion . . . that the demonic spirit in this young woman was indeed a territorial spirit or principality that had maintained the region in darkness."[3] Far from being inescapable, this conclusion seems highly speculative. In Acts 16:16, Luke tells us that a young slave girl in Philippi has a divination spirit. The Greek word for divination is *python*, because in Greek mythology a dragon guarded the oracle of Delphi in the region called Pytho. From this information, Greenwood infers that the spirit inhabiting the slave girl was a territorial spirit: "the reactions and activities that took place as a result of Paul's authoritative command affirm that the spirit working through this young woman was indeed a territorial spirit."[4] She lists the "reactions and activities" as "a city uproar, a raging gang, the incarceration of Paul and Silas, a violent earthquake that broke everybody's chains, and the salvation of the prison guard and his household."[5] The connection to the claim that the divination spirit was a territorial spirit is made using only an incredulous question, "Why would banishing a demon from one girl induce a city uproar and incite a hostile crowd against Paul and Silas?"[6]

Actually, Luke tells us why her masters were upset in verse 16. They made a lot of profit off of her ability to predict the future. Then, Luke tells us why they started a riot in verse 19: "when her *owners saw that their hope of gain was gone*, they seized Paul and Silas and dragged them into the marketplace before the rulers" (emphasis added). Greenwood notes this, but then provides

---

2. Ibid., 180–81.
3. Ibid., 180.
4. Ibid., 181.
5. Ibid.
6. Ibid., 180.

an explanation of the events that is not revealed by Luke. On the basis of her own experience, she makes much out of the claim that the city is thrown into an uproar. She writes: "I personally have prayed deliverance prayers over numerous persons, but never has my deliverance ministry resulted in a city tumult."[7] So, the inference seems to be that this particular spirit must have been uniquely powerful. Notice that this is based on an inference from Greenwood's experience and not anything that Luke tells us. There may have been authentic witchcraft in the city, but there is nothing to indicate the presence of especially powerful spirits. Nor is the miraculous rescue from prison evidence that a territorial spirit had been bound. In fact, Luke provides no logical or grammatical link between the casting out of the demon and the salvation of the jailer and his family, nor does he even mention the demon or the exorcism again. Finally, Greenwood misrepresents Paul's motivations. She writes: "Paul did not back off from this power encounter, but with boldness cast out a python spirit, also named a spirit of divination, from a slave girl."[8] Luke tells it differently. He intimates that it is only after "many days" when Paul has become "greatly annoyed" that he casts out the demon (v. 18)! So, Paul does not enter the city looking to encounter territorial spirits or demons and he does not cast out a demon at the first opportunity. Paul's mission is simply not focused on power encounters with demons. In short, this text is no evidence at all for apostolic endorsement about engaging territorial spirits. Powlison sums it up well in his critique: "Though mysteries remain about the slave girl's paranormal ability, the passage is crystal clear about many things. It offers a striking refutation of the premises and procedures of strategic-level spiritual warfare."[9]

In fact, much of the information about these territorial spirits and patterns for handling them is extrabiblical, and either anecdotal or from suspect sources (sometimes both). For example, C. Peter Wagner notes that "former Secretary of the Interior James Watt, through sensitivities acquired in his past association with the occult, perceives specific dark angels assigned to the White House."[10] Why should we trust someone with occult sensitivities? Later, he mentions Rita Cabezas, who "has discovered that directly under Satan are six worldwide principalities."[11] He mentions that her research is based on "her extensive psychological/deliverance practice and that it later evolved into receiving revelatory words of knowledge."[12] That ought to give one serious pause because; even if it were plausible that she received some new revelation,

7. Ibid.
8. Ibid., 181.
9. Ibid., 207.
10. C. Peter Wagner, "Territorial Spirits," in *Wrestling with Dark Angels*, eds. C. Peter Wagner and F. Douglas Pennoyer (Venture, CA: Regal, 1990), 80.
11. Ibid., 84.
12. Ibid.

none of the data are consistent with the Bible. It is clear that the Bible does not teach anything like the system she outlines. In both examples given here (and countless could be adduced from similar books), the structure of the strategic-level principalities is based on reports of former occultists or spiritual perceptions that cannot be tested against Scripture (or don't survive the test), neither of which is worth significant attention. Certainly, we should not reorganize our thinking about spiritual warfare in light of anecdotes.

Defiling the Land

Another aspect of strategic-level spiritual warfare is that sins of various regions defile the land, and that this must be remedied by what is called identificational repentance. In order to argue for the first point, strategic-level spiritual warfare proponents refer to passages in the Old Testament that speak about the land being defiled because of Israel's sin. They then generalize this specific threat of cursing to a specific people in light of a specific covenant to all people everywhere, so that God's covenant with Israel applies to the United States or Germany. The exegesis is simply faulty. Even if these specific curses applied to everyone, the Bible does not teach identificational repentance. In fact, proponents of this view admit that the term was not invented until the 1990s.[13] After spiritually mapping a location (combining historical information with revelatory spiritual insights), one discovers the sins of a nation. The argument is that these corporate sins require a special intercession called identificational repentance.

George Otis outlines this repentance in two stages: "(1) an acknowledgement that one's affinity group (clan, city, nation, or organization) has been guilty of a specific corporate sin before God and man, and (2) a prayerful petition that God will use personal repudiation of this sin as a redemptive beachhead from which to move into the larger community."[14] So far as it goes, prayers that people will turn from sin seem like excellent prayers. However, proponents misinterpret Scripture when they attempt to find biblical models of this type of repentance. For example, they cite the prayers of Nehemiah on behalf of the people as an example of this method.[15] Nehemiah is praying as priest in his designated role as an intercessor for that specific people, a role assigned him according to God's statutes for his people as laid out by Moses. There is nothing in Nehemiah to suggest that his actions are intended to be a pattern for Christian evangelism, nor is there any mention of dark spiritual powers or territorial spirits in the text. One reason that this hermeneutic is accepted in some circles in spite of these problems is that proponents often see

---

13. Wagner and Greenwood, "The Strategic-Level Deliverance Model," 181.
14. George Otis, *Informed Intercession: Transforming Your Community through Spiritual Mapping and Strategic Prayer* (Ventura, CA: Renew, 1999), 251.
15. Wagner and Greenwood, "The Strategic-Level Deliverance Model," 187.

themselves in prophetic or apostolic roles, and so descriptions of how an Old Testament priest behaved in keeping with the covenants that governed him become prescriptions for Christian practice. This is, quite simply, a mistake.

Summary

Strategic-level warfare is underlined with some good and helpful intentions. There is a focus on the spiritual nature of conflict, the significance of prayer, the power of God's authority, the urgency of the endeavor, and the importance of repentance. Unfortunately, the model is predicated on faulty hermeneutics, occult speculations, and anecdotes. Nonbiblical practices come to the forefront as techniques for engagement as if the biblical admonitions that we have been given were not enough. Hence, there is an underlying denial of the sufficiency of Scripture, which results in an unhealthy level of fascination with spirits and occult powers.

REFLECTION QUESTIONS

1. Why is it important that strategic-level warfare focuses on spiritual conflict?

2. Why is it hasty to develop a sophisticated theory of territorial spirits?

3. How does 2 Timothy 3:16–17 remind us of the sufficiency of Scripture for our spiritual practice?

4. How is occult learning unlike studying the sciences or arts?

5. How should we be encouraged by strategic-level warfare proponents' zeal for evangelism?

What Is the "War with the Flesh" Model of Spiritual Warfare?

The "war with the flesh" model of spiritual warfare focuses on the internal struggle between the flesh and the Spirit. The focus in this model is remembering one's new identity in Christ and using the power of the Holy Spirit to evade temptations to sin. Proponents of this view do not deny the influence of the Devil and his angels or the need to resist the Devil, but they focus on internal struggles primarily rather than external struggles against spiritual powers. As a result, they deny that spiritual warfare is a special kind of ministry distinct from the basic struggle of the Christian life. Whatever else spiritual warfare entails, if it is not at root centered on believing the truths of the gospel, clinging to one's identity in Christ, and resisting sin, then it will be a failed project.[1]

War with the Flesh

Sometimes, the fundamentals of spiritual warfare become neglected in conversations about dark powers and demonic temptations. The fact is, however, that Christians never get past their need for the gospel because it is an ongoing source of grace and renewal (Col. 1:6; Acts 20:32) and correction (Gal. 2:14). Furthermore, the war with the flesh is the most immediate conflict that Christians face. Unlike the pressures of the world or the temptations of the Devil, our evil desires are internal (James 1:13). But, what is "the flesh" exactly?

In the New Testament, "the flesh" is a term sometimes used to describe the predilections of our fallen human nature, in particular our sinful desires

---

1. A recent defense of this model dubs it "The Classical Model." See David Powlison, "The Classical Model," in *Understanding Spiritual Warfare: Four Views*, eds. James K. Beilby and Paul Rhodes Eddy (Grand Rapids: Baker Academic, 2012), 89–111.

and temptations. Hence, references to the flesh are often made in contrast to the Spirit (Gal. 5:17; Rom. 7:23). Even after we have come to Christ by faith and have been born again, Christians continue to experience internal struggles with sinful desires and ungodliness. The "war with the flesh" model is so called because it emphasizes that spiritual warfare is primarily focused on this ongoing internal struggle. Thus, in this model, "spiritual warfare is a pastoral, theological term for describing the moral conflict of the Christian life."[2]

In Romans 7, Paul describes this internal conflict in the life of a Christian.[3] He notes that the law awakens the sin that dwells within all of us to deceive us and lead to our destruction (v. 11). The desires that the Christian has to live contrary to God's laws are powerful and set against God's plans. Paul writes, "For I know that nothing good dwells in me, that is, in my flesh. For I have the desire to do what is right, but not the ability to carry it out. For I do not do the good I want, but the evil I do not want is what I keep on doing. Now if I do what I do not want, it is no longer I who do it, but the sin that dwells within me" (vv. 18–20). The spiritual conflict is not merely between the Christian and the Devil or the Christian and the world. There is a conflict within each person: "For I delight in the law of God, in my inner being, but I see in my members another law waging war against the law of my mind and making me captive to the law of sin that dwells in my members" (vv. 22–23). So, the world, the Devil, and the flesh are cooperating influences and enemies of Christian life and growth.

Paul is saying that—even though he has believed the gospel and been saved—the remnants of his past life have not completely dissipated and that they threaten to draw him backward away from Christ and into bondage to sin. He even says that the law of sin is "waging war" against what he knows and believes to be true. When the Christian is plagued by doubts or tempted to backslide, it may be that the enemy is tempting him to evil—but it may simply be his own sin warring against the truth. It may be both. In any case, the solution will be the same. Paul asks, "Who will deliver me from this body of death?" (v. 24). His answer: Jesus Christ, our Lord.

---

2. Powlison, "The Classical Model," 92.
3. There is some dispute about this passage even among conservative scholars. For a defense of this view, see Grant R. Osborne, *Romans*, IVP New Testament Commentary (Downers Grove, IL: InterVarsity Press, 2004), 180–82. He says, "It is more likely that the contrast between life under the flesh in 7:14–25 and life under the Spirit in 8:1–17 is a comparison not of the unsaved and the saved but of the Christian trusting the flesh and the Christian living in the Spirit." For an opposing conclusion, see Douglas Moo, *Romans 1–8*, Wycliffe Exegetical Commentary (Chicago: Moody, 1991), 468–77. Moo notes well that "this teaching about the inability of the Mosaic Law to rescue sinful people from spiritual bondage is the same," regardless of the dispute about how to identify the referent of "I" in Romans 7:14–25.

Because the Christian has union with Christ, he is free from the controlling power of sin. Hence, Paul can write confidently that God "will not let you be tempted beyond your ability, but with the temptation he will also provide the way of escape, that you may be able to endure it" (1 Cor. 10:13). If you are a Christian, you do not have to succumb to sin.

Nevertheless, Paul's comforting words are bracketed by two important warnings. In 1 Corinthians 10:12, he says, "let anyone who thinks that he stands take heed, lest he fall." In other words, pay attention! Our world is in the midst of spiritual war, and there are forces set against the Christian (Eph. 6:12). In 1 Corinthians 10:14, Paul commands "flee from idolatry." If, as Paul has said, the Christian can avoid temptation, then he should. The war with the flesh model centers on this point. Christians should be aware that their own flesh is set against them and their progress in the faith. Hence, they should be prepared to be ruthless in the treatment of their own sin and their pursuit of the glory of Christ.

A related aspect of this view is that it does not consider deliverance ministries to be a significant part of spiritual warfare. In fact, proponents of this view argue that even the exorcisms in the gospel accounts are primarily focused on the authority of Jesus, not the bondage of the oppressed or their sins. Furthermore, the New Testament provides no guidance or exhortation to its readers on how or under what circumstances to cast out demons or to engage hostile spiritual forces in some kind of offensive campaign. This realization is an important corrective in this view to some of the excesses of deliverance ministries. Of particular note is the example in Acts 16:16–18. These verses describe how Paul casts a "spirit of divination" (i.e., an occult spirit involved in fortune-telling) out of a slave girl because she was pestering Paul and Silas. In fact, Luke tells us that Paul cast out the demon because he had become "greatly annoyed" (v. 18). Luke mentions this story because it helps to achieve his purpose of telling about the advance of the gospel (Acts 1:8), not so that we can learn how to combat demons. Paul casts out the demon, not because it is necessary to his apostolic purpose (as he sees it), but because the demon is annoying. If narratives such as this text are to be prescriptions for spiritual warfare, then we would have to instruct deliverance ministers not to cast out demons until they were annoyed by the demoniacs! But, to dwell on such matters is to miss Luke's point. The real deliverance in Acts 16 comes in verse 31, when in response to his question, Paul instructs the jailer on how to be saved: "Believe in the Lord Jesus, and you will be saved."

Objections to the View

One risk of this view is that it might undercut the corporate nature of evil and the Christian struggle against sin. The World-Systems model, for all its weaknesses, does importantly draw our attention to the ways in which the organizing structures of societies are caught up in the ravages of sin and the enemy. The world is a mess, and the enemy is at work in it. Hence, it is important to be reminded that an individual's personal struggles with sin are not all there is to spiritual warfare even if they are the central and most important area of focus. Furthermore, the daily disciplines of the Christian life (e.g., prayer and Bible reading) are not the sole avenue for spiritual growth and maturity.

There is also the church. It is in the context of local gathered bodies of believers that we are encouraged and strengthened in the faith (Rom. 12:4; 1 Cor. 12:27; Heb. 10:24–25). Therefore, spiritual warfare is also a corporate endeavor and not merely an individual one. This view is correct that spiritual warfare is not a special brand of ministry, but we need to be sure that the context of the local body of Christ is kept central in our understanding of spiritual warfare. In particular, we can construe Paul's admonitions regarding church discipline to be avenues of spiritual warfare to the extent that they remind us about the deceitfulness of sin and encourage the body in the doctrine of our Lord.[4] Neither of these points are incompatible with the view, however.

Summary

Put simply, the woman who prays for God to strengthen her against worries about her children is engaged in spiritual warfare as really and truly as the man who reports an ecstatic battle with the Devil. We are sometimes led to believe that spiritual warfare is characterized by moments of great intensity when the veil across the spiritual realm is rolled back long enough for us to see the flashing sword of Michael as he wrestles the great dragon. The activity of spiritual warfare, however, is regularly manifest in the daily humdrum struggle against our petty foibles and persistent patterns of ungodliness. Mundane as such struggles may be, they are the real stuff of spiritual warfare and sanctification; and we err when we reserve spiritual warfare as a term to describe only the fantastic and extraordinary. If one wants to engage in spiritual warfare, one can start simply with an earnest prayer that the gospel will take root more fully in one's heart, so that with great boldness one may share the glorious work of our Savior.

---

4. For helpful reflection on church discipline and the role of church membership in perseverance in the faith, see Jeremy Kimble, *40 Questions on Church Membership and Discipline* (Grand Rapids: Kregel, 2017), esp. 175–79.

REFLECTION QUESTIONS

1. What is the "flesh"?

2. Why might it be difficult to view the daily struggles of Christian living as spiritual warfare?

3. Is it significant support for this view that we are never commanded to engage demons?

4. How might your church better engage in spiritual warfare?

5. How might your spiritual disciplines reflect your commitment to spiritual warfare?

Questions Related to
Spiritual-Warfare Practices

What Is the Full Armor of God?

Ephesians 6:10–20 is a key text in discussion of spiritual warfare. In verses 11 and 13, Paul commands his readers to put on "the whole armor of God." "Whole armor," or "full armor," is the translation of the Greek word *panoplian*. The word is only found in this letter, which raises questions about what exactly this armor is. In the context of the letter, it seems best to conclude that Christ is the full armor of God for the believer.

It is important first of all to note what Paul is *not* instructing his readers to do. It is not inviting believers to engage in some spiritual assault (say, by seeking to assault demons or demonic strongholds). The commands are similar here to those elsewhere in Scripture. Consider James 4:7, "Resist the devil, and he will flee from you" or 1 Peter 5:8–9, "Be sober-minded; be watchful. Your adversary the devil prowls around like a roaring lion, seeking someone to devour. Resist him, firm in your faith. . . ." The repeated call for "engagement" with the evil one is to resist and stand firm. This text is reminding the believer that he is already in a spiritual battle. John tells us that "the whole world lies in the power of the evil one" (1 John 5:19). Likewise, Paul says here, "we do not wrestle," not "we will soon wrestle."

Paul is also not explaining how the believer might engage in some offensive campaign against the Devil or his angels. The primary imperatives of the passage are "stand," "keep alert," and "pray." Of these commands, only the command to pray could be seen as offensive. Even then, the content of the prayer is to be supplication for boldness in proclaiming the gospel—not in cleansings or exorcisms of various kinds. Indeed, in the broadest sense, the battle in which believers are engaged is already won (Rom. 5:18–21)! The greatest spiritual power that believers have is "the immeasurable greatness of his power toward us who believe" (Eph. 1:19). The believer's strength in the Lord is based on the appropriation of what Christ has already done and is doing on the believer's behalf. Putting on the armor of God is roughly synonymous to putting on Christ, recognizing that in Christ we have every equipping to withstand the Devil with all perseverance.

One should also add the corporate nature of the struggle to this individual interpretation (personal faith in Christ and growth in holiness). This corporate nature shows that spiritual warfare is an activity of the church, and in particular focus seems to be the resistance of disunity that spiritual forces bring to bear on the church.[1] It is as easy to conceptualize spiritual warfare as a largely individual activity as it is to conceptualize the Christian life as a largely individual activity, but both conceptions are mistaken. Rather, Paul tells us in Colossians that God "delivered us from the domain of darkness and transferred us to the kingdom of his beloved Son" (Col. 1:11–13). God provides individuals an escape from temptation (1 Cor. 10:13), and hell will not prevail against his church (Matt. 16:18).

One of the major reasons that Ephesians 6:10–20 is taken to recommend assault against demons is because the metaphor of the armor of God is misunderstood. Some interpreters argue that Paul chose the armor metaphor on the basis of his knowledge of how Roman soldiers dressed.[2] There is a problem with this argument: It is based on psychologizing. In other words, the interpreter is trying to answer the question, "Why did Paul use an armor metaphor?" by telling us what Paul must have been thinking, given some historical information inferred from Acts. In certain cases, this method is plausible and appropriate. But, in this instance, it shortcuts two important observations. The first is that the motif of what theologians call "union with Christ" is pervasive in the letter; and the second is that the language Paul uses has a background not solely based on his knowledge and experience of Roman soldiers but in the writing of the prophet Isaiah.

Union with Christ

The initial verse of this section (v. 10) appeals to a repeated biblical and Pauline theme, namely, that in the Lord the believer is able to find strength.[3] Because this verse introduces the rest of the passage, it seems likely the armor of God should be interpreted in light of this controlling instruction to be strong in the Lord. So, when Paul commands us to "put on" the whole armor of God in verse 11, there is already a link between strength in the Lord and refuge in his armor (Neh. 8:10). Now, Paul has already made use of the terminology "put on" in his letter to the Ephesians. In 4:24, he commands them to "put on the new self, created after the likeness of God in true righteousness

---

1. See discussion of demonic assault on the church in Question 10.
2. "It is quite possible that Paul's vivid description of the armor may stem from the fact that, while writing this letter, he was in prison being guarded by Roman soldiers" (Harold W. Hoehner, *Ephesians: An Exegetical Commentary* (Grand Rapids: Baker Academic, 2002), 822–23. See also Ernest Best, *Ephesians*, International Critical Commentary (London: T&T Clark, 1998), 591.
3. See, e.g., Exodus 15:1; Deuteronomy 31:7; Nehemiah 8:10; Psalm 22:18; Isaiah 40:31; Zechariah 10:12; Romans 4:20; 2 Corinthians 10:9–10; Philippians 4:13; 2 Timothy 2:1.

and holiness." Indeed, Paul's prayer throughout the letter has been that the Ephesians might know "the immeasurable greatness of his power toward us who believe, according to the working of his great might" (1:19) and that the Father, "according to the riches of his glory . . . may grant you to be strengthened with power through his Spirit" (3:16).

This concluding exhortation then is a further exposition of Paul's call to "walk in a manner worthy of the calling to which you have been called" (4:1). The purpose of putting on the armor of God is specifically to be able to resist the schemes of the Devil. Paul does not say in this place what his schemes are, but we know from other texts that false teaching is one of the mechanisms by which the Devil leads people astray (from Adam until now) and introduces disunity to the church.

The idea that our blessing and protection come from our union with Christ is clearly established in Paul's introduction to the letter. We are blessed in Christ (1:3), chosen in him (1:4), have redemption and forgiveness in him (1:7) according to the plan in Christ (1:9), obtained inheritance in him (1:11), hope in him (1:12), and receive the seal of the Spirit in him (1:13). So, Paul's command at the beginning of this last section is not new, but rather builds on an important theme in the letter and, indeed, in the Bible.

Isaianic Background

The other important literary background for Paul's discussion is the book of Isaiah.[4] Of particular interest is Isaiah 59:15–20. In this text, Isaiah tells us that the Lord sees injustice without anyone to save, so "his own arm brought him salvation, and his righteousness upheld him. He put on righteousness as a breastplate; a helmet of salvation on his head; he put on garments of vengeance for clothing, and wrapped himself in zeal as a cloak" (vv. 16–17). The section concludes with the Lord's declaration that a "Redeemer will come to Zion" to the repentant (v. 20). The Lord himself is the one who brings salvation, and he is the one Isaiah describes as putting on the armor. So, it is actually the Lord who goes out to fight because the battle is his (Exod. 14:13; Deut. 20:1; 1 Sam. 17:47; 2 Chron. 20:15; 32:8). Paul has cited from this same passage in Romans 11:26–27, so it is a familiar passage to him. Given this background, we should understand the passage primarily as a call to rely on what we have been given in Christ, because Christ is enough even in the presence of messengers of Satan (2 Cor. 12:7–9).

---

4. For a helpful discussion, see Mark D. Owens, "Spiritual Warfare and the Church's Mission According to Ephesians 6:10–17," *Tyndale Bulletin* 67, no. 1 (2016): 87–103. See also Clinton E. Arnold, *Ephesians*, Zondervan Exegetical Commentary on the New Testament (Grand Rapids: Zondervan, 2010), 452; Frank Thielman, *Ephesians*, Baker Exegetical Commentary on the New Testament (Grand Rapids: Baker Academic, 2010), 418–31.

Hence, in Ephesians 6:14–17, the important features of this text are not the specific pieces of armor that Paul mentions. These items seem primarily to serve as vehicles for the traits they represent, such as truth, righteousness, and surety in the gospel. As an example, the word "belt" does not appear in Greek, but the phrase *perizonnymi ten osphun humon* ("gird" or "fasten your loins") makes the addition of "belt" helpful. The point is that we should gird ourselves with the truth of the gospel and the righteousness of Christ. We should stand in readiness to fulfill our Christian duties and resist the temptations of the evil one because of the gospel of peace. When we are assaulted by the enemy (through temptations, false doctrines, persecutions, or tribulations), we should know that our faith in Christ is what sustains us. The crowning mark of the believer is his salvation in Christ. The final item mentioned is the sword of the Spirit—the word of God. Here "word" is the rendering of *rhema*.[5] Because his power is available to the believer, the believer is able to stand against the Devil and therefore should be prepared to stand firm. Christ is our armor.

The first three pieces of armor (the belt, breastplate, and shoes) are not explained; that is, Paul does not say what the believer can do with them. When he speaks of the shield of faith, by contrast, he notes that faith can "extinguish" the assault of the evil one. If the believer recalls the truth that his righteousness was purchased by Christ, then he can stand in the ready peace of faith. The pieces are armor are mutually reinforcing and represent the power to live according to the blessings that accrue to believers because of Christ. It would be easy to be caught up with speculations about what each piece of armor was and how it was to function individually, but this speculation would likely cause one to miss the larger point.[6] Paul intimates that all these things belong to the Christian and are available to him to use. The exhortation is simply to remember, and to wear them.

Prayer

Paul's final exhortation is to pray "at all times" (v. 18). Here perhaps is the most significant portion of this passage regarding spiritual warfare, much more so than his reminder that we struggle with spiritual forces of darkness. When he mentions principalities in verse 12, he does so by way of reminder. The schemes of the Devil are enacted by real spiritual beings who want to derail the Christian life and the church. The conflict is deadly serious and ongoing. But, he offers no additional information about these entities or how to engage them, beyond exhortations to renew our mind with the gospel and pray. Both of those exhortations are common in Paul's writings.

---

5. "Man does not live by bread alone but by every word (*rhema*) that proceeds from the mouth of God" (Matt. 4:4).

6. Although not always, and some helpful pastoral works take this approach.

We are encouraged in the passage to stand firm and withstand the Devil, using faith as our shield. But, here, the believer is also called to pray for all the saints. This duty will require perseverance likely because the Devil opposes prayer. In particular, the prayers should be for all the saints and the proclamation of the gospel. It seems clear that because of his situation (being in chains), Paul requests prayer for his boldness in evangelism. He ought to speak in this way, especially given the truth of the gospel and its power that he has described in the letter to the Ephesians; yet, even the apostle asks for prayer and supplication for the right words to say. No member of the church is too grand to require prayer or the whole armor of God. Our best equipment in spiritual warfare is the gospel, which reminds us of what we have in Christ because we believe and of what is available to those who do believe.

Summary
Christ is the full armor of God to those who believe. In him, we are equipped with all we need to withstand the Devil, the world, and the flesh. To struggle well against the evil one, we need only remind ourselves of who we are in Christ, the power of his gospel, and to pray for endurance and boldness to proclaim "the riches of the glory of this mystery, which is Christ in you" (Col. 1:27).

REFLECTION QUESTIONS

1. Is it comforting to know that Christ is our armor?

2. How does the biblical background in Isaiah of Paul's language help us better understand this text?

3. How does the context of Paul's other comments in Ephesians help us better understand this text?

4. Why and for what does Paul encourage us to pray, in light of our spiritual battle?

5. How does Paul remind us that Christians are united in the struggles against principalities and powers?

What Is "Tearing Down Strongholds"?

In 2 Corinthians 10:4, Paul writes: "For the weapons of our warfare are not of the flesh but have divine power to destroy strongholds." In spiritual warfare discussions, the idea of strongholds sometimes refers to places in which particular demons have special authority, either within a person's life because of sinful attitudes or within a particular community or region because of false worship. In the context of Paul's discussion in 2 Corinthians, however, "strongholds" refers to false doctrines and beliefs rather than the abode of enemies.[1] One of the ways that the enemy battles against us is through false belief and deception. In 2 Corinthians 10, Paul is explaining how he engages in spiritual warfare against the tactics of the enemy.

"Strongholds"

The first thing to note is that, like in Ephesians 6, Paul describes Christian living as a kind of warfare in 2 Corinthians 10:1–6. He refers in particular to the fact that the "weapons" of the Christian have power to destroy (or tear down) "strongholds." On the face of it, strongholds (*ochuromatos*) means "fortress" or "castle." It refers to a fortified position.[2] In context, however, the "strongholds" of the enemy are their arguments. Paul writes that we "have divine power to destroy strongholds, *arguments and every lofty opinion*" (emphasis added). The phrase that follows the word "strongholds" is explanatory and is intended by Paul to clarify his meaning. In the same way that our warfare is not physical, neither are the strongholds of the enemy. Rather,

---

1. Tom White offers a good definition of stronghold: "an entrenched pattern of thought, an ideology, value, or behavior that is contrary to the word and will of God" (*Breaking Strongholds: How Spiritual Warfare Sets Captives Free* [Ann Arbor, MI: Servant, 1993], 24).
2. BDAG lists "a strong military installation, fortress" but also notes that it is used in 2 Corinthians 10:4 in parallel to *logismoi* or "sophistries" (Frederick W. Danker, et al., *Greek-English Lexicon of the New Testament and Other Early Christian Literature*, 3rd ed. [Chicago: University of Chicago Press, 2000], 746).

they are false claims "against the knowledge of God" (v. 5). So, the battle here is not primarily a combat against demons, but a struggle to dispel demonic lies about God and the gospel of Jesus Christ. In fact, the struggle for one's thought life is a consistent theme in Paul's letters, as well as in the rest of the New Testament (Phil. 4:6–8; 2 Cor. 10:5).

Paul works strenuously to explain the gospel even to the churches because "I am afraid that as the serpent deceived Eve by his cunning, your thoughts will be led astray from a sincere and pure devotion to Christ" (2 Cor. 11:3). The simile that he uses is instructive: It is the subtlety of the enemy that leads people from the truth. Some people boast that they do the same work that Paul does, but "such men are false apostles, deceitful workmen, disguising themselves as apostles of Christ" (2 Cor. 11:13). These false teachers, he says, are merely mimicking their leader, "for even Satan disguises himself as an angel of light. So it is no surprise if his servants, also, disguise themselves as servants of righteousness" (2 Cor. 11:14–15). Notice that the concern here is not about possession or occult attacks from the enemy, but something more "ordinary"—false teaching!

Examine Yourselves

The enemy and his servants often disguise their wrong-doing in an effort to mislead us and turn our attention from the truth of the gospel. His attacks are often attacks of cunning or subtlety (Gen. 3:1; 1 Cor. 11:3). Paul can conclude his letter, then, with an earnest appeal for the restoration of his people. He begs them to "examine themselves" to see if Christ is in them, and not to go on believing lies, such as that they can continue in sin or turn aside to other roads to salvation (2 Cor. 13:5). He requests that they tear down strongholds of the enemy (lies, false beliefs) so that he can use his authority to build them up and "not for tearing down" (2 Cor. 13:10).

Self-examination is crucial for determining whether we believe the truths of the Bible. Often, we can operate on hidden assumptions or lies that cause us to doubt God or to embrace sin. These things must be exposed to the light so that they can be torn down. In 2 Corinthians 2:10–11, Paul emphasizes forgiveness "so that we would not be outwitted by Satan; for we are not ignorant of his designs." Certainly, Paul talks elsewhere about the schemes of the Devil, such as in Ephesians 6: "Put on the whole armor of God that you may be able to stand against the schemes of the devil" (v. 11). In that text, "schemes" is a translation of *methodias*. In 2 Corinthians 2, however, Paul uses the term *noemata*, which is everywhere else translated "mind" or "thoughts." The translation "schemes" or "designs" as found in most English Bibles is interpretive, but the interpretation actually disguises a broader insight in Paul's letters: we are not unfamiliar with the thoughts of the Devil because we have the same thoughts and practices. James concurs:

You desire and do not have, so you murder. You covet and cannot obtain, so you fight and quarrel. You do not have, because you do not ask. You ask and do not receive, because you ask wrongly, to spend it on your passions. You adulterous people! Do you not know that friendship with the world is enmity with God? Therefore, whoever wishes to be a friend of the world makes himself an enemy of God. (4:2–4)

And, what is James' conclusion? "Submit yourselves therefore to God. Resist the devil, and he will flee from you. Draw near to God, and he will draw near to you" (4:7–8). We allow devilish strongholds to remain in our thinking, and those lead us to act contrary to the truth of the gospel. We must root out the lies of the enemy! Paul commands, "Do not be conformed to this world, but be transformed by the renewal of your mind" (Rom. 12:2).

Many commentators note that because Paul says we are not unaware of the Devil's schemes, we need to come to understand how the enemy attacks us. So far as it goes, I think this is a good point. However, it overlooks the fact that, apart from Christ, we are already blinded by the Devil and are sons of disobedience. As Paul says, we are *not* ignorant of his schemes. We need to focus less on his schemes and more on how to free ourselves from sin and false beliefs. This is why one of the explicit responsibilities of the pastor is to teach well, "patiently enduring evil, correcting his opponents with gentleness" (2 Tim. 2:24–25). Paul says that then "God may perhaps grant them repentance leading to a knowledge of the truth, and that they may come to their senses and *escape from the snare of the devil*, after being captured by him to do his will" (2 Tim. 2:25–26, emphasis added). This "capturing" is not possession. Rather, someone is ensnared by false teaching that leads to quarrelling (2 Tim. 2:23). The reality is that someone can be ensnared and be a servant of the enemy *and not know it* (John 8:44–47). That is the reason that we need to constantly be confronted with the truth of God's Word, and why we must be ruthless with our sin and false beliefs.

How to Tear Down Strongholds

Spiritual warfare is not easy, but it is simple. To tear down strongholds, we must: (1) study the Bible carefully, (2) pray, and (3) participate in Christian community. We must study the Bible so that we know the truth about God. We must pray to repent of our sins, ask God to protect us from the evil one, and make us bold to confess and share the gospel. We must participate in Christian community so that we can encourage and be encouraged in the faith as Hebrews says: "Take care, brothers, lest there be in any of you an evil, unbelieving heart, leading you to fall away from the living God. But exhort one another every day, as long as it is called 'today,' that none of you may be hardened by the deceitfulness of sin" (Heb. 3:12–13).

Summary

Strongholds are ways of thinking that are contrary to the gospel message, gospel hope, and gospel promises. Tearing them down requires exercising control over our thought life by the Spirit's power, and learning more about God through study of his Word. Because the enemy is set against the advance of the gospel, we must heed Peter's exhortation to "honor Christ the Lord as holy, always being prepared to make a defense to anyone who asks you for a reason for the hope that is in you" (1 Peter 3:15). By proclaiming the gospel and explaining it well, we tear down strongholds to the glory of God.

REFLECTION QUESTIONS

1. How can you begin to identify strongholds in your own life?

2. Are there any initiatives for corporate prayer that you could get involved with in your local church?

3. Why is self-examination critical in spiritual warfare?

4. Why is important to remember that deceit is a common tactic of the enemy?

5. How can you be bolder in addressing "every lofty opinion" in your evangelism?

What Is "Binding the Strong Man"?

The question in the chapter title refers to a passage in Mark (3:22–30), in which Jesus says that "no one can enter a strong man's house and plunder his goods, unless he first binds the strong man. Then indeed he may plunder his house" (v. 27). The metaphor is provocative, but the context of this saying makes it clear that Jesus is merely elaborating on his rebuke of the scribes, who accuse him of using demonic power to accomplish his miracles. Hence, the saying is a general principle, in this case applying to Satan. Jesus cannot be in league with Satan because Jesus is "plundering his house." In the context of Mark's gospel, this passage serves to emphasize the mystery of Jesus' identity. Yet, though he speaks to the scribes in parables (v. 23), Jesus' comments make it clear that he is empowered by the Holy Spirit in his ministry and not by the Devil (vv. 28–30).[1]

Luke contains another account with the same teaching (Luke 11:14–22). Jesus points out the folly of the scribes' accusation. Because the Jews also have exorcists, they cannot accuse him of using demonic power without it reflecting poorly on their own sons (v. 19). In contrast, Jesus says that "when a strong man, fully armed, guards his own palace, his goods are safe; but when one stronger than he attacks him and overcomes him, he takes away his armor in which he trusted and divides the spoil" (vv. 21–22). Once again, Jesus is making plain that he is opposing Satan and is more powerful than Satan is. Hence, he can say in rebuke, "Whoever is not with me is against me" (v. 23). It is important to recognize the literary function of these accounts so that we do seek to "apply" texts in a way foreign to the intent of the inspired authors. In no case are these texts expecting us to "bind" demons so that we can plunder their houses (say by preaching the gospel). Rather, they are rebukes of Jesus to those who refuse to recognize his divine authority. He is the one who binds the strong man.

---

1. Elizabeth E. Shivley treats this passage as a program for understanding the conflict between Jesus and the Devil in Mark's account (*Apocalyptic Imagination in the Gospel of Mark: The Literary and Theological Role of Mark 3:22–30* [Berlin: de Gruyter, 2012]).

Mark's Account

The accusation against Jesus is that he uses the power of Beelzebul, the prince of demons, in order to cast out demons (Mark 3:22). The scribes accuse him of this in response to questions from the people about who Jesus is. Matthew tells us that some of the people were asking whether Jesus was the Son of David—that is, the Messiah (Matt. 12:23). The discussion of the "strong man" is a parable which reinforces Jesus' rebuke of this accusation. The scribes' hostility is explained by the events that Mark has chosen to describe to this point in his book.

Notice that by Mark 3, Mark has already established some curious claims about this Jesus. This figure appears with almost no introduction (1:9) to fulfil the prophecy of John (1:7–8). He is revealed to be God's Son (1:11), who can resist the temptation of the Devil (1:13). Unlike the scribe, he teaches with great authority (1:21–22) and has authority over unclean spirits who recognize him as the Holy One of God (1:24). Mark punctuates all this activity with the declaration of the people, "What is this? A new teaching with authority? He commands even the unclean spirits, and they obey him" (1:27). His fame begins to spread (1:28), because he can heal the sick and cast out demons (1:34).

In chapter 2, men bring a paralytic friend to him because Jesus has become famous as a teacher and a healer. But Jesus says something truly shocking to the paralytic, "Son, your sins are forgiven" (2:5). Here we have the first instance of the scribes accusing Jesus of blasphemy, since they think that he is pretending to have divine authority which only God can have (2:7). Yet, Jesus heals the man "that you may know that the Son of Man has authority on earth to forgive sins" (2:10). After this, Mark explains a pattern of suspicion and accusation of the scribes against Jesus (2:16, 24), culminating in their planning to destroy him (3:6). Although the demons know that he is the Son of God (3:11), the scribes believe that he is only able to cast out demons because he has the power of the prince of demons (Beelzebul).

Jesus rebukes them with a question, "How can Satan cast out Satan?" (3:23). The implied answer is, of course, that he can't, which Jesus elaborates upon in the next few verses (vv. 24–26).[2] The reason that Jesus is able to cast out the demons is because he is able to "bind the strong man" (Satan). In other words, his authority and power over the Devil is what the exorcisms demonstrate—the exact opposite of the scribes' accusation to the effect that Jesus was in league with the Devil. In fact, Jesus warns them that they are running the risk of blaspheming God's Spirit, because they are attributing his works to the Devil by saying that Jesus "has an unclean spirit" (3:30).

---

2. See William L. Lane, *The Gospel according to Mark*, New International Commentary on the New Testament (Grand Rapids: Eerdmans, 1974), 142–43.

Luke's Account

This event serves a similar function in Luke's account. Like Mark, Luke is teaching us that Jesus is the Messiah. The accounts of his miracles and teachings are evidence of this fact. In Luke 11:14, we are told that Jesus cast out a demon that made a man mute, and he is accused "casting out demons by Beelzebul, the prince of demons" (11:15). These are people who have misinterpreted the sign through unbelief. "Others, to test him, kept seeking from him a sign from heaven" (11:16). These are people who missed the sign altogether. Jesus rebukes the people by saying:

> Every kingdom divided against itself is laid waste, and a divided household falls. And if Satan also is divided against himself, how will his kingdom stand? For you say that I cast out demons by Beelzebul. And, if I cast out demons by Beelzebul, by whom do your sons cast them out? Therefore they will be your judges. But if it is by the finger of God that I cast out demons, then the kingdom of God has come upon you. When a strong man, fully armed guards his own palace, his good are safe; but when one stronger than he attacks him and overcomes him, he takes away his armor in which he trusted and divides the spoil. Whoever is not with me is against me, and whoever does not gather with me scatters. (11:17–23)

Here Luke records more of the "parables" that Jesus spoke to the people during this time (Mark 3:23). In particular, Luke emphasizes that Jesus warns the people to consider carefully the sign that they have witnessed and what it must portend. Either Jesus is casting out demons by demonic or divine power. If, as Jesus points out, it makes no sense for him to cast out demons by demonic power, then the only conclusion left is that he does so with divine authority. Hence, the kingdom of God has come.[3] Already in Luke, the reader has been told to anticipate a stronger man (3:16)! The strong-man passage here reinforces that idea of the arriving kingdom and the kingship of Jesus. Jesus is the stronger man who "overcomes the world" (John 16:33). Hence, by the Spirit Christians (16:7) are protected from the evil one (John 17:15).

Summary

Jesus came to "destroy the works of the devil" (1 John 3:8). He is the "stronger man" (Luke 3:16; 11:22) who can bind the strong man and plunder his house. He does this by his divine power and authority (Matt. 12:28; Mark 2:10; Luke 11:20). By his substitutionary death and resurrection, he "disarmed

---

3. See discussion in John T. Carroll, *Luke: A Commentary* (Louisville: Westminster John Knox, 2012), 256.

the rulers and authorities and put them to open shame" (Col. 2:15). Because he has conquered sin and death (1 Cor. 15:55–57), any who call on him will be saved (Joel 2:32; Acts 2:21; Rom. 10:13). It is not necessary for Christians to identify spirits to bind so that the gospel can go forward, because Jesus has already overcome. We must simply live out his victory by obeying his gospel (Rom. 10:16; 1 Peter 4:17; 2 Thess. 1:7–8) and pray for perseverance (Col. 1:10–11; Eph. 3:16) and boldness in declaring the message of reconciliation (Eph. 6:19).

REFLECTION QUESTIONS

1. How do the differences in the accounts in Mark and Luke help to show the different emphases of the authors?

2. How does the strong-man parable relate to the scribes' accusation against Jesus?

3. Why is it important to realize that Jesus is the stronger one who binds the strong man?

4. In light of Jesus' victory, what would it mean to "plunder"?

5. Is it comforting to know that the Spirit who empowered Jesus' ministry indwells all who are united to him in faith?

What Is Spiritual Mapping?

Spiritual Mapping can refer to two different practices.[1] In some cases, spiritual mapping refers to demographic and anthropological research about the cultural and religious beliefs of a particular region of the world. The goal is to better understand the culture that one will engage with the gospel. Such research is a necessary part of missions. In other cases, however, it refers to the attempt to trace specific lines of demonic influence and power, often through reliance on information obtained from occult sources, so that believers can discover the strongholds of territorial spirits. The idea is to find out the regions over which demons exercise peculiar authority, so that the demons can be bound and evangelistic efforts in the region can be successful. This latter practice has no biblical support whatsoever, is dangerous, and should be abandoned.

Mapping Enemy Territory

The idea behind "supernatural" spiritual mapping originates in the work of George Otis, Jr., among a handful of other members of the charismatic movement, especially in the 1990s.[2] The definition of the term is relatively modest: "An attempt to see our (fill in the region to be mapped) as it really is, not as it appears to be."[3] Some authors, such as Cindy Jacobs, offer more specific definitions: "In my opinion, it is the researching of a city to discover any inroads

---

1. In a helpful history of "spiritual mapping" and its relation to Christian mission, Nadège Mézié refers to two types of spiritual mapping. One she calls "supernatural," associated with George Otis, Jr. and others. The other she calls "realistic," associated with a trajectory of "human geography" originated by the Jesuits ("Les *évangéliques* cartographient le monde. Le Spiritual Mapping," *Archives de sciences sociales des religions* 142 [2008]: 63–85).
2. George Otis, Jr., *The Last of the Giants* (Tarrytown, NY: Chosen, 1991), 85.
3. C. Peter Wagner, "Introduction," in C. Peter Wagner, ed., *Breaking Strongholds in Your City* (Ventura, CA: Regal, 1993), 14. He cites Otis, *The Last of the Giants*, 85, as his source for the definition.

Satan has made, which prevent the spread of the gospel and the evangeliza-
tion of a city for Christ."[4] This involves not only an attempt to identify both
local and corporate demonic strongholds ("a fortified place that Satan builds to
exalt himself against the knowledge and plan of God")[5] but also the "redemptive gift" that each city or culture has to offer.[6] In part, this mapping involves an
understanding that prayer has a geographical dimension.[7] Spiritual research is
able to confirm what the Spirit reveals, such as the names of specific demonic
entities who have been or are currently worshipped in a particular city as well
as locations of their shrines. There is also concern about previous bloodshed in
an area (based on 2 Sam. 21:1) and corporate guilt that requires identificational
repentance (modeled on prayers from Nehemiah or Daniel).

Yet another author offers this definition: "It is God's revelation about the
spiritual situation of the world in which we live. It is vision that goes beyond
our natural senses and, by the Holy Spirit, reveals the spiritual hosts of darkness to us."[8] In point of fact, God has revealed the spiritual situation of the
world already through the Bible, but this author is referring to ongoing revelation about specific circumstances in contemporary life, through dreams
and prophetic visions. Hence, he asserts: "Spiritual mapping plays the same
important role that intelligence and espionage play during war. It reveals the
conditions behind enemy lines. It is a spiritual, strategic and sophisticated
tool, which is powerful in God to assist in pulling down the strongholds of
the enemy."[9] Besides being a loose appropriation of 2 Corinthians 10, this
claim also evinces an overrealized account of the warfare metaphor, in particular the idea that the enemy is "over there" somewhere. It also leads to the
idea that the only reason that someone does not believe the gospel is because
they "simply cannot because Satan has blinded them and held them captive."[10]
Such a case can easily be made from 2 Corinthians 4:3–4. However, Paul does
not suggest spiritual mapping as a strategy for dealing with this situation. In
fact, he never makes mention of spiritual mapping at all. Rather, his encouragement is to continue in preaching the gospel (2 Cor. 4:5–6), and "the power
of God to salvation" (Rom. 1:14). Nevertheless, the wonderful aspect of this
focus is on the zeal and urgency that it produces for evangelism.

---

4. Cindy Jacobs, "Dealing with Strongholds," in *Breaking Strongholds*, 77. She also cites Otis'
   definition in addition to her own.
5. Ibid., 80.
6. "Redemptive gift" is a term suggested by John Dawson (*Taking Our Cities for God* [Lake
   Mary, FL: Creation House, 1989], 39). See C. Peter Wagner's discussion in "The Visible and
   the Invisible," in *Breaking Strongholds*, 56–57.
7. See Kjell Sjoberg, "Spiritual Mapping for Prophetic Prayer Actions," in *Breaking Strongholds*,
   97–119.
8. Harold Caballeros, "Defeating the Enemy with the Help of Spiritual Mapping," in *Breaking
   Strongholds*, 125.
9. Ibid.
10. Ibid., 127.

In certain respects, the historical research that is involved in the process is helpful because it produces a context from which to begin understanding a contemporary culture. Such cultural analysis is important because it provides a platform for shared understanding. Hence, it enables missionaries to communicate the gospel more clearly. But many of the specific practices, such as making maps with locations of occult sites, are simply foreign to the biblical witness. Unless we uncritically apply certain Old Testament proscriptions without reference to their literary and historical context, we rarely have even modest and tangential evidence to provide support for these methodologies. In fact, it is difficult to nail down exactly what the practices are, especially because practitioners lack a shared vocabulary even when it comes to the definition of spiritual mapping! All the definitions given in this chapter are derived from the same collection of essays, in demonstration of this point.[11]

Furthermore, after the activity of asking and answering historical, geographic, and social questions, the real progress in spiritual mapping is often attributed to a specific revelation of God. For example, one regularly reads accounts like: "While we were in prayer the Lord spoke and said, 'Tomorrow I will give you the man's first and last name in the newspaper.' He also told us on which page it would appear."[12] In other cases, the spiritual insights are based on reports from pagan religious authorities or local folklore.[13] In other cases, the insights are based on faulty appropriations of biblical texts (Jeremiah 33:3 is a common one). Sometimes, the fact that such texts are taken out of context is frankly admitted.[14] So, the whole process becomes quite piecemeal and subjective. Since it is based on some elaborate implications of often flimsy exegesis, it has little to recommend it. Of course, no one should short-change the significance of prayer in spiritual warfare and mission (see Question 32), but the prescription to break the power of a particular demon by facing the appropriate "ley lines" of the city is merely reverse engineering the supposed occult magic that caused problems for the city in the first place.[15] What counts most strongly against it is not that it contributes to a lessening emphasis on

---

11. Another is: "spiritual mapping combines research, divine revelation, and confirmatory evidence in order to provide complete and exact data concerning the identity, strategies and methods employed by spiritual forces of darkness to influence people and the churches of a given region" (Wagner, *Breaking Strongholds,* 177).

12. Caballeros, "Defeating the Enemy," 144.

13. Victor Lorenzo, "Evangelizing a City Dedicated to Darkness," in *Breaking Strongholds,* 175.

14. "I will be the first to recognize that this passage [Isa. 33:20–23], in its historical context, has little to do with strategic-level spiritual warfare or taking a city for God. Nevertheless, we felt it was God's prophetic word . . . so we set out to obey it and apply it as we sensed God's leading" (Wagner, *Breaking Strongholds,* 166).

15. See the description of spiritual mapping in La Plata in *Breaking Strongholds,* 190–92. Ley lines or "occultic power lines" are lines in a city that connect major occultic centers within the city. Spiritual mappers will identify major occultic centers (such as temples or monuments) and trace lines between them to organize prayer walking and intercessory efforts.

evangelism (far from it!) but that it places "prophetic" acts that are never endorsed or commanded by the biblical authors at the center of evangelistic efforts. It also flatly denies the sufficiency of Scripture, since a key component of
the methodology is to receive further revelations from God.[16] Finally, it makes
use of occultic conceptions of spiritual power.

Redemptive Gifts of Spiritual Mapping
Spiritual mapping is good insofar as it represents an earnest love for particular people and places, and a zealous desire to see the gospel received by
those people. Its emphases on the significance of prayer, the ultimate dependence of the church on God, the victory possible in God's power, the urgency
of evangelism, and boldness in spiritual warfare are all salient and needful.
But, many of the practices are not commended by Scripture and give far too
much credence to pagan religious ideologies. A common criticism against
those who reject spiritual mapping is that they do so because they are viewing
the world from a Western scientific rationalism. In fact, there may be some
truth to that. Certainly, we should not reject spiritual mapping because there
really are not such things as demons or Satan, etc. However, it is also true
that the preponderance of supposed elicit and explicit spiritual activity is occurring in areas where the folk religions are animistic. Hence, the argument
could as well be turned around: The filter of animism is the basis for the strong
associations between certain ritual activities (not endorsed by the Bible) and
perceived successes in the spiritual realm. Since the gospel is being preached
frequently by persons involved in the activities, it seems hasty to attribute the
success to innovations of the 1990s instead of the power of the Spirit in the
preaching of the gospel. The most inexcusable excess of the movement is its
startlingly poor and loose applications of biblical texts, which are often made
to represent directions for evangelism only because of a prior commitment to
the truth of spiritual mapping. It is odd, to say the least, that the gospel has
had such power for so long without these innovations.

Summary
If spiritual mapping refers merely to cultural and historical analysis, then
it is an important part of the social scientific research that makes for good
missiology. However, most often the term refers to a system of speculative investigations into the spiritual condition of a city or nation in ways that rely on

---

This borrows on the occult idea that spiritual powers flows in specific patterns throughout
the world.
16. "Work with intercessors especially gifted and called to strategic-level spiritual warfare,
seeking God's revelation of: (a) the redemptive gift or gifts of the city; (b) Satan's strongholds in the city; (c) territorial spirits assigned to the city; (d) corporate sin past and
present that needs to be dealt with; and (e) God's plan of attack and timing" (Wagner,
Breaking Strongholds, 231).

special revelation and occult speculation. That type of supernatural spiritual mapping is unwise and unbiblical.

REFLECTION QUESTIONS

1. What is spiritual mapping?

2. What is important in the cultural analysis stressed by spiritual mapping?

3. Why is ignoring the historical and literary context of biblical texts dangerous?

4. What assumptions about the nature of God's revelation are presupposed by spiritual mapping?

5. Are there methods in spiritual mapping that would be healthy to adopt? To reject?

What Is the Role of Prayer in Spiritual Warfare?

Prayer is the central activity of spiritual warfare because it is a means of communing with God, working his power in us through the Holy Spirit, and warding off the lure of demonic temptation. It is also plainly commanded in relation to spiritual warfare throughout the New Testament. But, even acknowledging as much, one needs to know both what the significance of prayer is for spiritual warfare as well as what one ought to pray. Scripture provides answers to both these questions.

Prayer in Spiritual Warfare

Prayer is frequently related to the central concern of spiritual warfare—warring against the flesh in the power of God's spirit according to his word—in Scripture. Nowhere is this more obvious than in the classic spiritual warfare passage, Ephesians 6:10–20. Paul connects the idea of the "sword of the Spirit, which is the word of God," with "praying at all times in the Spirit, with all prayer and supplication" (Eph. 6:17–18). But, the connection occurs in many other passages as well.

We are told to pray that we not enter into temptation and to be delivered from evil or the evil one (Matt. 6:13; 26:41; Mark 14:38; Luke 11:4; 22:40, 46). Jesus asks God for unity in Spirit in his church (John 17:20–21). Paul prays that the church would be built up in their faith: "it is my prayer that your love may abound more and more, with knowledge and all discernment" (Phil. 1:9); "asking that you may be filled with the knowledge of his will in all spiritual wisdom and understanding" (Col. 1:9); and "that our God may make you worthy of his calling and may fulfill every resolve for good and every work of faith by his power" (2 Thess. 1:11). There are numerous prayers for boldness and success in the preaching of the gospel (Matt. 9:38; 2 Cor. 5:20; Eph. 6:18–19; Col. 4:3; 1 Thess. 5:25; 2 Thess. 3:1; Heb. 13:18). We are taught that security lies in closeness to God, and this is maintained by prayer (Luke 21:36; Jude 20). Our repentance and faith is expressed by prayer (Acts 8:22). Finally, it is simply God's will that we "pray without ceasing, give thanks in all circumstances; for this is the will of God in Christ Jesus for you" (1 Thess. 5:17–18).

Since spiritual warfare is primarily caught up with the resistance of the enemy to the progress of the gospel in discipleship (both in making new disciples and in growing disciples), prayer for advancing of the gospel and increasing closeness to God is spiritual warfare—even if it never mentions principalities or powers! The object of attention and affection in our prayer life should be God and his will, and it is possible for us to be deceived by the enemy into focusing our attention on alternative methods of spiritual growth and transformation because, often, prayer feels like doing nothing. However, given the counsel of Scripture, it is clear that prayer is effective and crucially significant for spiritual warfare, and for Christian living in general.

What to Pray?

Given the commands of the apostles to pray, we should pray first of all for the things that they command us to pray. We should recite truths about God from the Bible and ask that God would help us to believe them and to have our affections rightly ordered toward those truths.[1] We should pray that God would strengthen us to obey his commands, and to give us perseverance to study his Word, to know what he commands of us. We should pray for our pastors and fellow church members, that they would grow in holiness and serve as members of Christ's church as they ought. We should pray for our leaders that they would pursue justice. We should pray for the lost (in general), that the gospel would be made known to them. We should pray for the lost (around us), that we might have courage to witness them with boldness. We should pray that the enticements of the enemy would not be more attractive to us than the beauty of God will. But most of all, we should pray because in making our requests known to God, we show our awareness of our dependence on him for all things.

A good place to start for studying prayer is the book of Psalms. It contains a messianic, eschatological orientation so that it is more than a random collection of prayers and songs but becomes for us an honest portrayal of suffering (Pss. 3, 22), longing (Pss. 83, 89), and victory (Ps. 47). It confesses God's righteousness (Pss. 5, 50), the beauty of his Law (Ps. 119), and his Messiah (Pss. 2, 110). In light of those things, it teaches us to praise him (Ps. 150). It is good as we make our requests known to God (prayer) that we remember whom we are beseeching, what his promises are, and what he has done for us in Christ.

---

1. See D. A. Carson, *Praying with Paul*, 2nd ed. (Grand Rapids: Baker, 2014), esp. 1–20 for a defense of this method of praying.

How to Pray?

Ceaselessly (1 Thess. 5:17). In particular, if we conceive of prayer as a part of our discipline for spiritual nourishment and growth in obedience to God (1 Tim. 4:7), we should set aside time daily to pray. Training is not haphazard, as our attempts to pray "throughout the day as we think of it" often are. Instead, prayer should be persistent and regular. In setting aside time to pray, we are following the example of Christ (Matt. 14:13; 26:36; Mark 1:35; 6:46) and obeying Paul's instruction.[2]

Scripturally. In other words, our prayer should not merely be heaped up words (Matt. 6:7–8) and we should not pray merely to be known as someone who prays (Matt. 5:5–6). Instead, we should pray following the pattern outlined for us in the Bible, referring to biblical truths so that when we ask that God's will be done (Matt. 6:10), we know for what we ask. Our prayers are more effective in conforming us to Christlikeness in this way (1 John 5:14; James 4:3).[3]

Earnestly. In Jesus, we have complete access to the Father (Rom. 8:15; Gal. 4:6; cf. Mark 14:36), so we should ask in light of the relationship that we have to him. Thus, we imitate Jesus (Luke 22:44) and obey his commands (Matt. 9:38; 1 Thess. 3:10).

Summary

Prayer is at the heart of spiritual warfare and the Christian life, because it confesses our dependence on God for renewal, sustenance, and strength. Contending with flesh and blood is difficult enough, but our battle is even greater than that (Eph. 6:12). But, "If God is for us, who can be against us?" (Rom. 8:31). We should pray for his strength (Eph. 6:10) and the proclamation of his word (Eph. 6:17–18). We should pray ceaselessly, scripturally, and earnestly, to be changed into in the image of Christ and to change the world in the light of his gospel.[4]

REFLECTION QUESTIONS

1. In what ways does the Bible connect the idea of prayer with temptation?

2. In what ways does the Bible connect the idea of prayer with proclamation of the gospel?

---

2. See E. M. Bounds, *The Complete Works of E.M. Bounds on Prayer* (Grand Rapids: Baker, 1990), 325–30.

3. For an example using the model of the Lord's Prayer, see Timothy Keller, *Prayer: Experiencing Awe and Intimacy with God* (New York: Dutton, 2014), 108–19.

4. For an introductory biblical theology of prayer, see Graeme Goldsworthy, *Prayer and the Knowledge of God* (Downers Grove, IL: InterVarsity Press, 2003).

3. What are some ways you can begin to make prayer a daily habit?

4. How can you begin to pray for the endurance and witness of missionaries whom your church supports?

5. How can you begin to pray for spiritual growth in your own life, and for opportunities to share the gospel?

Should We Practice Exorcisms?

The history of Christian exorcism demonstrates a great deal of flux regarding how and when to perform exorcisms as well as who is able to perform them. Nevertheless, there is a steady ritualized form of exorcism from the seventh century that is similar in its language to the Catholic rituals of the present. Protestant practices have been much more fluid, which is to be expected from a movement that is much less institutional and has a shorter history. Christians of all stripes have believed in the potential of demonization because they have believed in the reality of demons and the reality of their activity. The New Testament does not present anything like a sophisticated form of exorcism, whether as a ritual or as an office of the church or an ongoing charism.

Instead, the presentation of exorcism in the Scriptures are signs and affirmations of the authority of Jesus and the in-breaking of his kingdom in fulfillment of God's covenant promises. Hence, these accounts should lead us to glorify Christ. If we were able to determine an authentic instance of demonization, then exorcism (it seems) would be appropriate, but the remedy suggested by the biblical accounts is nothing more than prayer that recognizes the authority of Christ. Further, no emphasis on exorcism is given outside of Matthew, Mark, Luke, and Acts in the New Testament. Even mentions in Acts are relatively sparse and do not constitute a primary focus on ministry in the life of Paul (Acts 16:18).[1]

History of Christian Exorcism

As early as the late second century, exorcisms were part and parcel of the preparation of catechumens for baptism, and this settled into some regularity in the churches around the middle of the third century. Records of the baptismal rites of the period often involve the laying on of hands or adjurations

---

1. Or compare Paul's activity in Acts 19:1–10 with the activity of exorcists in 19:11–20.

against the Devil and evil spirits.[2] In fact, some church writers were convinced that every non-believer was possessed by a demon in need of exorcising. By the fourth century, these rites become more symbolic, although scholars debate the extent to which writers of the period (such as Augustine) saw the exorcism elements of the baptism ritual as literal expulsions of demons as opposed to symbolic declarations of the new freedom of the believer.

In most cases, it seems that the renouncing of the Devil was merely a declaration of allegiance to Christ rather than an act by which the Devil or one of his demons was to be expelled from a baptismal candidate. By the end of the fifth century, the baptismal rite had become quite elaborate in some churches, and the renouncing of the Devil was incorporated in the process. The priest or bishop would exhale on the candidate as a representation of the enemy being blown away from him (referred to as "exsufflation"). There were also ablutions (ritual washings) with salt and oil that were representative of the purging of evil. In some cases, however, these activities are representations of the protection against spirits that one's Christian status brings. The exorcisms were usually not *ekballistic* (casting out) so much as they were vocal renunciations of the Devil's influence and authority. The exorcism became more strictly organized by the sixth or seventh century, from which period we have records of pre-baptismal cleansing rituals. Normally, these unfolded over a period of seven days, in which the Devil was rebuked. These rituals were also not *ekballistic* either: The seven days were intended to symbolize the sevenfold gift of the Spirit.

At the same time, non-baptismal exorcisms were increasingly the purview of extraordinary people, rather than a lay ministry as it had been considered until around the middle of the third century.[3] Curiously, these rituals are not modeled on the much simpler "rites" presented in the New Testament. In particular, "casting out" language was not particularly common in organized rites, although it may have been in extemporaneous lay exorcisms. However, by the end of the fifth century, there was an established extra-baptismal rite of exorcism.

In the middle ages, there were significant revisions to the understanding of exorcism. In some cases it took on magical elements, whereas in others there was a greater diagnostic and intellectual curiosity regarding the nature of demons and demonic power. As the church expanded, exorcism often faded from a "front-line" practice associated with conversion and renouncing the Devil to a defense against encroachments from sorcerers and pagan religious peoples. Regardless, increased systematic theological attention to the importance of exorcism (particularly in its associations with baptism) raised questions about its effectiveness. Because the rite did not seem to prevent infant death or disease in the catechumenate (a person in training for baptism),

---

2. W. Telfer, *Cyril of Jerusalem and Nemesius of Emesa* (Philadelphia: Westminster, 1955), 70.
3. Eusebius, *Ecclesiastial History*, trans. Christian Frederick Cruse (Grand Rapids: Baker, 1981), 263–366.

there were questions about whether it could be considered a sacrament (i.e., efficacious through the unfolding of a particular rite).

In part, these developments are related to the increasing sense in which exorcism was reserved as an act associated with extraordinary saints and their ritual shrines. Because of a series of doctrinal disputes, the view of exorcism remained in a certain state of flux throughout the period. By the late 1300s, however, there were standard lists of diagnostic criteria for determining whether someone might be afflicted by a demon.[4] Even these were different in different regions and cultures. In fact, they also believed, on the basis of certain mystical commitments, in a type of divine possession, which could be indistinguishable from mental illness or possession of different kinds.[5] Hence, although the treatment for demoniacs became more ritualized and medicinal in one sense, in the years following the Reformation, the records indicate that there are cultural aspects to "possessed" individuals, which makes it even more difficult to assess in which cases someone was legitimately in need of exorcism. Perhaps, changes in the frequency of possession reflects a new strategy of the enemy. Of course, after the Enlightenment, exorcism waned considerably until certain Protestant movements resuscitated the idea in the twentieth century. Nevertheless, it has remained a traceable and systemic object of contention and fascination through most of church history.

How to Exorcise

The history of the exorcism in the Christian church reveals that there were disagreements about when and how to perform an exorcism. However, even from relatively early on, there were ritualized processes for dealing with demons. Generally, these involved a rebuke of some kind based on the spoken authority of Jesus. In many cases, the rituals were quite elaborate. Thus, the difficulty of distinguishing exorcism from the magic of the pagans has regularly been a struggle, and throughout much of church history the model for the exorcist was not Christ, but Solomon.[6]

---

4. Michael D. Bailey, *Magic and Superstition in Europe: A Concise History from Antiquity to the Present* (Lanham, MD: Rowman & Littlefield, 2006), 107–40. See also Nancy Caciola, "Mystics, Demoniacs, and the Physiology of Spirit Possession in Medieval Europe," *Comparative Studies in Society and History* 42, no. 2 (2000): 268–306. In part, some consensus was sought because of inadequate descriptions in earlier accounts of successful exorcism and healing. See Despina Iosif, "'I saw Satan fall like lightning from heaven': Illness as Demon Possession in the World of the First Christian Ascetics and Monks," *Mental Health, Religion and Culture* 14, no. 4 (2011): 326.

5. See Nancy Caciola, *Discerning Spirits: Divine and Demonic Possession in the Middle Ages* (Ithaca. NY: Cornell University Press, 2003), 31–78.

6. In part, the latter is based on the tradition found in the apocryphal *Testament of Solomon*. See Ra'anan Boustan and Micahel Beshay, "Sealing the Demons, Once and for All: The Ring of Solomon, the Cross of Christ, and the Power of Biblical Kingship," *Archiv für Religionsgeschichte* 16, no. 1 (2015): 99–130; and Peter Busch, "Solomon as True Exorcist:

In contrast to ritualized prayers, the *ekballistic* ("casting out") acts of Jesus are typically simple affairs. However, contemporary accounts of exorcism are more likely to resemble something from horror films involving an extended battle with the Devil rather than the simple commands that characterize the gospel accounts. Surely, this is a mistake.

One could take the pattern of the gospel accounts as a prescription for how to perform an exorcism, but no actual prescribed method for exorcism appears in Scripture. In other words, if one was committed to performing an exorcism, there would be no potential biblical model except for the acts of Jesus in the Gospels. None of the letter writers of the New Testament suggest anything about "healing" demoniacs nor is exorcism mentioned in any of the spiritual-gift lists in the New Testament letters. So, for all the elaborate history of exorcism in the Christian church, we really have no guide for such practices in the New Testament. Given the extraordinary diversity and confusion about exorcism in Christian history, we should probably focus our attention on the biblical accounts if we intend to develop a model.

On that score, however, it seems unnecessary to have a ritualized exorcism practice for three reasons: (1) the gospel accounts are not ritualized, (2) such rituals confuse Christian exorcism with magical practices, and (3) our prayers to God never require such ritualization.

If it is right that we have full access to the Father through the Son in the Spirit, then we can pray for the healing of the oppressed by simply asking. All ritualization runs the risk of being functionally godless—i.e., we run the risk of thinking that certain acts or spoken formulas work by some mechanical process so that the outcome is guaranteed. But, even in the gospel accounts, we see that exorcisms by the faithful do not always reach their full effect or any success at all (Mark 9:28–29). Rather, the incidents of exorcism recorded in the gospels are intended primarily to show Jesus' authority over demons, not to provide instruction in how we might similarly engage demons. Even Michael the archangel does not engage directly in dispute with the enemy (Jude 9), although Jesus does (Matt. 4:1). In fact, the instance of the disciples' failure to cast out a demon in Mark 9 is instructive. When they ask why they were not able to cast out the demon, Jesus replies that, "this kind cannot be driven out by anything except prayer."[7] There is a significant insight here.

Prayer (making our requests known to God) is an embodied expression of our dependence on God and, importantly, of our acknowledgement that we rely on him for our needs. It is our faith (trust) in God that is significant in

The Testament of Solomon in Its Cultural Setting," in *The Figure of Solomon in Jewish, Christian, and Islamic Tradition: King, Sage, and Architect*, ed. Jozef Verhayden, Themes in Biblical Narrative (Leiden: Brill, 2013), 183–95. The text of *Testament of Solomon* is available in D. Duling, "Testament of Solomon," in *The Old Testament Pseudepigrapha*, vol. 1, ed. James H. Charlesworth (New York: Doubleday, 1983), 935–88.
7. The Byzantine manuscripts add "and fasting."

this regard. When the father of the boy with the unclean spirit tells Jesus that his disciples could not cast it out, Jesus responds with, "O faithless generation" (Mark 9:19; Luke 9:41). When the man asks Jesus for his help, he says, "*if* you can do anything, have compassion on us and help us" (Mark 9:22, emphasis added). Jesus' response is telling. He repeats the "*if*" in an incredulous way. Of course, Jesus has the authority! Jesus instructs him that "all things are possible for one who believes," and the man asks for his help in believing (9:23–24).

In Matthew's account, we get another insight into Jesus' comment that prayer was needed to drive out this demon. Matthew records that Jesus says the disciples could not cast out the demon, "Because of your little faith" (Matt. 17:20). Rather than focusing on the method for casting out demons, we should focus on the one who has all authority on heaven and earth (Matt. 28:18). If we are to discover a "method" for exorcism in Scripture, it seems to me that it is prayer (and fasting). Not adjurations, incantations, ablutions, but a faithful, earnest request to God.

Who to Exorcise

A thornier problem is how to determine whether someone is authentically possessed by a demon. As a general rule, we should expect the possession to resemble the accounts given in Scripture. A curious observation from these accounts is that the question whether someone is possessed is never in doubt. In contrast, diagnostic lists used to verify the empirical signs of demonization have been regular features of Christian writings on possession for the better part of 1,600 years. Many of the symptoms of possession are similar to those presented in Scripture and, since those accounts are actual accounts of demonization, they seem to be our best guide. Even still, it remains a problem that many of the symptoms of the demonized (deafness, seizure, muteness) are likewise symptoms of disease, which the gospel writers treat differently than demonization (e.g., Mark 6:13). Our tendency in the West is to distinguish sharply between physical and spiritual maladies. But caution is needed here. We should not rule out the possibility of demonic activity, nor should we suggest it is the root of all troubles. Crucially, whether a demon is involved in a situation or not, helping a person who is struggling is a duty of the Christian community that should involve prayer for discernment, wisdom, and restoration. It seems to me that, in general, the presence of demonic possession would be remarkably obvious since that is the case in the New Testament, as opposed to "hidden demons" that are often referred to in texts on spiritual warfare.

Summary

The history of Christian exorcistic practice shows that it has received mixed emphasis at different moments of church history. Ritualized practices seem mostly to be an effort at providing a framework for interpreting "possession experiences" and for offering some comfort about the chances of success in exorcising demons. However, these practices are not commended by the New Testament and, frankly, resemble pagan magic more than simple Christian piety. The "formula" in the New Testament is merely prayer that relies on and pronounces the authority of Jesus. Given the pattern of the New Testament, we would expect possession to be obvious if it appeared, but the pattern of possession only makes significant appearances in the Synoptic accounts (Matthew, Mark, Luke) and in Acts. John's account and the epistles of the New Testament make no mention of exorcism, although they do insist on the reality of demons and spiritual warfare. The weapons of spiritual warfare are faith in Christ and the preaching of the gospel.

REFLECTION QUESTIONS

1. What is the difference between pre-baptismal exorcism and *ekballistic* exorcism?

2. How has the understanding of exorcism changed in church history?

3. Why should we avoid rigid ritualism in our understanding of exorcism?

4. Are there formulas for exorcism in the New Testament? What does this imply?

5. Why is prayer significant in exorcism?

Is It Possible to Bless Objects for Spiritual Warfare?

In a word, the answer to the question posed in this chapter is "no." However, some Christians hold that people, places, and objects can be specially consecrated by certain ritual acts, such that they are imbued with some special power or authority that limits the access of the enemy or spiritual forces to harm them or their possessors. These are merely beliefs in magic, which are not endorsed by the biblical authors. In fact, commands regarding magical practices are always negative, forbidding any participation in them. Nor are these censures limited to the Old Testament. Not only is it *not* possible to bless objects for spiritual warfare (because Scripture provides no guidance for how to do so), but it is also completely unnecessary.

Consecrating the Temple

Because the Old Testament describes practices and rituals for cleansing certain places and objects, some Christians infer that similar practices would cleanse places or objects in contemporary life. Frankly, this misunderstands God's gracious provision for his people as a kind of magical formula by which spiritual forces are compelled to act in specific ways. An examination of passages in the Old Testament regarding cleansing make it clear that none of the endorsed rituals guarantee certain spiritual results and that they are not patterns for the church to adopt.

In Exodus 40, Moses records the Lord's instructions on how he is to erect the tabernacle. In particular, Moses is charged with consecrating the objects in the tabernacle with oil:

> Then you shall take the anointing oil and anoint the tabernacle and all that is in it, and consecrate it and all its furniture, so that it may become holy. You shall also anoint the

altar of burnt offering and all its utensils, and consecrate the
altar, so that the altar may become most holy. You shall also
anoint the basin and its stand, and consecrate it. Then you
shall bring Aaron and his sons to the entrance of the tent of
meeting and shall wash them with water and put on Aaron
the holy garments. (Exod. 40:9–13)

Clearly, the preparation of the temple to receive the presence of the Lord
is a significant ritual, but nothing in this text suggests that similar prepara-
tions elsewhere would similarly render a site or object (or person) holy. In
other words, the provision is limited with respect to both the time and place
of God's choosing. In part this is because consecration of these elements and
of Aaron and his sons is a way of marking them for use in the ministry of
the Lord's tabernacle, and it is abundantly obvious that this happens based
on God's choice (Exod. 28:1–4). In fact, consecration or "making holy" has
primarily the connotation that something is made sacred, but this does not
reflect the sense that it contains a type of divine or heavenly deposit or is empowered in some way by this process.

In fact, the first instance we have in the Law of Moses of something being
consecrated or declared holy is the Sabbath day (Gen. 2:3). But, clearly this
does not mean that some "blessing" has accrued to the Sabbath day that wards
off sin or evil. Instead, the day is marked with a special significance, as attested
by way of the Sabbath command (Exod. 20:8). There he writes, "Remember
the Sabbath day, to keep it holy." The people are to do this, "For in six days
the LORD made heaven and earth, the sea, and all that is in them, and rested
on the seventh day. Therefore, the LORD blessed the Sabbath day and made
it holy" (Exod. 20:11). In other words, the logic of the command is, because
God has consecrated this day of his week-long creation, the people are commanded to continue likewise to mark it with special significance (by resting
from labor). The one who "profanes" the Sabbath is cut off from the people
(Exod. 31:14) So, holy objects are holy because they have been set apart for
God's purposes in specific ways that he has dictated, not because they have
some intrinsic divine power.

This understanding of consecration for ritual purposes in the Law is de-
cidedly different from the consecration of, for example, holy water in the early
church. Because of the association between baptism and washing, water became a sign of ritual cleansing by the fourth century.[1] In fact, there are extant
blessings for water and oil from some documents of this period, and the blessings are intended to imbue the liquids with curative properties. In some cases,
these blessings were associated with other substances as well (most commonly,

1. Thomas M. Finn, "Ritual Process and the Survival of Early Christianity: A Study of the
Apostolic Tradition of Hippolytus," *Journal of Ritual Studies* 3, no. 1 (1989): 69–89.

salt) and increasingly came to be seen as medicinal aids in tasks such as exorcism or warding off witchcraft. So, being set apart for ritual use slowly came to mean freed from corruption in a way sufficient to physically heal or dispel evil spirits. Certainly, by the seventh century, there was an agreement that priests were able to make water holy (i.e., imbue it with divine or semidivine power) in the Eastern Church. By the Middle Ages, the distribution of "holy" water for purposes as diverse as blessing homes and cattle was a common practice in the West. It seems clear that all this is a significant departure from the biblical idiom even if it is an understandable development. The Roman Ritual of the Catholic Church contains blessings for all manner of items and is still endorsed by the Catholic Church today.[2] Protestant churches, especially some branches of Pentecostalism, utilize a similar understanding of blessing in the sense that they hold that it is possible to bless certain places or objects with divine protection, but the methods of such churches are more enthusiastic and spontaneous than the rituals of Catholicism.

So far as it goes, there does not seem to be any reason that praying that God would protect certain people from the enemy and temptation, etc., is harmful. In fact, such prayer is endorsed by Jesus (Matt. 6:13). But, the simple piety represented by these petitions to God for his protection does not require the quasi-magical use of ritualized prayers and objects.

Consecrate Yourselves

Furthermore, the petition for protection against evil in the Lord's Prayer comes in the context of a request for his kingdom and personal holiness. And, the prayer for blessing or holiness—continuous with the Old Testament background—is pervasive in the New Testament. In other words, we must distinguish between two senses in which we use the word "blessing." Blessing can mean imbuing with divine or celestial power and protection, as in the example of holy water, or it can refer to setting something intentionally apart for God's purposes. The latter is the generically biblical way of describing consecration or holiness. This can be done through recognizing something's status or importance appropriately (Matt. 6:9; 1 Peter 3:15) or setting something or someone apart for God's service (Matt. 23:19; Gal. 1:15).

In the New Testament, however, we increasingly see the fullest sense in which someone is "made holy," which takes place when someone is purified from sin—not through ritual but through the Holy Spirit (Rom. 15:16; 1 Thess. 5:23) on the basis of knowing Jesus (John 17:17). But, even this holiness reflects the access to God and intentional commitment to his service. Jesus tells Paul that:

---

2. Philip T. Weller, ed., *The Roman Ritual* (Boonville, NY: Preserving Christian Publications, 2007). Volume 3 contains blessings.

> I have appeared to you for this purpose, to appoint you as
> a servant and witness to the things in which you have seen
> me and to those in which I will appear to you delivering you
> from your people and from the Gentiles—to whom I am
> sending you to open their eyes, so that they may turn from
> darkness to light and from the power of Satan to God that
> they may receive forgiveness of sins and a place among those
> who are sanctified by faith in me. (Acts 26:16–18)

Hence, we consecrate ourselves (not our things) by faith in Jesus and his
word (Eph. 5:26). The Christian church already has "every spiritual blessing in
the heavenly places" in Christ (Eph. 1:3). So, blessing external things for use
in spiritual combat is simply redundant—and frankly, it smacks of accommodation to animistic worldviews and syncretism.

Summary

The consecration of objects in the Old Testament does not imbue them
with divine power. Rather, it marks them as sacred objects for the service of
God in his temple according to his instructions. The same is true for the office
of the priests. The service belongs to them and not to others, not even kings (2
Chron. 26:16–21), because the sons of Aaron are those "consecrated to burn
incense" (2 Chron. 26:18). Likewise, consecration in the New Testament is the
purification from sin found by faith in Christ's blood and trust in his word. It
has no connotation of magic or apotropaic (protection from spirits) power,
aside from the power of God's spirit by which Christians may mortify their
flesh. Historical associations of the blessing of particular people or objects
with effusive divine power are later developments often based on accounts of
great saints or loose conceptual relationships between medicinal anointing
and healing (James 5:14). But, these latter are based on God's response to
prayer and not to anything specially imbued in the oil. Not only is there no
guide for blessing objects for spiritual warfare in the Scriptures, it is unnecessary. The blessing of Christ and prayer are sufficient.

REFLECTION QUESTIONS

1. How is consecration understood in the Old Testament with regard to the
   temple?

2. How does the purification of holiness relate to Jesus in the New Testament?

3. How do two different senses of the English word "blessing" confuse the
   discussion?

4. What does the Lord's Prayer teach us about preparation for spiritual warfare?

5. How does Ephesians 1:3–22 shed light on this discussion?

Questions Related to the Occult

What Does the Bible Say about the Occult?

The term "occult" refers to a spectrum of mystery religions, magical practices, and beliefs, such as alchemy, theosophy (meeting God by mystic revelation), spiritism, and other secret "wisdom." The word "occult" itself refers to something hidden or mysterious. The Bible does not describe the practices associated with the occult in any great detail, but the biblical authors uniformly and categorically reject participation in such practices.[1]

Pagan Magicians

The rejection of these pagan magicians and their practices is especially clear in the Law of Moses, and continues to be a major theme in the Old Testament that carries into the New Testament. The basic problem with the occult is that it attempts to discover and achieve knowledge and power through spiritual means other than those ordained by God. Part of the reason that occultism is so strongly forbidden in the Law is because association with occult methods of divination or spirits is a blatant display of distrust in God. In other words, it violates the first commandment ("I am the LORD your God, who brought you out of the land of Egypt, out of the house of slavery. You shall have no other gods before me," Exod. 20:2–3). The relationship between occultism of various kinds and pagan religious idolatry is apparent throughout Scripture and in any examination of occultism historically.

The fact that occult powers are real and can have supernatural effects is never in doubt in the Bible. This is reflected, for example, when Moses describes the power of the wise men of Egypt. They are able to turn their staffs

---

1. For book-length treatments of the occult from a Christian perspective, see Josh McDowell and Don Stewart, *Understanding the Occult* (San Bernardino, CA: Here's Life Publishers, 1982) and Dave Hunt, *Occult Invasion* (Eugene, OR: Harvest House, 1998).

into serpents (Exod. 7:11), turn water into blood (Exod. 7:22), call frogs into the land (Exod. 8:7), but they are unable to repeat the third plague (Exod. 8:18). The magicians are able to perform these supernatural acts according to *latehem* (= "their secrets" or "their secret arts"). The LXX renders the word as *pharmakeia*, which can refer to medicine (as in the English "pharmacy") but also sorcery. The text does not explain the mechanics of these secret arts, and, in fact, the point of these passages seems to be to point to the power of God, not the "power" of the wise men.

Clearly, however, these magicians were capable of counterfeit miracles, which is suggestive of demonic power (Matt. 24:24; 2 Thess. 2:9; 1 John 4:1). Furthermore, in explanation of why they cannot reproduce the plague of gnats, the wise men explain to Pharaoh that Moses' sign is "the finger of God" (Exod. 8:19). Jesus refers to the finger of God in relation to his ability to cast out demons to contradict the scribes' claims that he exorcises by the power of Beelzebub (Luke 11:20).[2] This suggests that the wise men's power is demonic. In other instances, wise men or magicians are unable to attain the wisdom or interpretative insight of the one who has God's help (Gen. 41:24; Dan. 1:20). So, while the Bible confirms that occult powers exist, and are probably powered by demonic influence, they are no match for divine power and authority.

Condemnation

The fact that these magicians are not a match for God's prophets is itself a condemnation of their power since no one should rely on something weak when they have access to someone strong. However, there are also regular, explicit condemnations of occult activity. In fact, sorcery is regularly associated with idolatry and pagan religion. Perhaps the best example of this condemnation is found in Deuteronomy 18:9–12:

> When you come into the land that the LORD your God is giving you, you shall not learn to follow the abominable practices of those nations. There shall not be found among you anyone who burns his son or his daughter as an offering, anyone who practices divination or tells fortunes or interprets omens, or a sorcerer, or a charmer or a medium or a necromancer or one who inquires of the dead, for whoever does these things is an abomination to the LORD. And because of these abominations the LORD your God is driving them out before you.

---

2. "But if it is by the finger of God that I cast out demons, then the kingdom of God has come upon you."

So, the nations are being pushed out of the land for these types of occult activity. Furthermore, such occult activities are not necessary for the people as they enter the land, because God will send his prophet to them (Deut. 18:15), which is ultimately a promise about the coming Messiah. In contrast, Paul writes that "what pagans sacrifice they offer to demons and not to God," and "I do not want you to be participants with demons" (1 Cor. 10:20).

In fact, even Saul's attempt to call on a departed prophet of God is censured because it violates God's command about how he will reveal himself and his purposes to his people (1 Sam. 28:6–19). Saul's consultation of the medium is the explicit reason given for his death:

> So Saul died for his breach of faith. He broke faith with the LORD in that he did not keep the command of the LORD, and also consulted a medium, seeking guidance. He did not seek guidance from the LORD. Therefore, the LORD put him to death and turned the kingdom over to David the son of Jesse. (1 Chron. 10:13–14)

Hence, "you shall not permit a sorceress to live" (Exod. 22:18). The same charge is given in Leviticus 20 in the context of child sacrifice. In fact, verse 6 states, "If a person turns to mediums and necromancers, whoring after them, I will set my face against that person and will cut him off from among his people." That is precisely what happened to Saul. The overarching idea here is that occult participation may not merely be a fun, spooky diversion—it might be consultation with demons or those empowered by them. The fact that it *can* be such is explicitly stated by the biblical authors, so there is no reason for a Christian to be involved in such pursuits.

In any case, Christians have something better than occult speculations: we have God. Why would we go to fortune tellers or astrologists when we have the word of God? Joseph says "Do not all interpretations belong to God?" (Gen. 40:8). Isaiah makes the same point:

> Bind up the testimony; seal the teaching [Law] among my disciples. I will wait for the LORD, who is hiding his face from the house of Jacob, and I will hope in him. Behold, I and the children whom the LORD has given me are sign and portents in Israel from the LORD of hosts, who dwells on Mount Zion. And when they say to you, "Inquire of mediums and the necromancers who chirp and mutter," should not a people inquire of their God? Should they inquire of the dead on behalf of the living? To the teaching and to the testimony! (Isa. 8:16–20)

These condemnations are not limited to the Old Testament. Paul reaffirms the demonic nature of pagan rituals (1 Cor. 10:20) and includes sorcery as a mark of the flesh (Gal. 5:19–21). Furthermore, conversion to Christianity involves giving exclusive allegiance to Jesus Christ. This is the explanation for the reactions of former sorcerers when they become Christians. When the sons of Sceva attempt to practice exorcism, using Jesus' name as a magic talisman, they are beaten by the demoniac that they were attempting to exorcise (Acts 19:13–16). Luke intimates:

> And this became known to all the residents of Ephesus, both Jews and Greeks. And fear fell upon them all, and the name of the Lord Jesus was extolled. Also many of those who were now believers came, confessing and divulging their practices. And a number of those who had practiced magic arts brought their books together and burned them in the sight of all. (Acts 19:17–19)

In other words, a sign of their repentance from sin was their turning away from such practices, which are fleshly. They involve false religion (Acts 19:26–27). Earlier in Acts, the magician Elymas sets himself against Paul and Barnabas in their preaching of the gospel. Paul condemns him by saying, "You son of the devil, you enemy of all righteousness, full of deceit and villainy, will you not stop making crooked the straight paths of the Lord?" (Acts 13:10).

Summary

The Bible condemns participation in the occult. It affirms that occult claims of power and knowledge are possibly true. Although some occultists are frauds or "entertainers," some are in league with demonic powers. It also teaches that participation in such activities is an abomination to God because it represents idolatry, a lack of trust in God to fulfil his promises, and a disregard for his commandments. Because it is rooted in demonic power, feigned or actual, it represents a practice of the flesh and not of those who walk in the Spirit. Hence, Christians should not participate in occult activities or give them any heed.[3]

REFLECTION QUESTIONS

1. What does the Bible say about the reality of occult powers?

---

3. For historical perspective on the occult, see Lawrence E. Sullivan, ed., *Hidden Truths: Magic, Alchemy, and the Occult* (New York: MacMillan, 1989).

2. Why does the Bible condemn participation in the occult?

3. How can we guard against wrong thinking about the occult, in our consumption of media?

4. Why is it important to remember that the Holy Spirit is greater than demons?

5. How can we pray for those involved in the occult?

QUESTION 36

What Is the New Age Movement?

The New Age movement is a grassroots cultural movement generated in the late twentieth century.[1] It emphasizes spirituality, in particular embracing certain meditative elements of predominately Eastern religions. Because it has no central organization or creed, one can only speak in generalities about its generic shape and emphases. Nevertheless, New Age as a movement is characterized by individualism and relativism.[2] It is not theistic (believing in and worshipping a god); instead it cultivates spirituality without religion with a focus on self-improvement and growth. Because its adherents reject that there is only one path to salvation or enlightenment or personal peace, the movement is not united by any formal religious commitments and does not have members or churches. The movement partakes of many ancient and long standing religious traditions known as esotericism, and so some scholars hold that the "new" in New Age is a misnomer.[3] However, the "new" generally is understood to refer to the age that the rediscovery of certain ancient techniques for transformation will generate. When a sufficient number of people reach higher stages of consciousness, for example, humanity will enter a new age in which it more perfectly represents the divine. This transition to this "New Age" corresponds to the change in astrological signs (a putative orientation of the constellations) to the sign of Aquarius.

Pantheism

In general, New Age articulates a view of the world in which a divine principle or energy suffuses everything that exists. This means that in some

---

1. Scholars generally hold that the phrase was coined in Alice Bailey, *Discipleship in the New Age* (New York: Lucis, 1944).
2. The United States boasts more than 2,500 different spiritual groups, many of which would fall under the umbrella of New Age. The diversity of doctrines and methods is dizzying.
3. Wouter Hanegraaf, *New Age Religion and Western Culture* (Albany: SUNY Press, 1997) is a seminal study of the New Age movement.

sense everything is god. A result of this conception is that each human person is god or is part of the divine principle or energy. Hence, the spirituality suggested by New Age is frequently self-focused. A major goal is often to contribute to self-transformation in ways that help one more perfectly realize his or her internal divinity. This also leads many to believe that all religions are essentially good in their core teachings and that they represent many different paths to the divine. Hence, this "religion" inherently promotes inclusivism because it argues that no particular religion or spirituality is better or more true or more apt to lead to salvation/transformation/nirvana than any other. It also follows from this that there is no set moral law. Rather, the divine energy that flows through everything simply *is*, a kind of impersonal force.[4]

Knowledge

Another common features of New Age belief is that mystical knowledge is attainable through certain ritual practices, such as transcendent meditation. Strictly speaking, transcendental meditation is a technique promoted by an Indian religious leader of the twentieth century, Mahesh Yogi. However, the term has come to represent a generic technique in which a mantra (secret, religious phrase) is repeated silently. The argument is that such activity done properly promotes greater health and well-being. These healing benefits also offer an opportunity for spiritual growth that can result in mystical experiences that can provide one with knowledge of the spiritual world behind material reality. If sufficient numbers of people were to have these transcendent experiences, then a New Age of spirituality would awaken that would lead to a more peaceful and just world. This knowledge is also not the purview of any particular religion or even any particular deity, since channelers or mediums sometimes claim to have access to multiple "gods" as diverse as Vishnu, Jesus, and Buddha. According to most New Age accounts, because these figures are all merely aspects of the divine, they do not see contradictions in holding to multiple religions or deities.

Channeling

Another technique in support of becoming more aware of the universe is known as channeling. Channeling is understood to be a method for communicating with nonhuman consciousness, understood either as angelic beings, spirits, or extraterrestrial beings. Although there is a general commitment to pantheism represented in the idea that the whole universe is a living entity, there is also an understanding of different levels of spiritual power, "angels" or "guides," between the divine and human consciousness. These beings often

---

4. Sometimes, this is described as the power behind all consciousness. See Hugh B. Urban, *New Age, Neopagan, and New Religious Movements* (Oakland: University of California Press, 2015), 224–25.

serve as spirit guides to provide wisdom or knowledge that assists people in their spiritual journeys. Some people claim to have a special gift for this type of communication, and sell their services to others. Often, the explanation for these beings is that they exist on "higher planes" of reality. In some cases, these are explained using misunderstandings of contemporary particle physics. In fact, an attempt to explain the underlying mechanisms of certain healing, communication, and transformative New Age practices are often based on references to quantum mechanics.

One goal for some New Age practitioners is to achieve a new state of consciousness that would allow them to shed their physical bodies and move to one of the higher planes. Because New Age generally affirms a belief in reincarnation, progress can be made on one's spiritual journey across lifetimes. In some cases, channelers or mediums claim to speak with the deceased, usually because the deceased person wants to communicate a message to one of the living. A related idea behind channeling is that death is illusory in some sense, since reincarnation is possible.

Channelers also teach that by applying their techniques they can generate good fortune, or even come to control reality, merely by using their thoughts and mental energy. Many New Age books hold that the divine consciousness that suffuses the universe is something into which they can tap to succeed in life, business, or romance. Some even attempt to explain the power of prayer in this way.

Critiques

The Christian critiques of the movement are probably obvious, but perhaps the essentials are worth restating. The movement flatly denies the existence of a personal, creator God. Since the fundamental dichotomy of the Christian worldview is that there is God and there is what God created, Christianity is fundamentally incompatible with New Age beliefs.

Likewise, Christianity make exclusive claims about how salvation is possible. Jesus says, "I am the way, and the truth, and the life. No one comes to the Father except through me" (John 14:6). Peter says that, "there is salvation in no one else, for there is no other name under heaven given among men by which we must be saved" (Acts 4:12). Paul says, "There is one God, and there is one mediator between God and men, the man Christ Jesus" (1 Tim. 2:5). Whatever spiritual "knowledge" is available outside the witness of Scripture is sufficient to leave men without excuse for their idolatry (Rom. 1:18–21), but provides no way for them to be saved because "faith comes from hearing, and hearing through the word of Christ" (Rom. 10:17). A syncretistic system like New Age is not compatible with Christian belief.

Finally, New Age promotes the idea that it is merely through ignorance of one's participation in the divine that men do not achieve higher levels of happiness. Meditation and internal reflection are promoted as means of self-improvement. But, the Christian worldview categorically rejects the idea that man, left to his own devices, is capable of material contribution to true moral improvement: "There is no one righteous" (Eccl. 7:20; Ps. 14:3; Rom. 3:10); "There is a way that seems right to a man, but its end is the way to death" (Prov. 14:12). Instead, "the fear of the LORD is the beginning of knowledge" (Prov. 1:7). It is not possible to attain to such knowledge if one resorts to spiritual beings in flagrant disregard of God's commands (Exod. 20:1–2; Deut. 8:6; 1 John 5:4).

Summary

New Age is not a religion, but is an umbrella term for a wide variety of esoteric practices and beliefs. In general, New Age affirms a universal divine energy that pervades all things, a commitment to expanding the internal spark of the divine through meditation and spiritual practices, and a goal of achieving higher levels of happiness through increased consciousness, often with the aid of high spiritual beings. New Age ideas are present in nearly all facets of American cultural life, often undergirding an interest in the spiritual nature of reality, the possibility of magic, and communication with the dead, as well as a fascination with angels and extraterrestrials. Christians should be cautious in consumption of such materials, carefully distinguishing between fantasy and the revelation of God.

REFLECTION QUESTIONS

1. Why is pantheism impossible to square with orthodox Christianity?

2. What drives a fascination with fortune telling and astrology?

3. Why is the idea of self-focused self-improvement so attractive in our culture?

4. How does the embrace of New Age beliefs reveal a desire to fulfill spiritual needs?

5. How can you begin to recognize the influence of New Age beliefs in your own consumption of media and entertainment?

What Is Wicca?

Wicca is the name for a spectrum of religious and spiritual practices that attribute their origins to the pre-Christian religions of Ireland, England, and Wales. In some cases, the religious movement is known as "Neo-Paganism," although increasingly Wicca is understood to be a subgroup within Neo-Paganism. Generally, Wiccans adopt this label because of negative connotations of the word "witch." It is one of the fastest growing religious movements in the United States.[1] Like many new religious movements, it does not possess an elaborate, corporate organization. Practitioners of Wicca refer to themselves variously as Wiccans, witches, and in some cases druids. Local groups are referred to as covens or circles, but many adherents (called "solitaries") do not belong to a group. While Wiccans are often associated with Satanists (in particular because of historical understandings of witches from the early modern period), contemporary Wiccans generally deny that they worship Satan or even believe in his existence. Wiccans understand Satan to be merely an artifact of Christianity, and they trace their own roots to the pagan religions of the West prior to the advent of Christianity in those locales.[2]

Because the movement has little to no institutional structure, it has been difficult for sociologists to study it as an independent religious group in spite of the fact that its rapid growth has made it an object of scholarly and popular interest. Witches and macabre (reminiscent of the grave) fascinations culturally associated with vampires and lycanthropes (people that can change into animals) are increasingly common features of American popular culture, but these

---

1. Barry A. Kosmin, Egon Mayer, and Ariela Keysar demonstrate a growth from 8,000 to 134,000 from 1990–2001 based on a sample of 50,000 (*American Religious Identification Survey* [New York: City University of New York, 2001], 13). The 2011 U.S. Census listed the number that self-identify as either Wiccan or Neo-Pagan as 682,000.
2. See discussion about debated origins in Ethan Doyle White, *Wicca: History, Belief, and Community in Modern Pagan Witchcraft* (Brighton: Sussex Academic Press, 2016), 13–23.

depictions often reflect a blend of tropes that are foreign in many respects to the Wiccan self-understanding.

Modern Witchcraft

Wicca is probably best understood as a nature religion. It shares some broad similarities with New Age beliefs in that it holds that the world is a living being. Wiccans argue, however, that the Earth in particular is divine. They revere or worship Gaia, who is the personified Earth, sometimes referred to as the Great Mother. A related core belief is that all life is sacred, in part because all life on earth shares a necessary relationship with Mother Gaia. This goddess is both a personal entity and the divine energy that suffuses all living things on Earth. As a result of these beliefs, Wiccans tend to be environmentally conscious and often attribute natural disasters to Gaia's displeasure with humans' disrespect for the earth. In other cases, however, these events are viewed as necessary actions by Gaia to maintain the ecosystem of the earth. At the same time, Wiccans believe that the divine is both male and female. Although the goddess has some precedence, a god (sometimes referred to as the Oak, the Sun King, or the Horned God) is seen by many Wiccans as her divine consort.[3]

Because Wiccans view all life as fundamentally interconnected, their central creed is the minimal ethical principle "harm none." Celebrations are generally based on significant seasonal events, which might be related to the harvest cycle, the lunar calendar, or the solstices. Samhain (Halloween) on October 31 is the beginning of the calendar. It is associated frequently with the pagan background behind Halloween. Yule (originally referring to the period of the calendar including December and January) is the celebration of the winter solstice in late December. In fact, Wiccans hold that many of the festivities associated with Christmas in American and British culture originally reflected the celebration of the winter solstice. The summer solstice in mid-June is a time of heightened magic, while the equinoxes in March and September, represent significant times of transition, in particular the exchange of ascendency between the god and goddess.

Magic

The practice of Wicca or "the craft" is often associated with the practice of magic. Wiccans see magic as a way to harness certain powerful symbols to focus one's desires and develop a more conscious awareness of the divine.

---

3. Although in other cases, he is seen as an equal, such as in the Gardnerian system, so named for its founder. See Gerald Gardner, *The Meaning of Witchcraft* (London: Antiquarian, 1971), 129. In more recent developments, the Goddess receives emphasis, partly because of a merging of Wicca with some strains of feminist thought. See Kristy Coleman, *Re-Riting Woman: Dianic Wicca and the Feminine Divine* (Walnut Creek, CA: AltaMira, 2009), 150–65.

In many cases, rituals are performed in association with significant seasonal events. Magic is understood to be a neutral power. Popular conceptions of magic express this by referring to "good" or "helpful" magic as white magic and to "evil" or "harmful" magic as black magic. Because Wiccans' creed is "if it harm none, do as you will" they do not generally use this scheme. Instead they stress the significance of one's intentions in using ritual powers. In fact, in some cases, a spell is nothing more than repeating one's goal up to ten times per day in a way similar to the mantra of Eastern meditation. Wicca relies heavily on a strong conception of one's intuition as an exemplar of the divine. Most magical practices are seen as ways to strengthen one's intuition so that it can serve them better.[4]

One of the specific principles in Wiccan magic is known as the Three-fold Law. This law is similar to the New Age adoption of a belief in karma, in which one's actions are always brought into balance. If you harm someone using magic, the Three-fold Law stipulates that you will receive three times the harm in return. On the other hand, good magic will bring three times the blessing. Because of this principle, Wiccans resent the accusation that they are practitioners of black magic or that they are evil. From their vantage point, doing evil acts would bring harm to them.

Magic for Wiccans is primarily about celebrating nature and increasing their awareness of the divine principle in all things, not about controlling people or the elements. However, many Wiccan manuals or guides for the practice of magic suggest that such control is possible.[5] Furthermore, rituals associated with the full moon are often intended to call the leader of the ritual to enter into direct contact with the divine spirit in order to access hidden knowledge akin to other forms of pagan divination. This ritual is often referred to as "Drawing Down the Moon." Most versions of the ritual involve the adoption of certain postures, an invocation of the goddess, as well as invitation for the light to enter into the person performing the ritual. The goal of this activity is a ritual possession that, though temporary, involves a trance-like state and the ability to answer specific questions asked by participants in the ritual. In some versions of Wicca, the person who performs the ritual actually becomes the goddess for the period of the ritual. From the Christian viewpoint, this clearly looks like a request to be possessed by a demon.

Critique

Wicca promotes the worship of a false goddess and an incorrect understanding of the divine nature. It also promotes moral relativism because evil,

---

4. Scott Cunningham, *Wicca: A Guide for the Solitary Practitioner* (St. Paul: Llewellyn, 1988), 18–20.
5. See Doreen Valiente, *An ABC of Witchcraft* (London: Robert Hale, 1986).

while something to be avoided, is merely another aspect of life. We avoid it primarily because it causes us pain and not because of some overriding moral principle. The idea that one can be led by intuition is popular in many new religious movements, but it also contributes to religious systems that are highly idiosyncratic. Hence, Wicca is in many respects a do-it-yourself religion and spirituality. Hence, we have to be careful in assuming that we have a grasp of what a particular Wiccan believes simply because he or she identifies as a Wiccan. In particular, the accusation that Wiccans are Satanists is mistaken because there are other religious movements that actively and knowingly worship the Devil (such as the Church of Satan). Whatever false god or demon Wiccans may contact through their rituals, they do not believe it to be the Devil or a demon. This, of course, does not make their rituals any less dangerous or idolatrous. However, we should be careful of overlooking distinctions between religious and cultural groups, since such distinctions are crucial to the groups' self-understanding and, therefore, to our ability to understand and witness to them.

Some of the practices associated with Wicca (such as repeating one's goals, or visualizing the achievement of one's goals) are innocuous. Others seem to be merely nonsense ritualistic actions that have no effect on the external world. But, the Bible is clear that not all occult activity is merely nonsense, and the request for ritual possession by the "divine" is an especially dangerous practice. It is important to be reminded that vestiges of pagan religious activity are present and growing features of contemporary Western spirituality and that our cultural fascination with paranormal activity increases the fascination with trends such as Wicca. In fact, the Midwestern United States has one of the densest concentrations of Neo-Paganism and Wicca, such that the religion is not as fringe and farfetched as it might otherwise appear.

Summary

Wicca is a nature-religion that believes that the divine goddess suffuses all things. It is not the same as Satanism. Wiccans are sometimes members of local covens, but the majority operate as individual practitioners. Although there are several branches of Wicca with more distinct beliefs, the Wiccan Rede ("harm none") and the Three-fold Law are the basic components of Wiccan religion. Wiccans are comfortable relying on intuition to guide their spiritual practices, and borrowing from alternative religions and spiritualties to achieve their goals. Ritual magic is commonplace, some of which involves request for possession by the goddess. Many elements of Wicca are part and parcel of pagan religious idolatry. We should pray for people involved in this type of witchcraft, and seek opportunities to teach the real Old Time Religion.

REFLECTION QUESTIONS

1. Why might an individualist religion like Wicca be attractive in America?

2. What major religious tenets do Wiccans share?

3. Why is participation in magic potentially dangerous and not merely harmless fun?

4. Given its rapid growth, how might you find out about the presence of Wicca in your region?

5. How can you practice discernment in your consumption of media, related to witchcraft?

Are There Such Things as Spiritual Curses?

The Bible does not deny that there are dark spiritual powers or that pagan religious figures are capable through witchcraft of cursing people. In fact, the Law forbids such practices (e.g., Lev. 19:31). However, the Bible does not generally speak of "curses" in the sense of witchcraft or occult activity. In this chapter, I will describe the language of curses in the Bible. Although spiritual curses are possible, "If God is for us, who can be against us?" (Rom. 8:31). Finally, I address the issue of so-called "generational curses."

The Language of Cursing in the Bible

Cursing appears in several different forms in Scripture. The most significant curse comes from God as a penalty for Adam's sin in Eden. This curse is described in Genesis 3:14–19. The serpent (who is the Devil) is cursed to wallow in the dust as the least of beasts, and God says that the seed of the woman will destroy him (ultimately, speaking of Jesus' defeat of the enemy). The woman is cursed with increased pain in childbirth, and God says that she will have tension with her husband because of her desires and his position. The man is cursed with difficulty and struggle in his work because the ground is cursed so that it no longer yields fruit easily, and God says that man will work by the sweat of his face until he dies.

The word for "curse" in this text is *arar*. In most instances, the subject of the verb is God so that curse has the sense of judgment, or the establishment of a penalty for wrongdoing.[1] This sense is important to recognize. In English, "curse" usually means some kind of ill word spoken about someone to cause their harm or discomfort, but there is no sense in which the "judgment" that

---

1. It is also the verb used when leaders of the people promise a penalty for some action (e.g., Josh. 6:26).

the curse renders to someone is based on the righteousness of the one pro-claiming the curse. In other cases, a curse is merely an expression of desire that something would happen. When God curses someone, by contrast, it is not capricious. In fact, the presentation of a commandment implies a penalty for violating it.

This fact emerges explicitly in connection with the covenant that God reaffirms with Israel through Moses, as recorded in Deuteronomy. In chapter 27, Moses pronounces a conditional curse from verses 15–26. The pattern is "Cursed be the one who does X," where the X is a violation of some aspect of the law Moses has rehearsed before the people. In each instance, the penalty for committing the sin is acknowledged (and endorsed!) by the people who respond to Moses by saying, "Amen." The final curse is summative of the rest of the law, "Cursed be the one who does not confirm the words of this law by doing them" (v. 26). The covenant curses, then, are the associated penalties for failing to live up to God's standard.[2] A particular facet of these curses, then, is their association with the breach of the Law.

Generational Curses

Christians often talk about "generational, spiritual curses." The concept is usually ascribed to the text of Exodus 20:4–6:

> You shall not make for yourself a carved image, or any like-ness of anything that is in heaven above, or that is in the earth beneath, or that is in the water under the earth. You shall not bow down to them or serve them, for I the LORD your God am a jealous God, visiting the iniquity of the fathers on the children to the third and fourth generation of those who hate me, but showing steadfast love to thousands of those who love me and keep my commandments. (see also Exod. 34:7; Num. 14:18; Deut. 5:9)

The idea of a generational curse is that the sins of the father are repeated by his children and their children unless something disrupts the "family bondage" of the curse. Often, it is held that the effects of this curse continue even after a member of the family comes to faith in Christ.

Like many popular theological terms, "generational curses" is not used with a single precise meaning in all contexts. Certainly, it is true that sons imitate their fathers, and that a father with a bad temper is likely to raise a son with one as well. It is not helpful to describe such patterns as generational

---

2. See also the use in Psalm 119:21: "You rebuke the insolent, *accursed* ones, who wander from your commandments."

curses, however, because this leads to misunderstandings about the nature of God's disclosure of his jealousy in Exodus 20.

Visiting the Iniquity

What does it mean that God "visits" the iniquity of the fathers on the children? The Hebrew term is *paqad*. In some English translations (e.g., NIV), this word has been unfortunately translated "punishing." By itself, the word *paqad* simply does not mean punish. Rather, it means "visit." When it appears with the preposition *al*, however, then it can mean punish (i.e., to visit upon = punish: e.g., Exod. 32:23). Now, the word *al* does appear in Exodus 20:5, so the translation "punish" might suggest itself as an accurate translation of the text. Nevertheless, the word *al* does not follow *paqad*, so the translation cannot be "punish" in this case. Instead, it should be "visit iniquity upon." Because the NIV has decided to render *paqad* "punish," it became necessary to add a preposition ("for") that does not appear in Hebrew in order to render the phrase intelligible in English. Hence, the NIV reads: "punishing the children *for* the sin of the parents." Adding "for" produces a misleading English text because the idea of the NIV is that God punishes children for what the fathers have done—this exact misunderstanding of God's justice is addressed by Moses in Deuteronomy 24:16[3] and the rebuke found in Ezekiel 18.

Charitably, it may be that the NIV translators intended for their rending to communicate the idea that the punishment of the fathers *has effects for* the children to the third and fourth generation. This sense may be reflected in the Good News Translation: "I will bring punishment on those who hate me and on their descendants down to the third and fourth generation." Here it is possible that the punishment is for the sins of the fathers and has effects for future generations. This idea is consistent with the pattern of God's judgment and does not suggest that God punishes children for what their fathers did. GNT avoids the idiomatic "visit," choosing to translate *paqad* as "bring" and reads the Hebrew *avon* ("iniquity") in a fuller sense ("the punishment of the iniquity"), which is a well-attested option (e.g., Ps. 31:11; Isa. 5:18). It is true that the punishment of sin has ramifications for future generations, as it is true that a person's sins have ramifications for future generations. The idea of "visiting the iniquity of the fathers upon the children" should be understood in this sense, which can be seen later in the Old Testament when someone righteous like Daniel finds himself in exile.[4] His fathers rejected God and were punished. A result of that punishment is that Daniel was sent into exile, but

---

3. "Fathers shall not be put to death for their children, nor children put to death for their fathers; each is to die for his own sin."
4. "Rather, this oft-repeated theme speaks of God's determination to punish successive generations for committing the same sins they learned from their parents" (Douglas K. Stuart, *Exodus*, New American Commentary [Nashville: B&H, 2006], 454).

this should not be construed as Daniel being punished for what his fathers did. Furthermore, it should not be understood to mean that children are bound by God to commit the same sins as their fathers. It is true that children often commit the same sins as the fathers, but that has nothing to do with this verse. Certainly, it is not the result of some specific generational curse.

The reason that children commit the sins that the fathers commit is because all men are sinners. There is no need to hypothesize for an added curse beyond the effect of the Fall, especially one rejected by later biblical teachings. The salvation for the sinner is found in Christ's blood alone.

Summary

In most instances, cursing is a pronouncement of judgment in the Scripture. Although we often use cursing to refer to speaking ill words about someone, this is not the primary way that the terminology is used in Scripture.[5] Instead, God is generally the one speaking the curse. The programmatic claim that God is just to punish sin "to the third and fourth generation" should not be construed as the claim that God places specific families or generations under corporate spiritual bondage. Nor should Christians be concerned about the need to specially remove such curses in order for the gospel to have effect or for sinners to be saved.

REFLECTION QUESTIONS

1. Why is it comforting to know that God will have mercy on a person from any family who turns to him in faith?

2. How does Ezekiel 18 help us better understand the passage in Exodus 20?

3. Does this question gives us good reasons to compare English translations when we study our Bible?

4. How might the confusion on this subject encourage us to be precise in our theological language?

5. In light of God's promises of blessing, what concern should we have about occult curses?

---

5. See Mark 11:12–25.

What Is Satanic Ritual Abuse?

The satanic ritual abuse scare of the 1980s and '90s was a concern about an international conspiracy perpetrated by a coalition of satanic cults that was putatively responsible for the systematic abuse, rape, or murder of thousands of people. The threat of this conspiracy was felt so widely in the 1980s in the United States that popular magazine polls suggested that 70 percent of respondents gave some credence to satanic ritual abuse.[1] Much of the original attention came from a book first published in 1980 entitled *Michelle Remembers*, a memoir that provides a personal and graphic account of child abuse. The "remembers" in the title refers to the fact that the author's memories of these events were "recovered" through a series of psychoanalytic therapy sessions provided by the coauthor of the book. The idea that certain memories are so traumatic that they are repressed and effectively forgotten is a basic assumption of most of these cases. The book spawned a cottage industry of similar texts.

Another development was a concern about a ring of childcare facilities that were engaged in systematic sexual and physical abuse of children including forced participation in satanic rituals, in particular a widely reported case from Austin, Texas. What people found compelling about the reports (beyond their morbid and sinister details) is that they were reported by young children during therapeutic intervention. Since many of the details shared by children were similar, and there seemed to be no reason to suspect that the children would lie (certainly, not about sexual and physical abuse), the reports garnered significant attention. In fact, in eventual court proceedings, such testimonies played the dominant role in securing convictions for the prosecuted. At the present, the majority of the evidence for such crimes has been discredited, and no evidence has come to light regarding a conspiracy of satanic cults.

---

1. This oft-cited poll is found in A. S. Ross, "Blame it on the Devil," *Redbook* (June 1994): 86–89.

Abuse in Daycare

More than 100 investigations into alleged satanic abuse at daycare centers occurred during the 1980s. Such cases were heavily reported in the media, including in a special report that claimed that upward of a million Satanists were involved in similar rituals.[2] This television special received the highest rating for a documentary to that point. One of the earliest cases focused on the McMartin Preschool. The daycare was accused of sexual abuse and of satanic rituals, including human sacrifice. The related court cases lasted nearly seven years, including a retrial; however, no convictions were forthcoming and the jury was hung on some of the counts.

In a similar case in Texas, Fran and Dan Keller were convicted of sexual abuse in 1992. The criminal investigation into the Kellers began because a three-year-old girl reported to her mother that Dan Keller had spanked her during one of her stays at the home daycare. During a session with the child's therapist, she reported much more heinous abuse of a sexual nature. Shortly after these reports, other children from the daycare also reported abuse, including accounts of being forced to drink blood, sexual abuse, forced prostitution, and murder of an adult, infants, and pets. The fact that the Kellers were said to sometimes wear robes and light candles during some of the abuse confirmed a connection with a broader development of satanic rituals. A local physician provided testimony that injuries sustained by the young girl were consistent with her reports of sexual abuse. The Kellers were convicted about a year after the initial report of abuse following a six-day trial and were sentenced to forty-eight years in prison. In 2013, the doctor who provided testimony that corroborated reports of abuse recanted his testimony, claiming that he made a mistake based on his lack of training in identifying sexual abuse in children. The Kellers were released after being in prison for twenty-one years. Not all concern centered on daycare centers. There were also frequently unsourced reports of satanic kidnappings of up to 50,000 children yearly.

FBI Analysis

Even by 1992, however, the National Center for the Analysis of Violent Crime, branch of the Federal Bureau of Investigation, reported only two hundred to three hundred "stereotypical child abductions per year," most of whom were teenagers.[3] Part of the challenge reported by Kenneth Lanning, the author of the report, in identifying authentic cases of satanic activity

---

2. "Devil Worship: Exposing Satan's Underground," *The Geraldo Rivera Show* (October 22, 1988).
3. Kenneth V. Lanning. "Investigator's Guide to Allegations of 'Ritual' Child Abuse" (Quantico, VA: National Center for the Analysis of Violent Crime, Federal Bureau of Investigation, 1992), 6.

was the incredible number of distinct religious groups and spiritualties labeled as satanic. If satanism is used to refer to the fact that the enemy is present in false religions, preaching false gospels and blinding the minds of the unbelieving (2 Cor. 4:4), then one could hold that all non-Christian religions are satanic. However, in these cases, satanism typically referred to conscious and intentional worship of the Devil, as opposed to unknowing worship of the Devil through idolatry. Similarly, ritual religious crimes are difficult to identify because crimes can have ritual aspects that the perpetrators deny have anything to do with religious concerns. He argues that, from a legal standpoint, the intention of the criminal is significant, since religious acts considered criminal by one group might not be so considered by another (he uses male and female circumcision as an example).[4]

Likewise, Lanning is suspicious that satanism is even comparable to a religion like Christianity, except insofar as there is significant and wide-ranging disagreement as to what members of both groups believe. He points out that self-identifying satanists, such as Anton LeVey, do not even believe in God or Satan. For them, "Satan" is a kind of talisman for embracing personal freedoms and release from cultural or religious bondage. In light of these concerns, he prefers to discuss this type of crime as "multidimensional child sex rings" rather than refer it to the acts of satanists, since satanists are often uninvolved and these crimes can be perpetrated by people with no expressed affiliation with Satan. Of course, this has to do more with sociological labels used to identify legally recognized subgroups than it does with discerning the spiritual forces at work in the world. But, given Lanning's position in law enforcement, this position is understandable, since crime must be labeled in a way that would allow violent offenders to be prosecuted. He notes four components of what he calls "these kinds of cases": (1) multiple young victims with (2) multiple offenders who use (3) fear as a controlling tactic in their (4) bizarre or ritualistic activity.[5] In addition to deep suspicions about therapeutic techniques that "recover memories," he is suspicious about the most central "satanic" elements of these criminal cases, such as accusations of cannibalism and human sacrifice. He writes: "We live in a very violent society, and yet we have 'only' about 23,000 murders a year. Those who accept these stories of mass human sacrifice would have us believe that the Satanists and other occult practitioners are murdering more than twice as many people every year in this country as all the other murderers combined."[6] His conclusion is "in none of the cases of which I am aware has any evidence of a well-organized satanic cult been found."[7]

---

4. Ibid., 10–11.
5. Ibid., 15–16.
6. Ibid., 19.
7. Ibid.

Present Status

Law enforcement, historians, and sociologists now largely investigate satanic ritual abuse as a surprising hoax, scare, or witch hunt because most believe the allegations to have been sensationalized by the newly forming twenty-four-hour media. Studies of the transcripts of many interviews with children in the daycare centers suggest that leading questions and the suggestibility of children have more to do with the accusations than evidence of trauma or abuse (although the conviction in the Keller case did rest on the physician's testimony of sexual abuse). We should be hesitant to ever diminish the seriousness of a child's report simply because it was a child's. The studies of these particular cases, however, show that some of the investigators offered misleading accounts of what the children actually reported.

For adult cases, psychologists are much more suspicious of the "recovered memory" therapeutic techniques that undergird many of the sexual abuse allegations. In fact, one of the authors of a seminal work in defense of recovered memories recanted her approval in her second edition.[8] One of the oddities of these developments is that many Christian psychologists seemed keen to adopt such beliefs even though in general they are resistant to trends in psychology.[9] Even if there is no evidence of a widespread series of cooperating satanic cults, the Bible reports that the word is under the authority of the enemy and Satan "seeks whom he may devour" (1 Peter 5:8).

Summary

Satanic ritual abuse refers to a series of alleged crimes in the 1980s and '90s that were thought to have been perpetrated by a covert ring of satanists. A few high-profile cases produced a public fascination, especially because of the gory descriptions of the alleged violence. In fact, law enforcement officials did not find evidence of any conspiracy or even relationship between the high-profile cases. Ultimately, the panic generated by the media exposure seemed to outpace the evidence available, and convictions have been overturned in most of the high-profile cases.

REFLECTION QUESTIONS

1. What is satanic ritual abuse?

---

8. The original is Dianna Russell, *The Secret Trauma: Incest in the Lives of Girls and Women* (New York: Basic Books, 1986). She expressed her view that most retrieved memories are in fact false in the second edition (New York: Basic Books, 1987), xxvi.

9. Even otherwise helpful "truth encounter" proposals for spiritual growth are marred by these assumptions. See the discussion in Robert J. Priest and Esther E. Cordill, "Christian Communities and 'Recovered Memories' of Abuse," *Christian Scholar's Review* (2012): 381–400.

2. What are some of the difficulties for law enforcement in identifying ritual abuse?

3. How does the episode of the 1980s and '90s show the need for discernment in the Christian community?

4. How does scapegoating satanists undermine the real threat of satanic activity?

5. How should the threat of abuse cause us to review our own practices in family life and Christian ministry?

What Are Tarot, Ouija, and Divination?

There is a dizzying array of occult methods for gaining knowledge. Divination generally refers to attempts to discover the future, but sometimes divinatory practices are used to get answers to specific questions through spiritual means. Two of the methods most widely known are tarot and ouija. Both reveal an unwillingness to rely on God for what we need.

Ouija

The ouija board is actually a brand of spirit board. A spirit board is a flat piece of (usually) wood that is engraved either with an alphabet or simple characters. The method of divination relies on a planchette, which is a smaller piece of wood (or sometimes precious stone or metal) that has a hole bored into it. The hole is large enough that a single character or letter can be glimpsed through it. Practitioners ask that the spirit of the board or a familiar spirit answer their question by guiding the planchette to the answers. The theory is that the spirit will guide the planchette to the appropriate letters or characters to spell out or reveal the answer.

Ouija is a brand of spirit board first produced in the United States at the end of the nineteenth century. The nineteenth century in the United States saw a significant increase in spiritualism, which was a broad series of techniques used for speaking with spirits. The ouija board capitalized on these occult interests. Capitalists saw the board as an improvement on the standard communication with spirits at the time. An older method had spiritualists calling out each letter and expecting a spirit to provide some clue when one should start. Often, this was signaled by a knocking sound (usually provided by someone on the other side of the wall). Not everyone believed that the spirit communication was real, so some of these events were seen as merely spooky fun.

Yet, there were sufficient stories of "successful" communication so that the possibility of speaking to spirits was a live option. The ouija board was approved for a US Patent after the inventors demonstrated the effectiveness of the communication by spelling the patent officer's name.[1] The horror classic *The Exorcist* indicated that the possessed girl in the film was so possessed after communing with a spirit through a ouija board, but until that time there is little evidence that the ouija was considered sinister. After the 1970s, they continued to be produced but were often considered dangerous. Of course, if they really allow communication with spirits, then they are really dangerous. In the 1970s, Christian authors routinely condemned the use of the board because (even if they were nonsense from a divinatory perspective) the sense was that they served as a kind of gateway drug to more illicit and dangerous occult activities.[2]

Part of the mystery of the ouija board is that it is unclear how they work. Actually, this is one of its selling points. Some hold that they really do spell out answers because of the guidance of spirits, but others hold that one of the players is simply moving the planchette. Of course, the latter is the simpler explanation. Psychologists have sometimes suggested that an effect called the ideomotor effect is in play. Essentially, on this analysis, a person's anticipation of a certain response actually produces small movements in their extremities.[3] In other words, people subconsciously move their fingers, and hence the planchette appears to move without their control.

Tarot

Another popular game/divination system is tarot cards. Tarot is a form of divination in which a series of cards are laid on a table. Skilled practitioners "read" the cards, in order to divine the future and tell fortunes. Tarot dates back at least until the fifteenth century in Italy, where it was a card game (like any standard game with jack, queen, and king).[4] By the eighteenth century, the cards became increasingly associated with divination and were produced as a form of cartomancy (divination through cards). In some cases, the entire card deck is still produced (either fifty-two or seventy-eight cards, depending on the style), but many readings are performed with only a class of (twenty-two of) the cards, known as the Major Arcana. These cards were originally trump cards in trick-taking games (such as the modern spades).[5]

1. See the account in Morgan D. Rosenberg, "Did the Spirits Move Him?" *Inventors' Digest* 32, no. 10 (2016): 8–11.

2. For example, Edmond C. Gruss, *The Ouija Board: Doorway to the Occult* (Chicago: Moody Bible Institute, 1975).

3. An early account is given by William James, *The Principles of Psychology* (New York: MacMillan, 1890). Some more recent research among cognitive psychologists elaborates similar ideas. Armin Stock and Claudia Stock, "A Short History of Ideo-Motor Action," *Psychological Research* 68 (2004): 176–88.

4. Although some suggest that it was rooted in astrological practice by this period already. See Helen Farley, "The Evolution of the 'Mother' in Tarot," *Hecate* 32, no. 2 (2006): 68–87.

5. Carlo Penco, "Dummett and the Game of Tarot," *Teorema* 32 (2013): 141–55.

In its cartomantic use, each of the Major Arcana cards has a symbolic meaning, and the order in which the cards are drawn and laid on the table can be interpreted narratively to describe some future events. Like ouija, tarot readers are often accused of being charlatans (certainly, some of them must be), who rely on tricks and manipulation of their clients to "discover" personal details. In other cases, the readings are so vague that their "meaning" is actually provided by the client. Since spirit communication is thought to be relatively tenuous even when successful, the vagueness of the readings is associated with the difficulties of communication across the veil and not with a deliberate attempt to provide a prophecy that could be fulfilled by any number of conditions.

According to practitioners, however, the success of the tarot is based on what is called, in the Hermetic wisdom tradition, the law of correspondence. Essentially, this law teaches that the pattern by which (in this case) the cards are drawn and laid out is partially determined by the astrological state of the heavens. There is some hazy relationship between "what happens above" and "what happens below." Each of the Major Arcana represents different esoteric or archetypical meanings, which seem to depend on who is preparing the text on reading tarot. A standard method is attributed to traditional astrological readings.

Other Methods of Divination

There are many less well-known methods of divination, all of which purport to discover the future or secret knowledge by reference either to spirits or by the esoteric law of correspondence. There is dactyloscopy, which divines the future through metal rings inset with precious stones. Each of the stones or crystals reflects certain symbolic meanings. There is rhabdoscopy or dowsing, which is divining through the use or a wand or rod. The purpose of this technique is to find buried treasure. Cereoscopy divines by the melting of wax, using a method similar to tasseography, which reads tea leaves or coffee grounds. Coscinoscopy uses a sieve to find criminals. Kleidoscopy uses keys for the same purpose. Metoposcopy reads the forehead, and chiromancy the hand.[6] The list could go on, but the basic principles are the same. These occult techniques are intended to reveal some information otherwise undiscoverable. In the past, a defense was made of some of the methods because there was an attempt to describe them as scientific. Since, the argument goes, they are based on some standard patterns in nature, they are not forms of witchcraft, but rather empirical studies. The occult symbology and complete lack of explanatory edifice count strongly against this argument, to say nothing of the fact that many such practices are drawn from or embedded in pagan religious ritual.

---

6. Paul Christian, *The History and Practice of Magic* (New York: The Citadel Press, 1963), 343–97.

Critique

Christians are indwelt by the Holy Spirit. That should be enough to ward off any desire to look for guidance on one's future decision from some occult sources. We have graciously been entrusted with the deposit of the gospel, the Scriptures, and been blessed with Christian community, and we should let discernment arise from and take place within those contexts only. To look elsewhere runs the risk of denigrating the sufficiency of Scripture or the power of God. Finally, and perhaps most simply, the secret arts (whatever they are, exactly) are regularly and flatly forbidden by God in Scripture. Whether they turn out to be nonsense or participation with demons is beside the point.

At the same time, certain periods of American history have shown incredible paranoia and fear from evangelical Christians in response to occult trends in popular culture and media. It is important that our response to reports of witchcraft or popular "friendly" presentations of the occult (such as witches and vampires in film and books) be measured against the knowledge that God is on the side of his people. This does not mean that we should not be consistent in our discernment of potential threats to the purity of our doctrines and practices. However, our reaction to culture should not be primarily promoted by fear or worry because worry reflects a lack of trust in God (Matt. 6:27; 1 John 5:5). Paul tells us to "not be anxious about anything, but in everything by prayer and supplication with thanksgiving let your requests be made known to God" (Phil. 4:6). Christ is our armor, and prayer is our spiritual weapon.

Summary

There are many types of divination in practice, but two of the most common, ouija and tarot, present themselves as games or diversions. There is some debate about whether these practices are based merely on psychological tricks or reliance on some occult power, but settling that debate is beside the point. Because God is sovereign, attempts to divine the future are illicit, since they confess a low view of God's promises to guide and instruct his people. Christians should think carefully about how they engage in even "harmless" pagan practices.

REFLECTION QUESTIONS

1. What might cause methods of divination to be attractive to people?

2. What does participation in divination reveal about a person's confidence in God?

3. Are there ways to distinguish between "harmful" and "harmless" magic?

4. Are there ways in which we practice superstitions, even if we do not practice divination?

5. How can we pray that we might grow in our confidence in God's plans?

Selected Bibliography

Bailey, Michael D. *Magic and Superstition in Europe*: *A Concise History from Antiquity to the Present*. Lanham, MD: Rowman & Littlefield, 2006.

Beilby, James K. and Paul Rhodes Eddy, eds. *Understanding Spiritual Warfare: Four Views*. Grand Rapids: Baker Academic, 2012.

Caciola, Nancy. *Discerning Spirits: Divine and Demonic Possession in the Middle Ages*. Ithaca, NY: Cornell University Press, 2003.

Carson, D. A. *Praying with Paul*, 2nd edition. Grand Rapids: Baker, 2014.

Chafer, Lewis Sperry. *Satan*. Chicago: Moody Press, 1919.

Christian, Paul. *The History and Practice of Magic*, 2 vols. New York: The Citadel Press, 1963.

Dickason, C. Fred. *Demon Possession and the Christian Life: A New Perspective*. Westchester, IL: Crossway, 1990.

Gardner, Gerald. *The Meaning of Witchcraft*. London: Antiquarian, 1971.

Garrett, Duane. *Angels and the New Spirituality*. Nashville: B&H, 1995.

Goldsworthy, Graeme. *Prayer and the Knowledge of God*. Downers Grove, IL: InterVarsity Press, 2003.

Gruss, Edmond C. *The Ouija Board: Doorway to the Occult*. Chicago: Moody Bible Institute, 1975.

Harper, Michael. *Spiritual Warfare*. London: Hodder & Stoughton, 1970.

Hunt, Dave. *Occult Invasion*. Eugene, OR: Harvest House, 1998.

Koyna, Alex. *Demons: A Biblically Based Perspective*. Schaumburg, IL: Regular Baptist Press, 1990.

Lewis, C. S. *The Screwtape Letters*. New York: Harper Collins, 2001.

McDowell, Josh and Don Stewart. *Understanding the Occult*. San Bernardino, CA: Here's Life Publishers, 1982.

Otis, George. *The Last of the Giants*. Tarrytown, NY: Chosen, 1991.

_____. *The Twilight Labyrinth: Why Does Spiritual Darkness Linger Where It Does?* Grand Rapids: Chosen, 1997.

Sullivan, Lawrence E., ed. *Hidden Truths: Magic, Alchemy, and the Occult*. New York: Macmillan, 1989.

Unger, Merrill F. *Biblical Demonology*. Wheaton, IL: Scripture Press, 1952.

Urban, Hugh B. *New Age, Neopagan, and New Religious Movements: Alternative Spirituality in Contemporary America*. Oakland, CA: University of California Press, 2015.

Wagner, C. Peter, ed. *Breaking Strongholds in Your City*. Ventura, CA: Regal, 1993.

Wagner, C. Peter and F. Douglas Pennoyer, eds. *Wrestling with Dark Angels*. Ventura, CA: Regal, 1990.

White, Ethan Doyle. *Wicca: History, Belief, and Community in Modern Pagan Witchcraft*. Brighton, UK: Sussex Academic Press, 2016.

White, Tom. *Breaking Strongholds: How Spiritual Warfare Sets Captives Free*. Ann Arbor, MI: Servant, 1993.

Wink, Walter. *Engaging the Powers: Discernment and Resistance in a World of Domination*. Philadelphia: Fortress, 1992.

Scripture Index